RACING
CHELTEI
FESTI
GUIDE 2013

Edited by Nick Pulford
Foreword by Alastair Down

Contributors

Richard Birch
Graham Dench
Dave Edwards
Paul Kealy
Andrew King
Steve Mason
Rodney Masters
Donn McClean
Kevin Morley

Jonathan Mullin
Tom Pennington
James Pugh
Dave Randall
Colin Russell
Tom Segal
Craig Thake
Johnny Ward
Nick Watts

Designed by David Dew
Cover artwork by Jay Vincent
Inside artwork by Nigel Jones and Stefan Searle

Published in 2013 by Racing Post Books, Raceform Ltd, Compton, Newbury, Berkshire, RG20 6NL Copyright © Racing Post 2013

ISBN 978-1-908216-76-2

Printed by Stones the Printers

GW00671143

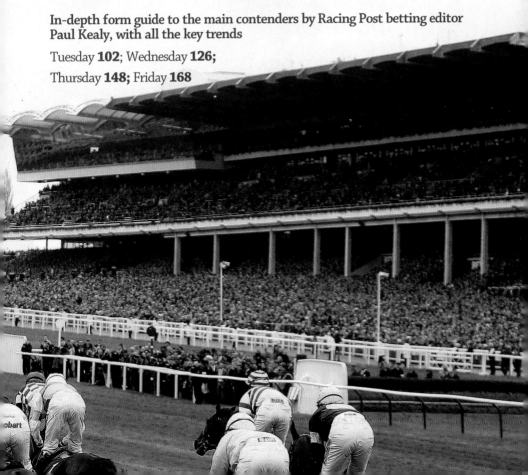

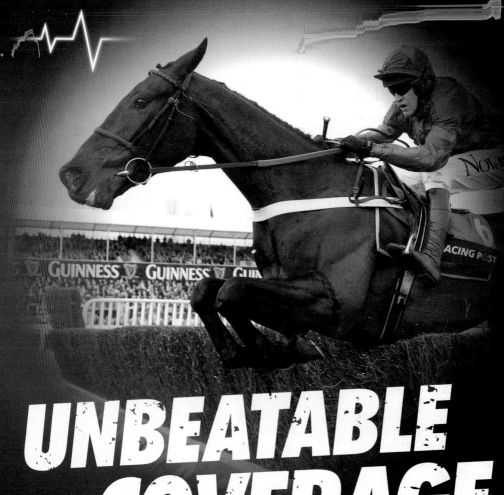

UNBEATABLE COVERAGE

DON'T MISS THE RACING POST EVERY DAY OF THE CHELTENHAM FESTIVAL

 RACING POST
THE **PULSE** OF THE FESTIVAL

The festival that belongs to everyone

THROUGHOUT the racing year many a meeting now carries the tag 'festival' but accept no counterfeit currency or pale imitations. It is the one and only Cheltenham Festival that makes March the month of magic marbled through with a smattering of madness.

Over the last 30 years no other British sporting occasion has soared on an upward curve quite as spectacularly as Cheltenham. Back in the 1980s it was something of a tweedy secret among the mud-pluggers with 70,000 racegoers attending its three days – now more than a quarter of a million ram the old place for four.

And for every enthusiast lucky enough to be on course there are ten back home riveted to the action in betting shop, bar and front room as the best jumpers in the islands follow in the footsteps of the sport's legends in the lee of Cleeve Hill.

Whether you watch from the lawn in front of the stands or on the television you can chuck that stiff upper lip away for the duration because every year without fail the festival shivers the spine with spectacle, excitement and emotion in the raw.

Nowhere else in sport generates an atmosphere quite like it. As the tired but triumphant wend their way back down the horsewalk in front of the stands there is an eruption of acclaim, admiration, affection and plain unvarnished joy.

To stand around the winner's enclosure as the Champion Hurdle winner or hero of the Gold Cup walks in to the roars of the faithful is to be at the centre of jumping's universe. All around you is the cacophony of the happy as hands and voices are raised in welcome and recognition of indelible triumph.

Perhaps the most compelling thing about the festival is the way it belongs to everybody. From Galway to Grimsby and Perth to Penzance, every section of society is caught up in the great escape of four fabulous days. It doesn't matter if you own a hedge fund or a hedge trimmer, are grand or 'gor blimey, young, old, beery or cheery, the festival is a brilliant celebration of sporting ties that bind.

Up that hill from the last, with every yard hard, horses become heroes. Heads will shake in wonder and wallets will wax and wane as for four days in March we are suddenly more alive and thrillingly involved than at any other time of the racing year.

There is no feeling quite like it for the simple reason that there is nothing to match it.

Alastair Down
Racing Journalist of the Year

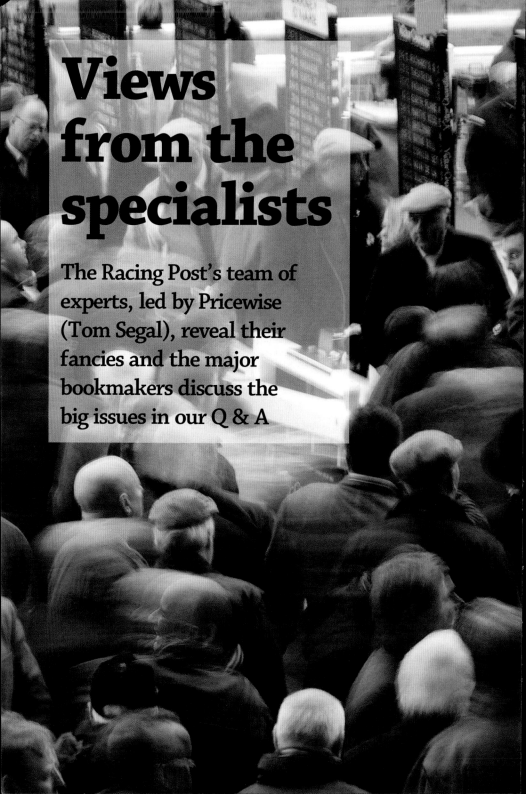

Views from the specialists

The Racing Post's team of experts, led by Pricewise (Tom Segal), reveal their fancies and the major bookmakers discuss the big issues in our Q & A

Go with the flow

Pricewise master Tom Segal expects River Maigue to go well on a crucial opening day

Two major factors have made this year's Cheltenham Festival an unappetising ante-post betting medium for many punters.

The first is the way bookmakers approach ante-post betting these days, which is the antithesis of how it used to be. In the past, the point of ante-post betting was to weigh up the risk of whether a horse was going to run in the attempt to obtain a bigger price. Nowadays the bookmakers work the other way round. They price everything up at a shorter price than they used to in the weeks before the festival but are much more competitive on the day. Why would anyone back Hurricane Fly at 13-8 now, when you are almost certain to get a bigger price on the day once you know he is running and what his opposition is?

The second problem for value-seeking punters is the prevalence of superstar horses who are extremely short prices for their respective Cheltenham races. While it is unlikely all the shorties will win, they have scared off a great deal of the opposition and punters aren't getting a great each-way price for any alternative. Having said that, the racing is so competitive at the festival that there will still be plenty of good bets to be had.

On the first day the key horses are going to be My Tent Or Yours, Simonsig and Hurricane Fly, and it is hard to come up with a good reason why the first two races of the festival won't go to Nicky Henderson.

On form My Tent Or Yours would have a good chance of winning the Champion Hurdle, let alone the Supreme, as you couldn't fail to have been impressed with his Betfair Hurdle romp. He has a couple of negatives, in that he can pull too hard and has no form at Cheltenham, which makes me think the 2-1 on offer at present is no bargain. Henderson has another string to his bow with **River Maigue**, who looked special when hacking up on heavy ground at Kempton over Christmas. More than Jezki, who ran below expectations at the festival last year, River Maigue may give My Tent Or Yours most to think about.

To be honest I can't see Simonsig being beaten in the Arkle. His jumping has been so fluent that it's likely Overturn will simply set the race up for him. This might be a good each-way race, however, as it looks certain to be run at a fierce pace with Overturn and Arvika Ligeonniere in the line-up and there might be scope for a big-priced horse to be held up off the pace before coming late to grab a bit of the pie. I'm hoping Ruby Walsh will ride **Fago** like he did Al Ferof when he beat Sprinter Sacre in the Supreme by coming late and fast. If that was to happen I could see him finishing at least second and rewarding each-way support.

It may sound strange given he has won 14 Grade 1 races, but I believe Hurricane Fly has a bit to prove after his disappointing effort in last year's Champion Hurdle. On that occasion he never travelled with much fluency and, while he has looked back to his best this season, he has only been beating Thousand Stars, a stablemate he always beats.

Zarkandar is better than he showed in last year's Champion

I'm not convinced his Champion win in 2011 represents brilliant form either and he's not getting any younger, so he could be worth opposing.

Zarkandar is a much better horse than he showed in the race last year and Rock On Ruby ran a great trial at Doncaster, so they are two I have the utmost respect for. At a bigger price don't rule out Cotton Mill running a big race too. He was giving Simonsig a race when coming down two out in the Neptune last year and, while My Tent Or Yours thrashed him in the Betfair last time, Cotton Mill beat the rest easily and that was his first run of the season on ground much too soft.

Sprinter Sacre is the best two-mile chaser I've ever seen, so forget about trying to back one against him in the Champion Chase, but do consider having a bet on **Unioniste** in the RSA as I'm sure he's miles better than he showed at Newbury last time and I don't think this is the right race for Dynaste.

Unioniste's best effort came at Cheltenham in a big-field handicap chase run at a strong pace and that form seems much more representative of his best level of ability than the small-field races he ran in prior to that and afterwards. The rigours of the RSA should suit him down to the ground and he is reminiscent of the last five-year-old to win the

Will Hurricane Fly regain his crown in the Champion Hurdle?

Richard Birch At his best he ought to win on the bridle. He was clearly below par last year and Willie Mullins seems more than happy with him this campaign, which is good enough for me. My Tent Or Yours will be a serious threat if he runs.

Nick Watts I don't believe he will, although his task has been made easier by the death of Darlan. The reason for his failure last year is hard to pinpoint and he has ground to make up on Rock On Ruby, who hasn't gone backwards since. Grandouet has always struck me as a Champion Hurdle winner as he travels so well and has a stronger finishing burst than many think.

Paul Kealy In a small field on soft ground I've no doubt Hurricane Fly would thrash any of his rivals. Put them all together in the same race, though, and he's more vulnerable. Last year's race was the strongest-run contest he's been in and he got beat fair and square. Rock On Ruby is the one to beat.

Donn McClean The stats say he is up against it as a nine-year-old former champion, but his performances on the racecourse and his trainer say he is as good as ever this year, and that could be good enough.

Tom Segal I have doubts about him now and his 2011 win may not have been quite as good as it looked at the time. Zarkandar and Rock On Ruby look solid and My Tent Or Yours, if he ran, would have a massive chance too.

Sir Des Champs will be suited by the rigours of the Gold Cup

race, Star De Mohaison, who was also trained by Paul Nicholls.

With no Big Buck's this year, the World Hurdle has a much better betting shape to it. Oscar Whisky was beaten in the race last year and again in the Cleeve, so he can be opposed, while Reve De Sivola might not be quick enough unless the ground is testing. **Solwhit** is the standout horse at the prices. Not only does he have as much ability as anything else in the race but he could improve again for the step up to three miles. If he's right, Solwhit won't get a better chance of winning at the festival. Get Me Out Of Here, who has been second three times at the festival, looks a danger at a big price.

I would be staggered if the winner of the Gold Cup doesn't come from the first four in the betting as Bobs Worth, Sir Des Champs, Silviniaco Conti and Long Run look a class above the rest.

There isn't a tougher horse in training than Bobs Worth and his Hennessy form looks right out of the top drawer. He is unbeaten at Cheltenham and has every right to head the market but I have a strong feeling we haven't seen anything like the best of **Sir Des Champs** so far this season. He is going to be ideally suited by the rigours of the Gold Cup and the stronger the stamina test, the better he will be.

£25 FREE BET

TO ALL NEW CUSTOMERS

Open an account with BetVictor and we'll match the value of your first bet with a free bet up to a maximum of £25*

FOR OUR **BEST ODDS** TALK TO VICTOR

BET**VICTOR**
Online and mobile

Vital statistics

**The festival
by numbers**

🐎*Royal Relief
(1972 and 1974) and
Moscow Flyer (2003
and 2005) are the only
two Champion Chase
winners to lose the
crown and regain it*

52

*The current losing
sequence of Paul
Nicholls-trained
chasers at the festival,
since Kauto Star's
2009 Gold Cup (below)*

🐎*All of the last 12
Arkle winners to go for
the Champion Chase
the following year have
finished in the first
three, although only
half of them have won.
The finishing positions
(since 1992) are
123123112121*

Z is for Zarkandar

Top Irish tipster Donn McClean has quality, if not quantity, in his list of ante-post fancies

If your ante-post portfolio is a little more sparsely populated than usual this year, you are not alone. At this stage most years, I usually need a glossary to find my way from the Albert Bartlett Hurdle to the other end of the alphabet. This year, there has been no need for an up-to-the-minute indexing system. Actually, three lines would do it.

It is difficult to know why this is, but it is probably down to a perfect storm of conditions. Of course, there is the proliferation of races, 27 of them in all, with the charity race masquerading as the 28th. Champion Chase or Ryanair? Neptune or Albert Bartlett? These options were not available until recently.

Trainers have more Cheltenham choice than ever before (it's a veritable Aunty Nellie's Sweet Shop of riches) with the result that those equine conductors are becoming less and less inclined to nominate a definite Cheltenham target until as close to start time as negates the value of non-runner no bet.

It's become fashionable to nominate two or three Cheltenham races as you stand in winner's enclosures up and down these islands, and say that the steaming beast behind you could run in any of them. Procrastination is the order of the day.

Then there are the big horses this year. Trainers appear to be keen to avoid the big horses in the big races, but they are noticeably leaving the door ajar. If Sprinter Sacre makes it to Cheltenham in one piece, he could face just four or five rivals in the Queen Mother. If, on the other hand, God forbid, something were to happen that resulted in him missing the festival, they would flow from the Ryanair Chase like the sands of an hourglass.

The fact that three trainers dominate the Cheltenham markets at this stage leaves ante-post betting even more unstable. Take Willie Mullins, for example, and his novice chasers. At the time of going to press, it is possible that Arvika Ligeonniere will run in the Arkle, Aupcharlie will run in the Jewson, Boston Bob will run in the RSA Chase and Back In Focus will run in the National Hunt Chase. That all makes sense at present.

Say, however, that something untoward were to happen to Arvika Ligeonniere. In that instance, Aupcharlie could run in the Arkle. Consequentially, Boston Bob could run in the Jewson and Back In Focus could run in the RSA Chase, leaving Vesper Bell perhaps to run in the four-miler. It's possible. And where would your ante-post Lucky 15 be then? There are dependencies and contingencies like this all over Seven Barrows and Ditcheat as well, which makes ante-post betting even more fraught with uncertainty than usual.

The other element at play is the fact that there appears to be a higher-than-usual clutch of talented novices who have both the novice races and the handicaps as options. Cantlow could go in the JLT or the RSA Chase, for example. Inish Island could go in the Albert Bartlett or the

Coral Cup, or nowhere at all. African Gold could run in the Albert Bartlett or the Pertemps, Alderwood could go in the Arkle or the Grand Annual, Cause Of Causes could run in the Supreme Novices' Hurdle or the County Hurdle or even the Coral Cup, At Fishers Cross could go in the Albert Bartlett or the Pertemps. Then you have My Tent Or Yours – Supreme Novices' or Champion? As above, riddled with uncertainty.

Here are my three bets so far, for what they're worth: Champagne Fever in the Neptune Hurdle at 7-1, Zarkandar in the Champion Hurdle at 8-1 and Reve De Sivola in the World Hurdle at 10-1. The **Champagne Fever** *(below)* bet looked clever before he got beaten in the Slaney Hurdle, looked decidedly unclever after he did, and still looks frustratingly unclever now, even though he has since gone and won the Grade 1 Deloitte Hurdle.

His position as the Willie Mullins number one for the Neptune has been usurped by Pont Alexandre, which makes reluctant sense. What makes it even more frustrating, however, is that both horses are owned by Rich Ricci, so it looks like Champagne Fever will now go for the Supreme and won't even run as the stable's number two in the Neptune.

At least **Zarkandar** and Reve De Sivola are intended runners at this stage. I like Zarkandar. He is one of those horses who has a really willing attitude, yet who only just appears to do enough, so it is difficult to get a handle on exactly how good he is. He has won eight of his 11 completed races, only once by more than two and a quarter lengths.

Winner of the Betfair Hurdle last season off a mark of 151 (2lb higher than My Tent Or Yours' mark this year), he had an interrupted preparation for last year's Champion, yet he stayed on best of all from the rear to finish a never-nearer fifth, seven lengths behind the winner Rock On Ruby.

Two things are in his favour this year compared with last year. Firstly,

Tipster forum

Can anything stop Sprinter Sacre in the Champion Chase?

Richard Birch He is clearly much the best two-mile chaser in training and victory appears a penalty kick. There doesn't appear to be anything able to get him off the bridle at the moment, a reflection not only of Sprinter Sacre's talent but also the paucity of top-class opposition.

Nick Watts Nothing can stop Sprinter Sacre. Visually he always looks stunning and this will be no different. He's the best we've seen since Moscow Flyer, although he doesn't have the contemporaries that Moscow did.

Paul Kealy When you think only nine runners have been declared and three of those head the market for the Ryanair, it's quite likely he'll have nothing to beat. He's an amazing horse who could be the best two-miler we've seen for years but in years to come when people who never got the chance to see him look back in the form book and see wide-margin wins over Kumbeshwar and Mad Moose, they'll think "so what?" The division is that weak.

Donn McClean Barring something untoward happening, it's very difficult to see him getting beaten. For the forecast, Mail De Bievre would be interesting if he were to be supplemented for the race, especially if the ground came up on the easy side.

Tom Segal Sprinter Sacre is the most talented chaser I've ever seen bar none and will win easily. Cue Card could be second if he runs.

he was a five-year-old last year and history tells us that five-year-olds really do struggle in the Champion Hurdle. He should be much better equipped to deal with the rigours of the race this year as a more hardened six-year-old. Secondly, his preparation has apparently gone more smoothly to date. All being well between now and then, he should be at concert pitch on Champion Hurdle day.

He has impressed in all three runs this season, first when giving 21lb and a neck beating to his better-fancied stable companion Prospect Wells in the Elite Hurdle, then when beating Grandouet and Rock On Ruby in the International, albeit in receipt of 4lb, and finally in the Kingwell Hurdle at Wincanton. Both of his International rivals can be expected to come on for the run there, but Zarkandar can too and he surely wasn't ideally suited by having to make his own running. If the Champion turns into a battle of guts and wills, you can be certain Zarkandar will not be found wanting.

If there is a horse in training that epitomises guts and wills, it is **Reve De Sivola**. A dual Grade 1-winning novice and second in the Neptune Hurdle, he didn't like steeplechasing but has proven himself anew this season as a top-class staying hurdler.

He looked good in winning the Long Walk Hurdle at Ascot in December and built on that performance by lowering the colours of Oscar Whisky in the Cleeve Hurdle. Both of those runs were on soft ground, but his Grade 1 win at Punchestown as a novice was on good ground, as was his big run in the Neptune Hurdle. He is adept on good ground as well and the Cheltenham hill plays to his strengths. There shouldn't be much between him and Oscar Whisky again on March 14, but he should be marginal favourite in front of Nicky Henderson's horse in my book, as opposed to the current situation in which they are the other way around.

Also in my book (fiction, no doubt), **Our Conor** should be clear favourite for the Triumph Hurdle. Dessie Hughes's juvenile ran the best Triumph trial this season to date when he won the Spring Juvenile Hurdle at Leopardstown on Hennessy day.

The Spring has been a really good Triumph pointer in recent years. Unaccompanied won it in 2011 before finishing second to Zarkandar at Cheltenham and last year Hisaabaat and Countrywide Flame were first and third in the Leopardstown race before the placings were reversed in their one-two in the Triumph.

This year's Spring looked strong beforehand with Our Conor, Diakali and Blood Cotil – probably the three best juveniles in Ireland – in the field. The pace was strong, the time was good and the right horses came to the fore, with Our Conor running out an impressive winner.

The son of Jeremy has a really good attitude and he is a leading Triumph Hurdle player now, but Diakali may still be a candidate. Willie Mullins's horse is bred to be well suited by the stamina test that the Triumph Hurdle invariably presents and he may be even better when he doesn't have to make his own running.

Other potential bets? **Aupcharlie** in the Jewson Chase, **Lyreen Legend** if he runs in the four-miler, **Sizing Europe** if he runs in the Ryanair, **Alderwood** if he takes his chance in the Grand Annual. No doubt they will wend their weary ways into the portfolio at some stage. Getting fuller now. Glossary to be added soon.

One and only

Nick Watts makes the case for his Neptune fancy and runs through his ante-post portfolio

One of the best races at Cheltenham this year could be the Neptune Investment Management Novices' Hurdle and it is advantageous for ante-post punters that there is little doubt the market leaders will, injury permitting, take their places in the race.

The 2m5f contest has long been the nominated target for Pont Alexandre and **The New One** (below) and it promises to be a fantastic clash between two outstanding novices. Many punters seem to prefer the claims of the Willie Mullins-trained Pont Alexandre, but I'm in the opposite camp on this one and happy to be so.

The New One was a high-class bumper horse whose defeat of My Tent Or Yours at Aintree on Grand National day looks a brilliant piece of form in light of the latter's romp in the Betfair Hurdle at Newbury.

Nigel Twiston-Davies's five-year-old has progressed well over hurdles. Early wins at Newton Abbot and Cheltenham promised much, but it is his two more recent starts that marked him out as something special, albeit for different reasons.

At Warwick in January, on his return from a short break, The New One looked a class apart in winning a Grade 2 by 16 lengths. It was an eminently winnable contest but he did it impressively, never once coming off the bridle.

He was beaten on his latest start at Cheltenham, but in my view left

Ante-post diary

🐾 **Summer** Two go into the Cheltenham portfolio in the hope they can come back from injury. Grandouet is too big at 14-1 for the Champion Hurdle. He's likely to start at half that price if he gets to the race. Last Instalment is more risky at 20-1 for the Gold Cup but his form is good.

🐾 **November** It's always interesting to try to work out which of last season's hurdlers will take to fences, and Dynaste is backed for the RSA at 14-1 just before a smart chase debut at Cheltenham. A worrying aspect to his display is the speed he shows – could he be a Jewson horse rather than an RSA one?

Empiracle goes in at 25-1 for the Champion Bumper – his win at Huntingdon last month gets better with each look.

Our Vinnie is interesting in the Albert Bartlett at 20-1 after good runs at Cheltenham and Cork. Dynaste wins easily again but over 2m4f for the second time. The Feltham, apparently to be his next target, will tell us more.

🐾 **December** My Tent Or Yours looked good when beating Taquin Du Seuil at Ascot last month and is 20-1 for the Supreme. Although he's very keen in his races, there's no disguising his engine and he goes into the portfolio.

Grandouet makes his comeback in the International Hurdle, his first race for exactly a year. It's not easy, but he gives Zarkandar a good race conceding 4lb on testing ground. It's game on for the Champion Hurdle.

Any doubts about Dynaste staying are removed when he hoses up in the Feltham. He's now around 5-2 for the RSA and that must have become the more realistic aim for him now.

Our Vinnie continues his progress at Limerick by beating Pride Ofthe Parish in a Grade 3, giving the runner-up 6lb. He looks tough, classy and is improving, and his odds of winning the Albert Bartlett are contracting.

My Tent Or Yours is beaten at a muddy Newbury by stablemate Chatterbox. He drifts in the betting for the Supreme but the defeat can't really be held against him – he's a speed horse and conditions are atrocious. There'll be other days.

January Rival D'Estruval, a 16-1 shot for the National Hunt Chase, is next into the portfolio. He is being deliberately kept back for this race, as he is best fresh, and his form early in the season was good. Four miles will be a new venture for him, but he looks a strong stayer and won't fail through lack of stamina.

The Last Instalment Gold Cup dream is over as he gets injured again – it's the other leg this time. It was risky and it didn't work out, but generally the portfolio looks okay.

My Tent Or Yours rekindles Supreme hopes with an easy win at Huntingdon, beating Population easily. He's never in danger of defeat and is in a different class.

The portfolio is getting larger and Bostons Angel is next at 12-1 for the Cross Country Chase, which looks good each-way value. He lost his way over normal fences but seems rejuvenated by banks courses and is a classy horse to be running in cross-country chases.

Our Vinnie finishes third behind Pont Alexandre in a Grade 2 at Leopardstown. He's beaten a long way, but the 2m4f trip isn't far enough for him and he had to give away weight all round.

with his reputation enhanced. The ground was pretty bad and it was a day for grinding out results rather than showing class. Quickening in those conditions was seemingly impossible but that's what The New One did when he swept into an effortless lead rounding the home turn. He took lengths out of his field and looked home and dry, only to falter close home and lose out by a neck to the talented stayer At Fishers Cross.

It's my belief that on a better surface The New One would have won that race comfortably. Sam Twiston-Davies possibly went a touch too soon but he won't make that mistake again and, if Cheltenham dries up in March, The New One's turn of foot will be hard to match.

Another novice with a killer turn of foot is the impressive chaser **Dynaste** *(above)*. We don't yet know if it will be the Jewson or the RSA for him, but the longer race must be favourite and he will take an awful lot of beating.

Forget the comparisons with Grands Crus – beaten at 6-5 in the RSA for the David Pipe stable last year – because Dynaste is a stronger stayer and more straightforward than his stablemate. He looked right out of the top drawer when pulverising Hadrian's Approach, Third Intention and Molotof (all of whom have franked the form since) in the Feltham.

It's true that Feltham winners tend not to win the RSA, but there seems no good reason for that – it's just one of those curious anomalies

in racing. Dynaste is the best jumper and the fastest horse in the RSA and should win.

The Gold Cup has a solid favourite in Bobs Worth but I can't help thinking **Captain Chris** could have a big run in him and he looks overpriced.

Critics will point to the fact that he can't go left-handed but I'm not sure that's completely true. After all, he's won twice at Cheltenham, including the 2011 Arkle, where he easily beat the following season's Champion Chase winner, Finian's Rainbow. Not bad for a horse who can't go anti-clockwise.

Last season was a write-off for him but he still managed fourth place in the Ryanair Chase and he has looked right back to his best this season, including when all but winning the King George.

Our Vinnie is a speculative investment for the Albert Bartlett but there are sound reasons for supporting him. He's a strong and improving stayer who has won two Graded events in Ireland this season and was placed behind Pont Alexandre last time out at Leopardstown.

Admittedly he was well beaten, but he was attempting the impossible in conceding weight all round over a 2m4f trip well short of his best. The return to three miles will suit him and his trainer Charles Byrnes has an excellent record in the race. At 16-1 he's a fair shout.

🐎 *In the past 20
years just three RSA
Chase winners were
unbeaten over fences
and Denman (below)
is the only one in the
past decade*

33-1

*Countrywide Flame
last year was the
longest-priced winner
of the Triumph Hurdle
since the inception
of the Fred Winter
Hurdle in 2005 (every
winner before that had
been 9-1 or lower)*

New star for Twiston-Davies

Richard Birch explains why The New One is his
Neptune banker and selects his other big fancies

When Nigel Twiston-Davies was interviewed by Mick Fitzgerald in the Newton Abbot paddock last October prior to the runners cantering to the start, nobody could fail to notice the trainer was extremely nervous.

Considering he has twice tasted Grand National success and landed the Cheltenham Gold Cup with Imperial Commander in 2010, the fact he was sweating up badly ahead of a minor novice hurdle worth just £2,924 to the winner was intriguing.

After his 2-7 favourite The New One had romped home by 26 lengths, Twiston-Davies confided that the son of King's Theatre is potentially the best horse he has trained and that he had been petrified in case anything went wrong at the outset of a season he believed could end in Cheltenham glory.

That's some accolade, and I have no hesitation in nominating **The New One**, who is firmly on target for the Neptune Investment Management Novices' Hurdle, as my festival banker.

I thought the immensely likeable five-year-old, who combines a Rolls-Royce's cruising speed with a Ferrari's change of gear, enhanced his big-race claims despite a narrow defeat by At Fishers Cross in his Cheltenham trial in January.

Run that event ten times and you can rest assured The New One would win eight or even nine of them. Things merely conspired against him and his excellent partner Sam Twiston-Davies on the day.

The New One will go into the festival with all guns blazing and it will be an expensive disappointment if he fails to shoot down his opponents.

The markets seem to have underestimated the chance of a repeat victory in the CGA Foxhunter Chase by **Salsify**, who beat Chapoturgeon with more in hand than the one-length victory margin implies in last year's race.

Salsify beat his main Irish rival, Tammys Hill, in his final prep in the Raymond Smith Memorial Hunters Chase and, still only eight, it is perfectly reasonable to assume there is further improvement to come. He is confidently expected to confirm superiority over both Chapoturgeon and Tammys Hill to retain his crown.

Surely no race this season has had an easier winner than the Huntingdon bumper **Empiracle** took by seven lengths without needing even a nudge of Nick Scholfield's hands. The son of Kris Kin remains the subject of glowing reports from his trainer Jeremy Scott and, while he will be taking a big step up in class when he tackles the Weatherbys Champion Bumper, his style of running is tailor-made for this race.

If he is the horse Scott believes him to be, Empiracle will tank along to the bottom of the hill and show the necessary turn of foot to leave connections dreaming of next season when attention is turned to hurdles.

Rival D'Estruval has been meticulously laid out for the National Hunt Chase by Pauline Robson since romping to victory in a Kelso

Saphir Du Rheu looks just the type for the Fred Winter

novice chase in December. While that performance was visually impressive, it was his previous effort when an eight-length Carlisle runner-up to the talented Bold Sir Brian that firmly established his claims for the four-miler.

Always best fresh, Rival D'Estruval will go straight to Cheltenham without a prep run and his slick jumping and bottomless stamina give him the perfect attributes for this race.

Hurricane Fly clearly wasn't right last season. Willie Mullins believes he has him back in tip-top shape this year and, if that is the case, his Stan James Champion Hurdle rivals might as well stay in their stables.

Simonsig, one of the most exciting recruits to chasing in years, has the Racing Post Arkle Chase at his mercy, while it is worth keeping the JP McManus-owned novice chasers **Cantlow** and **Colour Squadron** on side in their respective handicaps.

Cantlow has long been seen as the type to excel at the festival, while Colour Squadron has twice been a huge eyecatcher in Newbury novice chases this winter, giving the impression he is being prepared to peak in March. Both have low mileage and remain open to colossal improvement.

Saphir Du Rheu looks just the type for the Fred Winter Juvenile Handicap Hurdle. He seemed to be going much faster at the finish than at any other stage in the race when spreadeagling Taunton opposition, headed by reasonable yardstick God Of The Kop, and could be well treated.

🐎 **Richard Birch** Much as I love Overturn, it's hard to see Simonsig getting turned over in the Arkle. If Colour Squadron contested the Jewson I would be confident of his ability to outrun his likely big odds and secure a top-three finish. Dynaste has done nothing wrong over fences and must take the beating in the RSA.

🐎 **Nick Watts** Dynaste has left a deep impression and has the RSA at his mercy against essentially slower opponents. Simonsig will win the Arkle as I'm not convinced Overturn is completely suited by Cheltenham – he's nought from three at the track. Aupcharlie looks as if he'll be suited by a drop in trip and can win the Jewson if he heads that way.

🐎 **Paul Kealy** Simonsig's jumping hasn't been put under scrutiny in a fast-run race and he's achieved much less than Sprinter Sacre had going into last year's Arkle yet is a similar price. I hope Overturn wins because he's a legend and jumps brilliantly. Aupcharlie (*below*) looks the one for the Jewson and I expect a good run at a price by Houblon Des Obeaux in the RSA.

Watch out for Alderwood

Johnny Ward has last year's County Hurdle winner high on his list of likely Irish handicappers

George Orwell's Animal Farm comes to mind when assessing the prospects of Irish handicappers at the festival. All Irish horses will be equal, but some will be more equal than others. That is to say, the key will be the marks allotted by the British handicapper.

Punters aplenty will be waiting to see how a few Irish horses are dealt with. An obvious one is **Alderwood**, last year's County Hurdle winner who went on to win a Grade 1 novice hurdle.

The record of Irish horses in Cheltenham handicap chases is worryingly bad and many are clearly harshly weighed for the festival. Alderwood ran off 135 on his only Irish handicap chase start and was beaten just over two lengths by a horse who seemed plenty high in the weights, so he really should not be any higher than 140 for the Grand Annual.

Intriguingly, he won the County Hurdle off 139. Tom Mullins knows that whatever he did to get the horse primed for Cheltenham last year can be relied upon again. He is likely to improve on his Irish maiden chase efforts, all of which were on heavy, and he jumps fine.

The profile of **Toner D'Oudairies** is quite similar to Alderwood's. He ran a blinder at the festival last year, travelling powerfully to finish a neck second off 137 in the Martin Pipe, when he traded at 1-3 in running. His best run over fences was his last one when second at Leopardstown and he looks really interesting if he goes for the Pulteney Novices' Handicap Chase. Ireland has won this race just once since its inception in 2005, but Toner D'Oudairies is capable of improving that record.

Ireland has won five of the last six County Hurdles and **Ted Veale**, a heavily backed third in the Boylesports Hurdle in January, is interesting. That race was won in 2011 by Final Approach, who followed up at Cheltenham, while 2008 County winner Silver Jaro had been third at Leopardstown.

Ted Veale was having his first try in a handicap at Leopardstown and shaped really well. He tanked through the race, prompting one in-running punter to back him at around 8-11, but got tired in the closing stages. Yielding ground at Cheltenham should be fine, as he stays a bit further too.

The Fred Winter is a race dear to me, as I backed its first winner, Dabiroun. I was in college at the time and a fiver each-way at 20-1 went a long way. Ireland snared the race again with What A Charm in 2011 and two wins from eight is a decent return, especially considering we hardly ever win the Triumph. Not many Irish runners for 2013 come to mind just yet but **Fatcatinthehat** is of interest.

Trainer Willie Mullins has other options for the Triumph and it would make sense if Fatcatinthehat was aimed at the handicap. He likes decent ground and has shown a decent level of ability on the Flat.

Hurdling has generally been straightforward for him, save for a fall when clear at the last at Punchestown. He has plenty of pace and the main

Fahamore looks the right type for the Pertemps Final

Tipster forum

Which novice chasers stand out in the Arkle, Jewson and RSA Chases?

Donn McClean It is difficult to see past Simonsig *(below)* in the Arkle. I think the Jewson is the perfect race for Aupcharlie. He just hasn't got three miles in two attempts this term, but he has bags of pace, is a super jumper and goes well on good ground. We know he can handle the track and Cheltenham Festival conditions. The pacy Dynaste may be vulnerable in the RSA Chase, which can turn into a real grueller, and that would suit Boston Bob or Back In Focus, whichever Team Mullins/Wylie choose to run. Super Duty could go well in the RSA at a big price if he takes his chance.

Tom Segal Simonsig wins the Arkle easily. Connections of Dynaste would be wise to opt for the Jewson as that race looks his for the taking, while Unioniste will be better in a strongly run race and his exquisite jumping will stand him in good stead in the RSA.

concern for Cheltenham is that he has a tendency to jump to his right.

Smaller Irish trainers can win at Cheltenham and there were memorable scenes last year when Salsify, nurtured in the small County Cork yard of Rodger Sweeney, beat 21 rivals under the trainer's son Colman to land the Foxhunter.

Salsify is a smart handicap chaser running against point-to-pointers, at least to this eye. He is capable of being ridden like a non-trier and sluicing through the field as if in a video game – visit the Racing Post website and see how far back he was for much of the Foxhunter last year. Encouragingly, he did much the same when scoring at Leopardstown in February at the expense of the useful Tammys Hill. Salsify ought to take a hell of a lot of beating at Cheltenham.

Eddie Harty is another trainer to note at the festival. He won the Supreme Novices' Hurdle with Captain Cee Bee, who memorably edged Binocular in a one-two for JP McManus, in 2008. The Harty-trained **Fahamore** is in the betting for the Pertemps Final and gives the impression of a reliable and progressive handicapper – exactly what you need in such a competitive race.

DON'T MISS A BEAT

Website Study form, compare prices and place bets
all in one place from our superb interactive cards

Twitter
@RacingPost
is the feed to
follow for all
the breaking
racing news

Facebook
/racingpost
Have your say
– vote on the
big topics and
enter exclusive
competitions

RACING POST

Tuesday, January 29, 2013

**PRICEWISE ON THE
RACING POST ARKLE**

Ante-post special with
form, ratings, trends and
running plans

**SIMPLE FOR
SIMONSIG?**

Find out who Tom Segal believes is the
value bet to topple the hot favourite

CARDS & FORM
Lingfield (AW)
Wolverhampton (AW)

MONDAY'S RESULTS
Kempton (AW)
Wolverhampton (AW)
Cagnes-sur-Mer (FR)

THE FESTIVAL
Ante-post Pricewise:
Racing Post Arkle

iPad Download our
great iPad app and
get the next day's
edition from 8pm
the night before

RACING POST

THE PULSE OF THE FESTIVAL

What do you
fancy for the
novice hurdles?

Richard Birch My Tent Or Yours tanked through the Betfair Hurdle like a future champion and will be a stone-cold certainty if he runs in the Supreme. The New One is my banker of the meeting in the Neptune and it's hard to see At Fishers Cross (below) finishing out of the first three in the Albert Bartlett.

Nick Watts Having put up My Tent Or Yours at 20-1 for the Supreme I see no reason to change tack after his romp at Newbury. However, my bet of the meeting is The New One in the Neptune. If the ground is anywhere near decent it wouldn't surprise me if he beat Pont Alexandre easily. Our Vinnie is a good each-way shout in the Albert Bartlett, while Our Conor was impressive at Leopardstown and can win the Triumph.

Paul Kealy I don't know what to make of My Tent Or Yours, but I'm not prepared to anoint him a superstar until he does it in a fast-run race. I'm a huge fan of Melodic Rendezvous, almost as keen on The New One in the Neptune, find At Fishers Cross pretty solid in the Albert Bartlett and like Our Conor in the Triumph, but not enough to back him at 6-1.

Horses for a special course
Dave Randall identifies a group of festival candidates with good Cheltenham form

If significant previous Cheltenham form is defined by a win or place at any meeting on the course, or a top-six finish at a previous festival, then 29 of the 54 winners at the last two Cheltenham Festivals arrived with such credentials. That offers compelling evidence of the importance of Cheltenham form, especially when taking into account that Irish raiders are unlikely to have had the opportunity to gain those credentials before the festival.

Irish-trained winners accounted for seven of the 25 who didn't already possess significant Cheltenham form, as they were venturing to race in Britain for the first time. An alternative pointer to consider with such runners is whether they have strong form at left-handed, undulating Navan.

This article aims to identify horses with a well-established or developing affinity with Cheltenham. Sometimes, as with Bobs Worth, the love affair is obvious, but with others some educated guesswork is required using factors such as Racing Post Ratings, running styles and ground preferences.

BOBS WORTH The long-time Gold Cup favourite has Cheltenham form figures of 1111. He won two 2m4½f novice hurdles in January 2011 before landing the Albert Bartlett Novices' Hurdle and the RSA Chase (at a then peak RPR 166) at the 2011 and 2012 festivals. His ready success in the Hennessy Gold Cup at Newbury in December took him to an RPR of 174 and his uncomplicated style – he simply travels, jumps and stays effectively – is perfectly suited to Cheltenham. It may prove a blessing in disguise that he was forced to miss a slog through the mud in the Argento Chase at Cheltenham in January after a tracheal wash produced less than positive results.

CLOSE HOUSE It is always comforting if your chosen horse for a Cheltenham Festival handicap is trained by David Pipe and even more so when, as in the case of Close House, there is good course form there too. The six-year-old son of Generous has some eyecatching form and significantly two of his best three RPRs were achieved at Cheltenham, first when he was 23-lengths fourth behind Simonsig in last year's Neptune Novices' Hurdle after staying on well up the run-in, and then when he opened his current campaign with a fine second in a 2m5f handicap hurdle at the Open meeting in November. He improved again to score over 2m6f at Wincanton on heavy ground in December and a step up to 3m for the Pertemps Final looks the logical move. Pipe won that contest with Cheltenham specialist Buena Vista in consecutive years in 2010 and 2011 and Close House is a best-priced 14-1 for this year's renewal.

MELODIC RENDEZVOUS A previous good run at Cheltenham is often in the background of Supreme Novices' Hurdle winners (three

Module, a Cheltenham winner, is interesting for the Jewson

of the last five British-trained scorers had such credentials) and it is encouraging when it is as good as the win posted by Melodic Rendezvous over 2m1f in December. Showing excellent progress from his debut hurdles victory at Exeter in October, the Jeremy Scott-trained gelding quickened inside the final furlong and stayed on strongly despite the heavy ground to earn an RPR of 133. Having franked the form by landing the Grade 1 Tolworth Novices' Hurdle at Sandown and a Listed novice hurdle at Exeter, he looks capable of improving if he gets a decent surface at the festival.

MODULE "He's been running against the best in France, is a really progressive horse and will make a cracking chaser next season. He's probably a 2m5f horse." Those were Tom George's thoughts following Module's British debut success in a 2m1f handicap hurdle at Cheltenham in January 2012 on pretty decent ground, when he skipped up the hill to earn an RPR of 141.

He failed to make his intended target in last year's Coral Cup but may be able to make up for lost time at this year's festival over fences. He fell four out when going strongly on his chase debut at Exeter in October before recording good wins on heavy ground at Newbury and Leicester. The obvious target is the Grade 2 Jewson Novices' Chase.

MONKSLAND Cheltenham may be the key to unlocking the potential of this lightly raced six-year-old when he returns to the track for the World Hurdle, for which he has been among the favourites since Big Buck's was ruled out by injury. On his only previous visit he was third – the worst placing in his form figures of 1113121 under rules – but it was an excellent third behind Simonsig in last year's Neptune Novices' Hurdle over 2m5f and he had legitimate excuses for not making more of a race of it. He was caught in a pocket when attempting to take closer order after four out and was hampered when Cotton Mill ran out and unseated his jockey in front of him at the second-last. He rallied to record a then peak RPR of 148 and has improved again in his second season over hurdles. He saw out three miles well when landing his second Grade 2 hurdle of the season at Leopardstown in December and is open to further improvement under potentially ideal conditions at Cheltenham.

ROCK ON RUBY Last year's Champion Hurdle winner has Cheltenham form figures of 12213 and it is notable that on the first four of those runs he matched or bettered his previous-best RPR. The clear pick of those displays came in that strongly run Champion Hurdle last March (RPR 171) and, although his worst figure (RPR 157) came on his most recent visit to Cheltenham in December, it was on unsuitable heavy ground and in the circumstances third place in the International Hurdle was a respectable effort. He is tactically versatile, ideally suited by a decent surface and stays 2m5f, and he looks unlikely to be out of the frame given his ability to travel into his races over the 2m½f trip of the Champion.

THE DRUIDS NEPHEW The six-year-old son of King's Theatre

Monksland heads for home at Down Royal

Essential info

A quick guide to festival betting

In the shops Most betting shops open earlier during the festival, usually at 8.30-9am

Free bets Many bookmakers offer free bets for new customers during the festival, but remember to check the terms and conditions. For a great range of free bets, go to racingpost.com

Compare the odds Find the best odds on your selections from a range of bookmakers by using the odds comparison table at racingpost.com

Early prices Be quick if you want to take an advertised price on the morning of the race – most firms hold their prices for a maximum of 15 minutes when their shops open and some offer no guarantee

Each-way Bookmakers often extend their place terms during the festival. In the big handicaps, it can pay to look for firms offering a quarter the odds for the first five places. The standard each-way terms are a quarter the odds for the first four places

Best odds Several firms offer 'best odds guaranteed', which means they will match the SP if you have taken an early price and your selection wins at bigger odds

Non-runner no bet Most bookmakers offer this concession from early March – some earlier on the bigger races. In this case, your stake is returned if your selection doesn't run.

Specials A vast range of special bets is available at the festival, including perennial favourites such as top trainer, top jockey and the number of Irish winners

posted a then peak RPR of 137 with an encouraging 18-length sixth in last year's Albert Bartlett Novices' Hurdle on his only previous visit to Cheltenham. An Irish point winner on good ground, he won over hurdles on good ground over 2m5f at Kempton in January last year. He recorded his best RPR yet on his third outing over fences this term when winning by ten lengths over 2m5f on soft ground at Wincanton in January. He has shown a tendency to jump left in his three chases on right-handed tracks and there is the prospect of further improvement back at left-handed Cheltenham. This solid jumper has an interesting profile for the Pulteney Novices' Handicap Chase and makes each-way appeal at around 16-1 off a mark of 135.

FAR WEST Few horses will turn up at the festival with such impressive form at Cheltenham this season as Triumph Hurdle candidate Far West, who has won twice at the track by an aggregate of 26 lengths. He recorded a peak RPR of 145 at the November Open meeting and did not have to run to that level in an easier contest the following month (RPR 141). Rolling Star recorded an RPR of 149 at Cheltenham trials day on his British debut for Nicky Henderson, but 6-1 favouritism may have been going a tad far and the Paul Nicholls-trained Far West is preferred on likely better ground.

CANTLOW It is hard to be sure which race Cantlow will contest at the festival, but his two-length third in last year's Pertemps Final (with a then peak RPR of 147) will entitle him to respect whichever race is chosen by trainer Paul Webber. He posted an RPR of 149 on his fourth start over fences at Taunton in January and, despite his novice status, would make some appeal off a mark of 143 in the JLT Specialty Handicap Chase.

Festival Q & A

The major off-course bookmakers offer their views of the leading contenders and the betting markets

Is Bobs Worth a deserving Gold Cup favourite?

Bet365 *Pat Cooney* His Hennessy win is the best performance over fences this season, so he merits his place as market leader on that form. Silviniaco Conti fits in the 'done nothing wrong' category and I think The Giant Bolster will be a lively outsider. Ignore his winter form and base his claims on spring form and he'll be on the premises.

Betfred *Matt Hulmes* Bobs Worth looks very solid at the top of the market. He's unbeaten at Cheltenham and running left-handed, he stays, jumps well and is the horse to beat. Sir Des Champs should be even better if he gets better ground. He could be the biggest danger to the favourite. Silviniaco Conti has shown all his best form on flat tracks. At a bigger price Cape Tribulation has the staying qualities and course form to outrun his odds.

BetVictor *Rob Joyce* Bobs Worth has excellent form at the track, is bombproof with regard to ground, jumps soundly if not spectacularly and stays forever. He's entitled to improve again on his Hennessy win on better ground and ticks the right boxes. I'm convinced it's a two-horse race with Sir Des Champs.

Blue Square *Alan Alger* The form of his Hennessy win puts him right there with a market leader's chance. He's unbeaten at Cheltenham and always seems to find that little bit more in his races, which is essential for this type of race in which the pace keeps building. The market tells you his biggest dangers are Silviniaco Conti and Sir Des Champs, and Long Run will be thereabouts at the finish.

Boylesports *Alan Reilly* We have taken a positive view of Bobs Worth all winter and have been most keen to keep him on our side ever since he tanked up the straight in the Hennessy. Nothing has happened to change our view. Sir Des Champs jumped better in the Irish Hennessy, but he needed to if he is to be considered a genuine Gold Cup horse. Better ground will be critical for him. If allowed to take his chance First Lieutenant could be the each-way value in the race. Although well held by Bobs Worth at Newbury, he jumps for fun and has to be thereabouts.

Coral *James Knight* Bobs Worth's form is solid, but he's not one to back ante-post, having missed the Argento with a setback. I think he'll be the same price or bigger on the day. I'm not sure there is much more to come from Silviniaco Conti and Sir Des Champs is short enough on what he has achieved. I'd be looking to the likes of The Giant Bolster and Imperial Commander at the prices.

Ladbrokes *Brian Miller* Bobs Worth is a worthy favourite in what is shaping to be a tremendous renewal of the race. His Hennessy win showed us he has improved from last year. Nigel Twiston-Davies has done an amazing job to get Imperial Commander back on the track and he is perhaps the best each-way value in the race.

Paddy Power *Brendan Duke* Bobs Worth is the most likely winner. If the likely better ground at Cheltenham doesn't sharpen up Sir Des Champs' jumping then I can only see Silviniaco Conti putting it up to Bobs Worth. Long Run will be placed at best, with Imperial Commander a prime candidate to bounce. The guaranteed stamina and festival form of Cape Tribulation makes him the most attractive of the outsiders.

William Hill *Kate Miller* Bobs Worth is a worthy favourite. Lightly raced with form in the book, proven around Cheltenham, the best festival trainer there has ever been and untapped potential too – what's not to like? At the prices I can see The Giant Bolster running another big race, but my personal pick and the most likely winner is Sir Des Champs. He has won at the last two festivals and is being primed for the Gold Cup by master trainer Willie Mullins.

Will Hurricane Fly regain his crown in the Champion Hurdle?

Bet365 He's the most likely winner, but he got warm in the preliminaries before the race last year and I'll wait to see him at the start this time. I can't see his price shortening between now and the off, so it's prudent to wait. A blanket will probably cover Grandouet, Rock On Ruby and Zarkandar at the finish, with Rock On Ruby possibly the biggest threat to Hurricane Fly.

Betfred The main doubt about Hurricane Fly is his disappointing run last year. Maybe he was given too much to do, but he has been beating the same small fields on appalling ground in Ireland and there is not much value left in his 6-4 quote. Zarkandar and Rock On Ruby look certain to be thereabouts at the business end and don't give up on former champion Binocular. The Irish Champion Hurdle was never going to suit, and it was only a satisfactory run, but reports suggest he is looking as good as ever at home.

BetVictor Hurricane Fly is the one to beat, although he hasn't really told us a great deal despite winning three Grade 1s this winter as they were all sub-standard small-field races on soft or heavy ground. If he isn't quite at his best I think Zarkandar is rock solid. I was disappointed with Rock On Ruby, despite winning, at Doncaster.

Blue Square I opposed Hurricane Fly last year on the basis of his price and once again it looks like there will be better bets elsewhere. Zarkandar would be my bet at the current prices. If it turned up really soft I would want to be against Rock On Ruby.

Boylesports Hurricane Fly's chances have improved not by what he has achieved on the track this season, but by the tragic losses of Darlan and arguably Go Native. Has he done anything more this season compared with last season? I'm not sure. He faces some stiff competition from Rock On Ruby and it'll be harder still if connections decide to run My Tent Or Yours.

Talking point

Trends against leading Cup fancies

Will it prove a blessing or a curse that Gold Cup favourite Bobs Worth was forced to miss a slog through the mud in the Argento Chase, which was his intended prep for the big day at Cheltenham?

The question arose after a tracheal wash prior to the Argento revealed Bobs Worth was not quite 100 per cent. It had been trainer Nicky Henderson's intention to give the Cheltenham specialist a prep run at his favourite track but now he heads to the Gold Cup after only one run this season – his impressive victory in the Hennessy Gold Cup.

In two respects, it will be a magnificent training feat by Henderson if Bobs Worth is successful. Conventional wisdom has always been that Gold Cup contenders should have at least two races as part of their build-up, the last of which should be in late December (most often the King George VI Chase) or around four to six weeks before Cheltenham.

That approach has held firm even with modern training methods, but Bobs Worth will buck the trends if he can return victorious from his layoff since December 1 and land the Gold Cup on only his second run of the season.

Another strong Gold Cup trend confronts Silviniaco Conti. Paul Nicholls's main hope lacks any course experience, yet most winners of the Gold Cup (and indeed of the festival's other big prizes) have performed well at a previous festival or at least won at one of the track's other meetings. The last Gold Cup winner without course experience was Imperial Call in 1996 and the only other in the past two decades was Jodami in 1993.

Coral Hurricane Fly looks too short to me and I'm not sure beating up the same horses again and again in Ireland has proved he is back to his best. Rock On Ruby and Zarkandar look much better bets at the prices.

Ladbrokes It will take a mighty effort to stop Hurricane Fly. Willie Mullins repeatedly stated he was never happy with him last season and the horse seems to have left whatever was troubling him behind. I like Zarkandar – others in the race may travel better but he keeps finding and he would be my pick.

Paddy Power It's extremely rare for any Cheltenham winner to regain their crown and on that basis I'll say Hurricane Fly won't win. I don't think last year's malaise was satisfactorily explained, so it could recur. Rock On Ruby looks solid, but if My Tent Or Yours runs he will win.

William Hill Hurricane Fly is the most likely winner. His preparation has gone well and he appears to have got over whatever was ailing him last March. Is he a good bet at the prices? Not for me. Rock On Ruby has been brought along steadily all season and he will be hard to keep off the podium. There is little between the terrier-like Zarkandar and Grandouet on the book and both will surely feature in the finish. From those at the head of the market, the only one I would be against is Hurricane Fly – and that is based purely on his price.

Can anything stop Sprinter Sacre in the Champion Chase?

Bet365 No. He's one of the favourites I'll be cheering on, as he's a joy to watch. The 'betting without' market may offer some value, with perhaps Wishfull Thinking the type to come from off the pace to be best of the rest.

Betfred This looks destined to be the biggest winning margin of the

*Sprinter Sacre
leads Simonsig and
Finian's Rainbow
at Seven Barrows*

Talking point
Past glories are
difficult to rekindle
....

The history books illustrate the difficulty of regaining one of the big Cheltenham titles once it has been lost, yet this year Hurricane Fly tries to regain the Champion Hurdle crown he took in 2011, while 2010 winner Binocular is also back for another attempt; Long Run (the 2011 winner) and Imperial Commander (2010) make fresh bids for the Gold Cup; and 2011 winner Sizing Europe could oppose Sprinter Sacre in the Queen Mother Champion Chase.

The list of winners who have regained the titles is short. Kauto Star in 2009 became the only horse to take back the Cheltenham Gold Cup after a two-year gap since his previous triumph and only one hurdler has done likewise in the Champion Hurdle (Comedy Of Errors in 1973 and 1975). Two Champion Chase winners – Royal Relief (1972 and 1974) and Moscow Flyer (2003 and 2005) – have regained the title.

In those three feature races, 39 horses have tried in the past 20 years to bridge a gap of two or more years since their previous triumph (including the three title-holders of 2000 who returned two years later after the foot-and-mouth outbreak) and only Moscow Flyer and Kauto Star have been successful.

Among the big names to have failed when well fancied are Kauto Star (on two more occasions), Denman (twice), Binocular (in last year's Champion Hurdle), Hardy Eustace, Istabraq, Master Minded and Viking Flagship.

Moscow Flyer and Kauto Star were both favourite for their second triumph, but 15 of the attempts that ended in defeat were at odds of 5-1 or lower.

festival as he looks a lot further clear than the ratings would suggest. It's hard to gauge which horses will turn up to take him on, but Sanctuaire has no other festival entries, shows his best form in the spring and could take second if he's on a going day

BetVictor No. He's different class to the opposition, although Sizing Europe, if he bypasses the Ryanair, might give him a race.

Blue Square Sprinter Sacre looks to have only the fences in opposition. I don't think any of the others will get near him. The restrictive price of the favourite should produce a fantastic each-way bet on last year's winner, Finian's Rainbow.

Boylesports Quite simply, no. He could be the best two-miler we've ever seen. For Barry Geraghty to compare him to Moscow Flyer at this stage of his career speaks volumes.

Coral It's hard to see him being threatened now that Flemenstar is out. It's a shame as I'm not sure we've found out how good Sprinter Sacre really is yet and this is likely to be another procession. Mail De Bievre could be the most interesting opponent if he is supplemented.

Ladbrokes He looks a very special horse and deserves the superlatives lavished on him this season. Sizing Europe, if taking this option, looks sure to run a solid race again.

Paddy Power Only an act of God can stop Sprinter Sacre. I'm loath to call Wishfull Thinking solid, but with Sizing Europe and Finian's Rainbow likely to duck the challenge he might be the one left standing to follow Sprinter Sacre home.

William Hill No horse is unbeatable, but his price assumes he's been and won a Champion Chase before, which he hasn't. Until he wins a Champion Chase it's nonsense to compare him with the best.

🐎The winner of the
County Hurdle has
been Irish-trained in
five of the past six
seasons

🐎David Pipe has
had a winner, two
runners-up, a third
and a fourth from ten
runners in the Fred
Winter

1998

The last year in which
the winner of the
Grand Annual Chase
carried more than 11st,
when Edredon Bleu
won with 11st 6lb

🐎Riverside Theatre
(below) last year
became the first horse
to take the Ryanair
Chase with his first
win over fences at
Cheltenham. Six of the
previous seven winners
had already landed a
Graded chase at the
course

What do you fancy for the World Hurdle without Big Buck's in the field?

Bet365 I like Monksland. He won well on soft ground on his first try at three miles and has the potential to improve again. Better ground would also help. It looks a wide-open contest and I wouldn't rule out a rejuvenated Get Me Out Of Here at a price.

Betfred Although he still has a bit to find on the figures, Monksland stands out at the head of the market. He is one of the few who has definitely had this race as his target all season and his excellent victory at Christmas proved he is improving all the time. Reve De Sivola looks the likeliest danger. At a fair price Get Me Out of Here may put in a performance.

BetVictor Willie Mullins could run Quevega if she comes out of the Mares' Hurdle in one piece and he did win two races with Simenon at Royal Ascot last year. Given our non-runner free bet option she has been the best-backed horse in the race.

Blue Square Get Me Out Of Here and Smad Place are my fancies at decent each-way prices. Smad Place was up against it as a five-year-old last season and he can improve on his third place.

Boylesports It looks like being a re-run of the Cleeve Hurdle. Tactics will be key, as Reve De Sivola arguably stays better than Oscar Whisky. Like many, the chances of Oscar Whisky will improve on better ground. They are very hard to separate.

Coral As long as the ground isn't too soft, Oscar Whisky probably just about has the class to win against this lot – assuming Quevega goes for the easy option again. She would have an outstanding chance of winning the World Hurdle if they fancied giving her more than an exercise gallop in the mares' race.

Ladbrokes In an open race I would go for Oscar Whisky. He is high class at two and a half miles but proved he stays three miles at Cheltenham despite being out of his ground. If the ground does eventually dry out, his turn of foot could be decisive.

Paddy Power Bog Warrior seems to have recaptured his novice chase form and his jumping suggests he prefers going left-handed. If his trainer is happy with the ground he will do for me.

William Hill It's a race with more than a whiff of a result about it. Smad Place could well outrun his odds and it wouldn't surprise me if he took the crown after his good third as a five-year-old last season. If spring arrives in time for the festival Get Me Out Of Here could be an unexpected player.

What do you fancy for the novice hurdles?

Bet365 My Tent Or Yours looks a banker for the Supreme, Pont Alexandre is the hot horse for the Neptune and Ballycasey has a solid chance in the Albert Bartlett. All three represent top stables and are sure to be in peak condition on the day. We'll look to oppose At

Fishers Cross in the Albert Bartlett if it's good ground – soft ground looks essential for him.

Betfred The best of the novices could be in the final race, the Albert Bartlett. I really like Ballycasey, who has not come off the bridle in his two novice hurdles and could be Willie Mullins's only runner in the race from a department that has immense strength in depth at his stable. The Neptune could be a decent duel between two impressive novices in Pont Alexandre, who has won with imperious ease twice in Ireland, and The New One, who lost out only to a battle-hardened stayer last time out and will be better suited by the quicker Old course. JP McManus holds the key to the Supreme and I believe Jezki may come out on top. Un Atout may be the overrated horse in the novice hurdles as he could be caught out for speed if the ground dries out.

BetVictor My Tent Or Yours looked a future Champion Hurdle winner at Newbury and he looks a banker in the Supreme. I fancy Taquin Du Seuil for the Neptune and Ballycasey for the Albert Bartlett. Pont Alexandre could be anything but all his form has been on soft or heavy ground and he showed a slight tendency to jump out to his right last time. He looks worth taking on, although he could be special when sent over fences.

Blue Square Jessica Harrington says Jezki will be better on drier ground and he's likely to get that at the festival. On the clock he'll take a lot of beating in the Supreme. In the Albert Bartlett I like At Fishers Cross, particularly after the way he handled the hill at Cheltenham last time. If he goes for the Neptune I'd fancy him there instead, with Champagne Fever the alternative in either of the races where At Fishers Cross doesn't turn up. In the Triumph the form of the trial that Far West won in November looks the best on offer.

Boylesports My Tent Or Yours should win the Supreme if connections take the novice route. Rolling Star has long been touted as the Seven Barrows Triumph horse and didn't disappoint on his debut when winning with a fair bit in hand. Ballycasey has been aimed at the Albert Bartlett for some time and his stablemate Pont Alexandre has done all that has been asked of him to be favourite for the Neptune, although at the price I'd be a layer. I think The New One's form is the best to date.

Coral My Tent Or Yours is possibly the most talented hurdler in training and should win the Supreme. Our Conor looked a bit special at Leopardstown and can win the Triumph. The Neptune and Albert Bartlett can go to The New One and At Fishers Cross.

Ladbrokes I've always been a big fan of Jezki, whose trainer insists he will improve on better ground. He's shown a high enough level of form already and any improvement would make him difficult to beat in the Supreme. In the Neptune you would have to side with Pont Alexandre, who won really well last time, doing it the hard way against a strong headwind in an exceptional time. At Fishers Cross looks an ideal sort for the Albert Bartlett. Our Conor was most impressive at Leopardstown in the Spring Juvenile Hurdle, but the Triumph looks too hard to call at present.

Talking point

Take short prices at your peril

Runners priced at 3-1 or lower once again returned a level-stake loss in 2012 – the ninth consecutive festival at which it proved costly to back the hottest fancies.

Fifteen runners were priced in that bracket last year and only five were successful – Sprinter Sacre at 8-11 in the Arkle, Quevega at 4-7 in the Mares' Hurdle, Simonsig at 2-1 in the Neptune, Sir Des Champs at 3-1 in the Jewson and Big Buck's at 5-6 in the World Hurdle.

The shortest-priced failures were Hurricane Fly (4-6 in the Champion Hurdle), Sizing Europe (4-5 Champion Chase), Grands Crus (6-5 RSA Chase) and Boston Bob (6-5 Albert Bartlett Novices' Hurdle).

Backers at short prices are on shaky ground away from the Grade 1 and 2 races – the last winner at 3-1 or lower in lesser company was Heads Onthe Ground in the 2007 Cross Country Chase (there have been 18 losers in that category since then).

The festival's handicaps rarely reward backers at short prices, with only one winner from 13 runners at 3-1 or lower in the past decade.

Races restricted to amateur riders can be costly too, although last year two of them were won by favourites (Teaforthree at 5-1 in the National Hunt Chase and Sunnyhillboy at 13-2 in the Kim Muir). In the amateur races in the past decade, none of the seven runners sent off at 3-1 or lower was successful.

Among the Grade 1 races, the Champion Bumper often has an overbet favourite and the last seven market leaders have finished 0833062 (two were 5-2 and two 3-1).

Vital statistics

Paddy Power My Tent Or Yours looks the best two-mile hurdler in training and even in a cracking renewal of the Supreme he should win comfortably. Pont Alexandre looks a serious talent and has an action that suggests better ground will not be an issue. Ballycasey brings strong bumper form to the Albert Bartlett and has done nothing wrong this term. Our Conor has a great attitude and that, combined with his slick jumping, can see him home in the Triumph. Both Jezki in the Supreme and Rolling Star in the Triumph will need to brush up their jumping to justify tight-looking prices.

William Hill It's very hard to knock the chances of My Tent Or Yours in the Supreme. Of his likely rivals, I have regard for Melodic Rendezvous and if that one goes for the Neptune he will be a major player. Pont Alexandre looked awesome in his wins in Ireland on bad ground but may be vulnerable on better going at the festival. Chatterbox is an interesting novice and would be a big runner if he goes for the Neptune. In the Albert Bartlett, you've got to like At Fishers Cross. He impressed me, and Tony McCoy, when outstaying The New One on trials day in January.

Which novice chasers stand out in the Arkle, Jewson and RSA Chases?

Bet365 The Arkle is a match between Simonsig and Overturn – the rest don't count. The Jewson is the ideal race for Captain Conan. He looks a true two-and-a-half-miler. The RSA has just the one class horse for the trip and that's Dynaste.

Betfred Overturn looks a real decent Arkle candidate and can serve it up to Simonsig. He will battle all the way to the line and the favourite will have to be every bit as good as people think to get past. The Jewson seems to be the weakest of the three novice chases, but it provides a good opportunity for Aupcharlie. At a price in the RSA I like the claims of Jim Culloty's Lord Windermere. He has run two solid races in Graded company over a slightly shorter trip.

BetVictor Simonsig is as exciting as Sprinter Sacre, Boston Bob showed guts as well as ability when winning the Dr PJ Moriarty at Leopardstown and Dynaste can defy the appalling record of Feltham winners in the RSA.

Blue Square Tom George's Majala looks a nice each-way bet in the Arkle. In the Jewson we can forgive Arvika Ligeonniere's fall last time out and he can at least place. They might take each other on in the Arkle and I'd want to be with Majala at the prices. The RSA Chase could go the way of Rocky Creek, whose Warwick win was mightily impressive.

Boylesports Although he goes into the Arkle with less than the desired experience Simonsig is very hard to oppose. Oscars Well will need to jump much better to have a chance in the Jewson but is capable and Aupcharlie shouldn't be ruled out as he felt the impact of a hard race at Christmas when beaten at Naas last time.

Coral I can't really see Simonsig not winning the Arkle. Dynaste looks

Majala is fancied at a big price in the Arkle by Blue Square

a more convincing stayer than Grands Crus, but Hadrian's Approach might get much closer to him than at Kempton as the stiffer track will suit. The Jewson is open – I'd run Unioniste as I think he will get outstayed in the RSA.

Ladbrokes Simonsig has done nothing but impress but I think Overturn can win the Arkle. He jumps well and keeps finding at the business end of a race. I have a suspicion that Oscars Well could run a big race in the Jewson. He has always had the potential to make a good chaser and this might be the ideal race for him. I'd be happy to row in with the favourite Dynaste in the RSA.

Paddy Power Simonsig will win the Arkle. Aupcharlie will improve on the likely better ground and shouldn't be far away in the Jewson. Only stamina failure can get Dynaste beaten in the RSA and unlike Grands Crus he wasn't curling up in the closing stages of the Feltham.

William Hill Most years Overturn would be a justifiably short-priced favourite to win the Arkle. He possesses all the attributes you look for in an Arkle winner, but this is no ordinary year - the mighty Simonsig

Talking point
Can Bobs Worth follow up RSA win?

Going from RSA Chase victory to Gold Cup success was a feat last achieved by Denman in 2007 and 2008 and Bobs Worth has followed a similar path in his bid to complete the double.

Like Denman, he ran well in a staying novice hurdle at the festival (he won the Albert Bartlett, whereas Denman was runner-up in what is now the Neptune) and then returned the following year to take the RSA. Since then, he has emulated Denman by landing the Hennessy in his first season as a senior chaser.

The gruelling nature of the RSA Chase meant it was once viewed as a graveyard for Cheltenham Gold Cup hopefuls, but the recent record is more than respectable. Three of the last ten RSA winners to attempt the double have been successful, going back to Garrison Savannah (1990 and 1991), and the overall record in that period is 136P31P195. In addition, two placed horses from the RSA Chase (Mr Mulligan and Long Run) have won the Gold Cup the following year.

If we take the betting as a guide to which RSA winners had enhanced their reputation leading up to the Gold Cup – as Bobs Worth has done – the record looks even better. Four of the previous year's RSA winners were sent off at less than 10-1 and finished 1P13.

The most high-profile failure was Florida Pearl, who in 1999 was the only RSA winner in recent history to go off Gold Cup favourite (5-2) but was only third behind See More Business. But the other two shortest-priced RSA winners (Denman at 9-4 and Looks Like Trouble at 9-2) were successful.

is around. He was always going to be a chaser and has been faultless to date. Dynaste travels, jumps and has a turn of foot – he's hard to fault for the RSA. Captain Conan is the one to beat in the Jewson. Although he wasn't impressive at Sandown, he is proven at Cheltenham.

What are the biggest losers in your book?

Bet365 We're looking okay at present, but we have three concerns. Sir Des Champs in the Gold Cup is our main headache – we've laid him at an average price of 7-1 – followed by The New One (laid at 12-1 in the Neptune) and Jezki at 7-1 in the Supreme.

Betfred Our biggest losers currently are Cinders And Ashes in the Champion Hurdle, Dynaste in the RSA Chase and Silviniaco Conti in the Gold Cup.

BetVictor Mail De Bievre in the Gold Cup – we were happy to see him labour in the Denman Chase at Newbury – and Pont Alexandre in the Neptune. If My Tent Or Yours and Simonsig have already won on the first day I'm concerned about the liabilities going on to Hurricane Fly in the Champion Hurdle.

Blue Square Punters have really got stuck into Hurricane Fly in the Champion Hurdle. In the Supreme we have seen plenty of interest in Jezki. It looks like our festival is make or break on day one.

Boylesports Golantilla has been the talking horse in Ireland for several months and since it was confirmed he would be joining Tony Martin the gamble has really taken off to such an extent that he is by far our worst result. Sir Des Champs is a similar take-out figure.

Coral We have been against Hurricane Fly for most of the season, so he is our worst result by design.

Ladbrokes Jezki in the Supreme, The New One in the Neptune and Sir Des Champs in the Gold Cup. We aren't uncomfortable with any of our current positions, although we face some possible hefty payouts.

Paddy Power Hurricane Fly followed at some distance by Sir Des Champs, Boston Bob and The New One. We're not massively worried – we wanted to lay them.

William Hill We have four main losers in the books on the principal races – Hurricane Fly in the Champion Hurdle, Sir Des Champs and Bobs Worth in the Gold Cup and Rolling Star in the Triumph. From a bookmaking perspective, we took on 'The Fly' in 2012 and got a result. In the Gold Cup we are happy to have the front two in the book and the Triumph looks an open renewal, so our Rolling Star position is not a major concern.

Who are the ones to watch from Ireland?

Bet365 I like the way Our Conor travels in his races and he has a big chance in the Triumph. Salsify looked back in business at Leopardstown and will be tough to beat in the Foxhunter. I'm still undecided about Boston Bob's chase form and he may be vulnerable in his chosen race at the likely prices. The only Irish banker is Quevega, and they'll also win the Cross Country Chase.

Betfred Our Conor looked very good at Leopardstown and has done nothing wrong. I can see Jezki being the traditional Irish opening-race steamer, or perhaps Golantilla in the Bumper.

BetVictor I'm taken with Golantilla in the Champion Bumper, although it looks a hot race. Willie Mullins has been well supported to be the leading trainer and he looks to have a strong hand. Our Conor was impressive at Leopardstown and wherever you look you see fancied Irish horses. The Supreme used to be an Irish benefit but Jezki and Un Atout will have to be outstanding to beat My Tent Or Yours. Champagne Fever didn't impress at Leopardstown and I can't have Our Vinnie at any price in the Albert Bartlett.

Blue Square I like Arvika Ligeonniere and Jezki. Quevega is always the Irish banker and she will once again take plenty of beating in her race. The gambles that develop on the day of the race are usually worth taking on.

Boylesports Alderwood. If he gets better ground he will have a great chance in the Grand Annual. Pont Alexandre could be overrated and represents no value in the Neptune. We're desperately looking to get Golantilla beaten in the Bumper.

Coral Willie Mullins has a really strong team and he should be only slightly bigger than Nicky Henderson for top trainer. Quevega should win and Our Conor looks strong in the Triumph. Some of the lads in the office like Rebel Fitz at a price in the Champion Hurdle.

Ladbrokes Quevega will be many people's idea of the banker in the Mares' Hurdle. Pont Alexandre and Ballycasey are two at better prices.

Paddy Power Pont Alexandre strikes me as the Irish banker, but I suspect it's Hurricane Fly who will capture hearts and minds. A repeat of last year's effort should see Salsify home in the Foxhunter. Jezki and Hurricane Fly are vulnerable.

William Hill With the likes of Hurricane Fly, Quevega, Sir Des Champs, Pont Alexandre, Boston Bob and Ballycasey, Willie Mullins has a serious battalion of equine talent. Of those at the head of the markets, the one I feel could struggle is Ballycasey in the Albert Bartlett. My Irish banker is Salsify in the Foxhunter. His recent win at Leopardstown from a strong field is the best hunter chase form in Britain and Ireland.

Give us a value bet for the festival

Bet365 I'm hoping First Lieutenant misses the Gold Cup and goes for the Ryanair Chase. He's good enough and the trip may just be perfect.

Betfred Get Me Out of Here at 20-1 for the World Hurdle. He loves the place and has the ability to spring a surprise. I'm interested in Fruity O'Rooney for the three-mile handicap chase off a mark 1lb lower than when he was second in the race last year.

BetVictor Leave the best till last – Oh Crick in the Grand Annual. He won the race in 2009 and is beginning to look well handicapped.

Blue Square I like Tom George's Majala in the Arkle and 33-1 looks a big price. Historically it's not a race for an outsider to win but he looks a good bet to snatch a place with the front two in the market taking up plenty of the percentage.

Boylesports Shutthefrontdoor in the Pertemps. He won with an awful lot in hand at Carlisle last time.

Coral Willie Mullins for top trainer. If you can get 2-1 or bigger that's good value.

Ladbrokes Rocky Creek in the National Hunt Chase.

Paddy Power It should be China Rock in the Ryanair but connections seem intent on a quixotic tilt at the Gold Cup. I hope the bottomless stamina of Back In Focus carries him home in the four-miler.

William Hill Barbatos in the Coral Cup. His trainer is a shrewd operator who knows his horse is well handicapped and will have him primed to run for his life.

What's your best bet of the festival?

Bet365 Sam Winner in the Pertemps Final. He showed he retains his ability with a fluent win at Kempton last time. He's going to look well weighted on his best form and the three-mile trip could be ideal.

Betfred Rival D'Estruval has been laid out for the National Hunt Chase, which has been attracting better horses in the last couple of years. He has shown good form in staying novice chases in the north on testing ground and looks sure to relish the marathon trip.

BetVictor Salsify in the Foxhunter. There will be plenty of dead wood in the race and he looked back to his best when beating an excellent yardstick in Tammys Hill last time.

Blue Square Smad Place comes back to contest the World Hurdle as a six-year-old having already been placed at five. There is no Big Buck's this year and he can take advantage at a big price.

Boylesports Salsify to follow up in the Foxhunter. Age is on his side and he showed at Leopardstown that he retains his ability. He travels so well in his races and could improve again on better ground.

Coral I'm looking forward to seeing how short some of JP McManus's horses are in the handicaps – Colour Squadron certainly caught the eye last time at Exeter.

Ladbrokes Ballycasey in the Albert Bartlett.

Paddy Power Pont Alexandre because he will win.

William Hill At Fishers Cross in the Albert Bartlett. He is a thoroughly genuine, highly progressive young stayer with a terrific record that includes an impressive win in January at Cheltenham.

Henderson holds the aces

Racing Post Ratings expert Steve Mason expects Long Run and Bobs Worth to run well

GOLD CUP With the exception of War Of Attrition, all the winners this century went into the race with an RPR of at least 170. Unless Irish Hennessy winner Sir Des Champs (169+) can make the step up into the elite bracket, that trend looks likely to continue.

Admittedly no staying chaser so far this season has run up to the ten-year average winning mark of 178 but Silviniaco Conti (175+), Bobs Worth (174) and Long Run (174) have all run to a level that suggests such a figure is within their compass.

King George winner Long Run already boasts several figures in excess of 178 and, while the disappointment of last season's below-par third in the race is still a concern, he is probably the one to beat.

Given the brutal nature of his gutsy King George win, it is probably a blessing that he missed his intended clash with Silviniaco Conti in the Denman Chase at Newbury. The harder than expected race he had at Newbury last season probably did him no favours in his attempt to defend his Gold Cup crown.

He went straight from an admittedly rescheduled King George to Cheltenham when triumphant in 2011 and he looks the pick of the prices of the quartet at the head of the market.

Stablemate Bobs Worth is tailor-made for the race and will surely run well. The form of Denman Chase winner Silviniaco Conti reads well but lack of course experience has to be a negative.

Of those at bigger prices, last season's runner-up The Giant Bolster (170) looks the best each-way option.

CHAMPION HURDLE A typical winner needs to be capable of running to an RPR of around 170 and all bar a couple of winners this century took a figure of at least 162 into the festival.

It will be surprising if the winner doesn't come from the accompanying top ten list, although Betfair Hurdle winner My Tent Or Yours (163+) would be a serious contender if connections opt to run him in this race rather than the Supreme Novices' Hurdle.

The 2011 winner Hurricane Fly (173) ran below expectations when only third in last season's race, but that was on his second run back after a delayed reappearance and things seem to have gone much more smoothly this time around.

His season has pretty much mirrored his 2011 campaign and his easy success in the Irish Champion Hurdle saw him earn his sixth RPR of 170 or above.

Among his probable rivals only Binocular (170) and last year's winner Rock On Ruby (171) have posted figures of a comparable level and Hurricane Fly thoroughly deserves his place at the head of the market.

Grandouet (166) and Zarkandar (164) may still be capable of breaking through the 170 barrier but both are plenty short enough in the betting.

Rock On Ruby may have finished behind that pair on his reappearance

Gold Cup

This year's top rated	RPR
Long Run	180
Finian's Rainbow	175
Silviniaco Conti	175
Bobs Worth	174
Captain Chris	170
The Giant Bolster	170
Sir Des Champs	169
First Lieutenant	168

How the past ten winners rated

Year	Winner	Win RPR	Pre-race RPR
2012	Synchronised	173	171
2011	Long Run	181	181
2010	Imperial Commander	182	177
2009	Kauto Star	185	184
2008	Denman	184	183
2007	Kauto Star	175	184
2006	War Of Attrition	173	167
2005	Kicking King	177	177
2004	Best Mate	174	178
2003	Best Mate	178	176

10yr winning average RPR: 178

Champion Hurdle

This year's top rated	RPR
Hurricane Fly	173
Rock On Ruby	171
Binocular	170
Oscar Whisky	170
Peddlers Cross	170
Overturn	167
Grandouet	166
Zaidpour	166
Thousand Stars	165
Zarkandar	164

How the past ten winners rated

Year	Winner	Win RPR	Pre-race RPR
2012	Rock On Ruby	171	166
2011	Hurricane Fly	171	169
2010	Binocular	172	172
2009	Punjabi	167	164
2008	Katchit	165	162
2007	Sublimity	167	148
2006	Brave Inca	171	170
2005	Hardy Eustace	168	170
2004	Hardy Eustace	170	156
2003	Rooster Booster	173	170

10yr winning average RPR: 170

Champion Chase

This year's top rated	RPR
Sprinter Sacre	178
Finian's Rainbow	175
Sizing Europe	174
Sanctuaire	171
Cue Card	170
Realt Dubh	169
Somersby	169

How the past ten winners rated

Year	Winner	Win RPR	Pre-race RPR
2012	Finian's Rainbow	175	167
2011	Sizing Europe	176	166
2010	Big Zeb	172	171
2009	Master Minded	169	186
2008	Master Minded	186	168
2007	Voy Por Ustedes	167	167
2006	Newmill	172	155
2005	Moscow Flyer	182	181
2004	Azertyuiop	176	179
2003	Moscow Flyer	174	168

10yr winning average RPR: 175

World Hurdle

This year's top rated	RPR
Oscar Whisky	170
Peddlers Cross	170
Grands Crus	169
Reve De Sivola	167
Quevega	*166
Bog Warrior	164
Monksland	161
Smad Place	161

Includes 7lb mares' allowance

How the past ten winners rated

Year	Winner	Win RPR	Pre-race RPR
2012	Big Buck's	170	176
2010	Big Buck's	174	176
2009	Big Buck's	176	166
2008	Inglis Drever	174	170
2007	Inglis Drever	169	167
2006	My Way De Solzen	166	159
2005	Inglis Drever	167	165
2004	Iris's Gift	176	173
2003	Baracouda	176	176

10yr winning average RPR: 171

in Cheltenham's International Hurdle in December, but on better ground he would be a strong fancy to come out best of the three on the big day.

Testing ground would be a concern for last year's winner and, while goodish going is the norm at the festival, there has been nothing normal about the weather since last year's meeting.

Perhaps the best value for those looking for an each-way option to the favourite is the 2010 winner Binocular. He was very much ridden to beat Hurricane Fly in last year's race and he might well have done that but for making a mistake at the last hurdle.

Given his indifferent record first time out, he ran as well as could have been expected behind Hurricane Fly on ground more testing than ideal in the Irish Champion Hurdle and the RPR of 162 he earned that day puts him right in the mix with horses much shorter in the betting. At his best he was a 172 horse and is probably still capable of running to figures in the high 160s.

Of the other highly rated entries, Oscar Whisky (170), Peddlers Cross (179), Overturn (167), Zaidpour (166) and Thousand Stars (165) are far from certain runners.

Last season's Triumph Hurdle winner Countrywide Flame (161) still has to prove he is up to this level but is open to further improvement if he gets the strongly run race he needs.

CHAMPION CHASE Sprinter Sacre (178+) dominates the market and it will be a major surprise if he doesn't add to last season's hugely impressive Arkle success.

He has yet to match the figures posted by Master Minded (186) and Moscow Flyer (182) but it seems a case of when, rather than if, his rating catches up to his reputation as the best two-mile chaser of the past 20 years.

Lack of opposition is a hindrance in terms of returning a big rating, but connections will not be complaining and a long odds-on success looks the most likely scenario.

If Finian's Rainbow (175), Sizing Europe (174), Cue Card (170) and Somersby (169) all lined up, it would have the makings of a vintage Champion Chase. However, they are all near the head of the market for the Ryanair and it looks long odds-on that most of them will swerve a clash with Sprinter Sacre.

Of the likely runners available at bigger odds, Kempton winner Sanctuaire (171) looks the best option. He failed to perform behind Sprinter Sacre in the rescheduled Victor Chandler Chase on heavy ground at Cheltenham, but a reproduction of that previous Kempton form will surely see him make the first three.

WORLD HURDLE A large entry and plenty with big ratings if you are prepared to go back far enough. Only a handful have posted figures in excess of 160 this season, however, and a couple of those are far from certain to line up.

Reve De Sivola *(right)* (167) and Oscar Whisky (170), first and second in the Cleeve Hurdle, head the home defence and, on the evidence of that course-and-distance trial, there should not be much to choose between the pair.

Oscar Whisky seemed not to get the trip in last year's race, but lack of stamina did not appear to be an issue on trials day and, although he didn't perform right up to his best, he ran well enough to suggest a more positive ride on better ground could see him reverse the placings.

However, that is no foregone conclusion and Reve De Sivola, clearly rejuvenated by the switch back to hurdles and seemingly getting on particularly well with Richard Johnson, will be hard to keep out of the frame.

Testing conditions would suit Bog Warrior (164), who is unbeaten in three starts since switching back to hurdles. He is not a definite runner, however.

Quevega (166) would be a major player but will presumably head for the Mares' Hurdle again and pick of the Irish entry could be the Noel Meade-trained Monksland (161). His current rating falls 10lb below an average winner of the race, but in the absence of Big Buck's this doesn't look a strong renewal.

RYANAIR CHASE The Sprinter Sacre factor could lead to this being the most open Grade 1 at the meeting. With no fewer than 14 of the current entries rated in excess of an average winner of the race, it has the makings of a cracker.

The 2012 winner Riverside Theatre (172) will need to jump and travel better than he did last year and has questions to answer after a disappointing run in the King George.

Stablemate Finian's Rainbow (175) would surely be defending his Champion Chase crown if Sprinter Sacre were not in the same yard,

Ryanair Chase

How the past winners rated

Year	Winner	Win RPR	Pre-race RPR
2012	Riverside Theatre	171	172
2011	Albertas Run	168	170
2010	Albertas Run	170	167
2009	Imperial Commander	169	161
2008	Our Vic	168	171
2007	Taranis	160	158
2006	Fondmort	164	165
2005	Thisthat'tother	164	162

8yr winning average RPR: 167

neptun

My Tent Or Yours (second left) already has an RPR that betters any Supreme-winning mark of the past 20 years

but he is another with a question mark hanging over him after two poor runs this season.

There are no such worries about 2011 Champion Chase winner Sizing Europe (174) and, while he has little hope of seeing out the trip in the Gold Cup, the intermediate distance of this race should not present a problem. Connections may yet opt to take on Sprinter Sacre on the Wednesday, but he would warrant serious consideration if taking the 'easier' route.

Cue Card (170) had his stamina limitations shown up in the King George and, in a normal year, last season's Arkle runner-up would presumably head for the Champion Chase. He appeared to prove his stamina at the Ryanair trip when winning the Ascot Chase but he will find it tougher to dictate from the front at Cheltenham.

Last season's RSA favourite Grands Crus (168) has endured a series of problems this season and could still head back over hurdles in the day's feature race, but he remains a potential 170+ chaser and the distance of this race is probably his optimum.

NOVICE HURDLES A figure in the low to mid-150s is normally sufficient to land a typical Grade 1 novice hurdle at the festival, but the signs are this could be a vintage year.

With an RPR already superior to any winning figure for the race in the past 20 years, hugely impressive Betfair Hurdle winner My Tent Or Yours (163+) will surely take all the beating if he runs in the festival curtain-raiser.

To put his rating into some sort of perspective, only Back In Front (160), Hors La Loi (159) and Captain Cee Bee (159) returned winning figures anything like on a par with his current lofty mark and you would be hard pushed to argue 163 is likely to represent the ceiling of his ability.

Connections have the option of running in the Champion Hurdle, but this race looks the logical target.

Tolworth Hurdle winner Melodic Rendezvous (155) probably upped

Supreme Novices'

How the past ten winners rated

Year	Winner	Win RPR	Pre-race RPR
2012	Cinders And Ashes	151	145
2011	Al Ferof	155	142
2010	Menorah	150	153
2009	Go Native	152	149
2008	Captain Cee Bee	159	144
2007	Ebaziyan	150	116
2006	Noland	150	137
2005	Arcalis	146	143
2004	Brave Inca	152	145
2003	Back In Front	160	149

10yr winning average RPR: 153

his game again when beating a below-par Puffin Billy (150) at Exeter but could run in the longer Neptune if the ground dries out, while the Willie Mullins pair Un Atout (153) and Champagne Fever (150) are entered for all three Grade 1 hurdles.

Dual Grade 1 winner Jezki (149+) looks a certain runner but is very tight in the market and a better option at the prices could be the Paul Nicholls-trained Dodging Bullets (155).

He was having only his second start over hurdles when fourth in last year's Triumph Hurdle and has made good progress this season, most recently finishing ahead of Countrywide Flame and Cinders And Ashes when third to Darlan in the Christmas Hurdle. He looks a decent each-way alternative to the favourite.

Crack Irish novice Pont Alexandre (156) heads the ratings for the staying novices and at this stage the Neptune looks the likely target for the impressive all-the-way Leopardstown winner.

At Fishers Cross (154) just touched off The New One (154) at Cheltenham on trials day and the pair look the pick of the home team for the Neptune and Albert Bartlett.

The New One looks set to clash with Pont Alexandre in the Neptune while At Fishers Cross sets a decent standard for the longer race.

Challow Hurdle winner Taquin Du Seuil (150) has found only My Tent Or Yours too good in an impressive novice campaign. He is entered in the Neptune and Albert Bartlett and should make his presence felt in whichever race he lines up.

Not for the first time in recent seasons, French imports dominate the British juvenile scene and top of the pile is Cheltenham trials day winner Rolling Star (149+), who already boasts an RPR in excess of a typical winner of the race. The Nicky Henderson-trained runner looks the one to beat.

Paul Nicholls has his customary strong team and the pick at this stage is Far West (145+), winner of all four starts since joining the yard.

Ruacana (136) falls a level below the best of the British-trained

Neptune Novices'

How the past ten winners rated

Year	Winner	Win RPR	Pre-race RPR
2012	Simonsig	162	153
2011	First Lieutenant	151	145
2010	Peddlers Cross	156	148
2009	Mikael D'Haguenet	159	158
2008	Fiveforthree	149	136
2007	Massini's Maguire	149	147
2006	Nicanor	155	146
2005	No Refuge	148	145
2004	Fundamentalist	157	148
2003	Hardy Eustace	153	149

10yr winning average RPR: 154

Triumph Hurdle

How the past ten winners rated

Year	Winner	Win RPR	Pre-race RPR
2012	Countrywide Flame	145	137
2011	Zarkandar	149	143
2010	Soldatino	143	144
2009	Zaynar	157	141
2008	Celestial Halo	149	133
2007	Katchit	154	136
2006	Detroit City	153	135
2005	Penzance	141	127
2004	Made In Japan	140	120
2003	Spectroscope	137	121

10yr winning average RPR: 147

Arkle Chase

How the past ten winners rated

Year	Winner	Win RPR	Pre-race RPR
2012	Sprinter Sacre	176	171
2011	Captain Chris	168	156
2010	Sizing Europe	166	165
2009	For'plasterer	162	157
2008	Tidal Bay	168	154
2007	My Way De Solzen	165	158
2006	Voy Por Ustedes	162	160
2005	Contraband	158	154
2004	Well Chief	157	133
2003	Azertyuiop	170	165

10yr winning average RPR: 165

RSA Chase

How the past ten winners rated

Year	Winner	Win RPR	Pre-race RPR
2012	Bobs Worth	166	162
2011	Bostons Angel	155	152
2010	Weapon's Amnesty	165	150
2009	Cooldine	168	160
2008	Albertas Run	162	157
2007	Denman	165	169
2006	Star De Mohaison	153	141
2005	Trabolgan	160	155
2004	Rule Supreme	161	154
2003	One Knight	159	151

10yr winning average RPR: 161

juveniles but his run in a Grade 1 at Leopardstown helps punters to get a handle on the relative level of the Irish form and suggests impressive winner Our Conor (146+) will be right in the mix.

NOVICE CHASES There's not quite the strength in depth of last season but the standard at the top level is very high with Simonsig (167+) and Dynaste (165+) already rated above the level of an average winner of their respective races.

A vintage winner of last year's Neptune, winning pointer Simonsig has looked even better over fences and, although missing his intended prep race at Newbury was not ideal, lack of experience looks unlikely to catch him out as he bids to land the Arkle on only his third run over regulation fences.

Last season's Champion Hurdle runner-up Overturn (162+) has been electric over fences in three starts this season and looks capable of at least matching his hurdle mark of 167. He rates a realistic alternative to Simonsig but it will be surprising if the Nicky Henderson-trained grey is beaten.

Arvika Ligeonniere (156) looks the pick of the Irish two-mile novices but blotted his copybook when falling at Leopardstown in January. Like Overturn, he enjoys forcing the pace and the way the race is run could pan out nicely for Simonsig.

RSA Chase favourite Dynaste has put together the sort of flawless novice campaign that resulted in stablemate Grands Crus being sent off at cramped odds for the same race last year.

Admittedly the Feltham Chase he won so impressively at Kempton on Boxing Day has not proved to be the best of RSA trials, but the fact that Grands Crus failed to build on a similarly impressive win last season shouldn't really be used as a stick to beat Dynaste with.

He should stay the trip of the RSA and, while the shorter Jewson looks the easier option, he will surely take his chance in the Grade 1.

All bar one of the last ten winners of the race went to the fesival with an RPR of at least 150 and Paul Nicholls has three decent candidates in the shape of Rocky Creek (155), Unioniste (155) and Sire Collonges (154). The last-named will need the ground to dry out and Rocky Creek may prove the pick of the trio if he goes to the festival.

Boston Bob (146) has yet to reproduce his smart hurdling form over fences and has the option of going for the Jewson but may struggle to cope with stablemate Aupcharlie (153) over the shorter trip.

The latter was outstayed by Back In Focus (153) over three miles at Leopardstown and the former Howard Johnson trained eight-year-old may prove the best of the Willie Mullins RSA possibles.

Bobs Worth rock solid

Dave Edwards (Topspeed) says the Hennessy
winner has one of the most reliable time lines

GOLD CUP The prolonged wet spell this winter has made slowly
run races a recurring theme and consequently many of the big-race
contenders have a big disparity between their optimum career rating
and this season's best. Working out which pieces of form are most
reliable is one of the key puzzles facing punters.

In the past decade five Gold Cup winners boasted a pre-race figure
above 165 and just three went to post with less than 160, so clearly a
rating in excess of that has to be pretty high on the wish list.

Among the market leaders Silviniaco Conti (157), First Lieutenant
(157) and Sir Des Champs (155) fall short of that benchmark and,
while they still could be big players, time-wise the odds are stacked
against them.

The Hennessy at Newbury in December is one race in this most
difficult of winters that was truly run and on that evidence Bobs Worth
(164) is justifiably favourite. He was only six seconds slower than the
Newbury standard and, with his Cheltenham record, he looks rock-solid.

Imperial Commander (180) holds the distinction of the highest
Topspeed Gold Cup rating this century and heads the overall ratings
based on his imperious performance when defeating Denman in 2010.

There was plenty to admire about his second to Cape Tribulation
in the Argento Chase on trials day at Cheltenham in January, on his
return from a 22-month absence, but even allowing for the testing
ground a time nearly a minute slower than standard takes some lustre
from the performance.

Three of his best four efforts on the stopwatch have been at
Cheltenham and probably too much has been made of the fact that he
is 12. The number that really counts is his optimum Topspeed rating
of 180. He is arguably too big a price given his achievements and has
place prospects if he avoids the 'bounce'.

Silviniaco Conti has won five of his eight chase starts, including
Wetherby's Charlie Hall and the Betfair at Haydock, both in modest
times. He has done nothing wrong but his victories have been gained
in small fields where he has largely been in his comfort zone.

Long Run, the 2011 winner and third last year, has posted figures
over 150 in six of his last eight starts. He was all out to beat Captain
Chris in the King George at Kempton, in a time 3.5sec slower than the
novice Dynaste clocked in the Feltham. That speaks volumes, as both
times were modest compared with the rest of the card.

CHAMPION HURDLE Precision hurdling and a blend of speed
and stamina are essential requirements and in the past decade eight
winners went to post with a Topspeed rating above 150 and five had
155-plus. Course experience allied to a big number is invaluable and
among the principals only Zaidpour, Raya Star, Thousand Stars, Oscar
Whisky and Rebel Fitz did not earn their personal bests at Cheltenham.

Gold Cup

Topspeed figures	Career best	Season best
Imperial Commander	180	96
Bobs Worth	164	164
Long Run	163	102
The Giant Bolster	162	146
Finian's Rainbow	159	120
Captain Chris	158	150
Silviniaco Conti	157	155
First Lieutenant	157	157
Champion Court	156	116
What A Friend	156	104
Sir Des Champs	155	109

How the past ten winners rated

Year	Winner	Win TS	Pre-race TS
2012	Synchronised	164	151
2011	Long Run	157	163
2010	Imperial Commander	180	173
2009	Kauto Star	172	176
2008	Denman	178	157
2007	Kauto Star	144	168
2006	War Of Attrition	153	133
2005	Kicking King	158	160
2004	Best Mate	165	168
2003	Best Mate	168	166

Champion Hurdle

Topspeed figures	Career best	Season best
Rock On Ruby	167	138
Overturn	163	-
Khyber Kim	163	-
Hurricane Fly	161	143
Binocular	163	110
Zarkandar	159	143
Grandouet	158	145
Peddlers Cross	153	70
Zaidpour	152	125
Raya Star	151	151
Thousand Stars	150	134
Cinders And Ashes	149	101
Rebel Fitz	149	149
Oscar Whisky	147	146

How the past ten winners rated

Year	Winner	Win TS	Pre-race TS
2012	Rock On Ruby	167	160
2011	Hurricane Fly	149	153
2010	Binocular	163	158
2009	Punjabi	155	160
2008	Katchit	157	157
2007	Sublimity	145	139
2006	Brave Inca	173	51
2005	Hardy Eustace	152	155
2004	Hardy Eustace	155	124
2003	Rooster Booster	164	154

Champion Chase

Topspeed figures	Career best	Season best
Sprinter Sacre	165	159
Sizing Europe	165	138
Somersby	165	148
Finian's Rainbow	159	120
Cue Card	156	155
Sanctuaire	150	138
Wishfull Thinking	149	132
Realt Dubh	147	120
Tataniano	147	113

How the past ten winners rated

Year	Winner	Win TS	Pre-race TS
2012	Finian's Rainbow	159	154
2011	Sizing Europe	146	166
2010	Big Zeb	168	159
2009	Master Minded	161	185
2008	Master Minded	185	143
2007	Voy Por Ustedes	159	160
2006	Newmill	163	155
2005	Moscow Flyer	145	177
2004	Azerytuiop	148	161
2003	Moscow Flyer	162	140

World Hurdle

Topspeed figures	Career best	Season best
Solwhit	167	133
Celestial Halo	166	123
Quevega*	165	-
Fiveforthree	161	-
Any Given Day	159	122
Peddlers Cross	153	70
Get Me Out Of Here	152	110
Reve De Sivola	152	130
Smad Place	152	118
Zaidpour	152	125
Oscar Whisky	148	146

*Includes 7lb mares' allowance

How the past ten winners rated

Year	Winner	Win TS	Pre-race TS
2012	Big Buck's	161	154
2011	Big Buck's	119	147
2010	Big Buck's	139	147
2009	Big Buck's	131	147
2008	Inglis Drever	175	162
2007	Inglis Drever	141	162
2006	My Way De Solzen	145	122
2005	Inglis Drever	148	162
2004	Iris's Gift	161	160
2003	Baracouda	161	147

Rock On Ruby heads the ratings on the strength of his success 12 months ago and there seems little obvious reason why he can't put in a repeat performance. He did not get the credit he deserved last year, but he increased his advantage on the climb to the line and won strictly on merit. The winning time was 2.6sec quicker than the Supreme, indicating that Cinders And Ashes has about 35 yards to find. He confirmed his wellbeing at Doncaster in February and time-wise sets the bar pretty high.

Hurricane Fly has a phenomenal strike-rate (16 from 19), although his winning Topspeed figure of 149 in 2011 was the second-lowest of the past decade. He has continued to mop up Grade 1 races in Ireland but most of them are run at a moderate pace against the same rivals. His overall timeline suggests he is vulnerable given searching end-to-end fractions and it is significant that his Champion Hurdle defeat last year was the only time he earned a figure above 160. He was taken out of his comfort zone then and, as only Comedy Of Errors has regained the hurdling crown, he has history as well as some smart opponents against him this time.

The Neptune has proved a useful pointer to the following year's Champion in the past but only Cotton Mill is entered this year. When he veered and unseated his rider at the second-last in the Neptune, he was probably on course to earn a speed figure of about 150. His best in completed starts is just 103, which is light years away from what will be needed.

Zarkandar finished fifth last year and has the potential to improve. The 2011 Triumph Hurdle winner is seven from nine over hurdles and has done nothing wrong this term.

CHAMPION CHASE Remarkably Sprinter Sacre boasts a pre-race figure of 165 without having been posed a serious question and a figure higher than that has been required to win the Champion Chase only twice in the past decade. If push comes to shove at Cheltenham, he could achieve a figure reminiscent of the Master Minded era.

In both outings this season he has annihilated his rivals and, despite winning the Tingle Creek on the bridle, still earned 159 on the clock. No fireworks were necessary when he romped home in the rerouted Victor Chandler at Cheltenham in January and he is simply head and shoulders above the opposition.

Sizing Europe has an excellent strike-rate of 66 per cent over fences and his optimum figure was earned in this race in 2010. His recent figures, however, like those of Somersby, suggest both have plenty to find.

WORLD HURDLE The winning speed rating often does not reflect this race's championship status in the staying division but that may be attributable to the fact that just two horses, Big Buck's and Inglis Drever, have landed seven of the last eight renewals. Such was their dominance that they breached the 160 mark only once each in that period – a level that had been reached earlier in the past decade by Baracouda and Iris's Gift.

Although billed as a test of stamina, the race often does not heat up until the second circuit and that style of racing usually results in a

moderate overall time.

Nine of the last ten winners had a pre-race figure of at least 147 and most of the field have attained that fairly modest level. The absence of Big Buck's makes it a wide-open race.

Several of the leading players on the clock have questions to answers over the trip, although if the race unfolds in its customary manner that could play into their hands.

Both Solwhit and Celestial Halo gained their best figures over two miles and in the event of a slow early pace they could have too much speed at the finish.

Quevega has won the Mares' Hurdle for the last four years and, although connections will probably be tempted to go for a nap hand, she would be well worth her place in this field.

Proven stayer Reve De Sivola has not looked back since reverting to hurdles this term but he couldn't match strides with Peddlers Cross in the 2010 Neptune. Peddlers Cross has not achieved much since but at his best could upset the applecart.

RYANAIR CHASE A pre-race figure above 150 has been the custom and there is no shortage of runners with that on their record. Albertas Run has an enviable festival record, including two wins and a second in this race, while Nicky Henderson has a strong hand with Riverside Theatre and Finian's Rainbow. Cue Card looked the real deal over 2m1½f at Exeter in November and again in the Ascot Chase. He can be forgiven his lacklustre effort in the King George and his recent Ascot victory suggests he's capable of figuring in the finish.

Cue Card has a good chance in the Ryanair after impressing over the 2m5f trip in the Ascot Chase

Ryanair Chase

Topspeed figures	Career best	Season best
Sizing Europe	165	138
Somersby	165	148
Riverside Theatre	162	75
Albertas Run	161	-
Finian's Rainbow	159	120
Grands Crus	159	87
First Lieutenant	157	157
Champion Court	156	116
Cue Card	156	155
Sir Des Champs	155	109
Rubi Light	153	135

Arkle Chase

Career-best Topspeed figures

Arvika Ligeonniere	144
Oscars Well	141
Baily Green	140
Majala	136
Changing Times	134
His Excellency	131
Captain Conan	129
Fago	126
Benefficient	125
Simonsig	125

RSA Chase

Career-best Topspeed figures

Unioniste*	140
Sire Collonges	136
Tofino Bay	133
Restless Harry	132
Rocky Creek	132
Houblon Des Obeaux	130
Third Intention	129
Mikael D'Haguenet	126
Brass Tax	125
Mountainous	125
Dynaste	124
*Includes 2lb for age	

Supreme Novices'

Career-best Topspeed figures

Cause Of Causes	132
Champagne Fever	131
Ifandbutwhynot	131
Too Scoops	131
Jezki	130
Bright New Dawn	129
Melodic Rendezvous	129
Forgotten Voice	128
Rule The World	126
Annie Power*	125
Waaheb	124
*Includes 7lb mares' allowance	

Neptune Novices'

Career-best Topspeed figures

Cause Of Causes	132
Champagne Fever	131
Ifandbutwhynot	131
At Fishers Cross	130
Bright New Dawn	129
Melodic Rendezvous	129
She Ranks Me*	127
Rule The World	126
Annie Power*	125
Caid Du Berlais**	125
Romeo Americo	124
Waaheb	124
Pont Alexandre	123
Glens Melody*	122
The New One	122
Unika La Reconce*	122
*Includes 7lb mares' allowance	
**Includes 9lb weight-for-age	

Baily Green could punch above his weight in the Arkle

ARKLE CHASE Since 1994 a rating above 150 has been needed to lift this prize on 13 occasions but the weather has put a huge dampener on pre-race time performances this season and no runner has yet hit that mark. Hot favourite Simonsig has beaten just eight rivals in his two wins and his best rating is a modest 125. In three starts Overturn has accounted for just nine opponents and 116 is his best. Top-rated Arvika Ligeonniere blotted his copybook with a fall last time out and that is not the best festival preparation. Baily Green has more experience than most and, while he appears exposed, could punch above his weight at massive odds.

RSA CHASE Last year's winner Bobs Worth maintained the pre-race benchmark requirement of 126 and this narrows the prospective winners down somewhat. Favourite Dynaste is just shy of the yardstick but has not put a foot wrong in three wins. Paul Nicholls is responsible for three of the top five on ratings and has a strong hand. If the ground is really soft, Tofino Bay would enter the equation.

SUPREME NOVICES' HURDLE Since 1994 the time of the opener has been slower than the Champion by more than a couple of seconds on just four occasions. A figure above 140 has been necessary to land the last nine runnings but a low pre-race figure has not been a hindrance. Betfair Hurdle winner My Tent Or Yours heads the market but the pedestrian pace of the Newbury handicap sets alarm bells ringing. He is well down the pecking order on the stopwatch and on soft ground Melodic Rendezvous looks a viable proposition.

NEPTUNE NOVICES' HURDLE Simonsig was the first winner for six years not to boast a pre-race figure above 129 but his winning rating of 155 was up with the race best. The poor weather means not many fulfil the pre-race criteria but Melodic Rendezvous is on the borderline and on good ground could run here instead of the Supreme. The New One has a host of admirers but lags behind on the clock and is far from certain to turn the tables on his Cheltenham conqueror At Fishers Cross.

Young blood

Tom Pennington of the Racing Post Bloodstock
team picks out some key runners on pedigree

SUPREME NOVICES' Significant interest surrounds the dual Grade
1-winning hurdler Jezki, who was snapped up by JP McManus for the
reported sum of €500,000 in January, but he must break the Cheltenham
Festival duck of his sire, Milan (0-7 with his festival runners).

Nicky Henderson has two leading fancies. The most exciting is My
Tent Or Yours, who is out of a half-sister to the top-class Flat performer
Conduit and is closely related to Irish Oaks winner Petrushka. His sire
Desert Prince has had one winner from six festival runners (17%), 2005
Fred Winter scorer Dabiroun, and the combination of quicker conditions
and a strongly run race should play to the six-year-old's strengths.

Henderson could also be represented by River Maigue, who is by
Zagreb, a sire yet to have a runner at the March showpiece. Zagreb's
progeny tend to have a preference for slow ground, so possible quick
conditions could be against River Maigue.
Advice: My Tent Or Yours win

NEPTUNE NOVICES' The New One can bolster King's Theatre's
strong festival record – he has had eight festival winners from 53
runners (15%), including last season's Ryanair Chase hero Riverside
Theatre and Albert Bartlett Novices' Hurdle scorer Brindisi Breeze.
Sixth in last year's Champion Bumper, The New One will be suited by
the course and a quicker surface.

Puffin Billy has the talent to provide Heron Island (0-5) with his
first festival winner. The five-year-old certainly has the pedigree,
being a half-brother to dual Grade 3 winner Zuzka and descending
from a family that includes Mole Board, who finished fourth in two
Champion Hurdles.
Advice: The New One win, Puffin Billy place

TRIUMPH HURDLE Far West has been impressive this season but
may lack the required speed for the Triumph, even though his sire
Poliglote produced last year's Arc winner Solemia.

Poliglote has sired two festival winners (22%), Coral Cup (2m5f)
winner Spirit River and National Hunt Chase (4m1f) winner Butler's
Cabin, and his progeny also have a preference for slow ground – high-
class French performers Saint Du Chenet and Nikita Du Berlais have
excelled in such conditions this season.

The Willie Mullins-trained Blood Cotil has good credentials. He is by
Enrique (25% winners to runners at the festival), sire of 2010 Champion
Hurdle winner Binocular, and has speed as well as stamina. His dam
is a half-sister to the Group 3-winning miler Boxing Day and he is also
related to Gabrial, who was third behind Frankel in the Sussex Stakes.

Mullins's other main fancy, Diakali, is a son of Sinndar (0-9), sire of
the Mullins-trained Mourad, who has twice been placed at the festival,
in the Triumph and World Hurdle.
Advice: Diakali win

Sire watch

Hits and misses
at the festival

☞ Bob Back has sired six
festival winners from 62
winners (10%), three of
whom have won at 3m
or further – a statistic
that bodes well for Gold
Cup favourite **Bobs
Worth** (dual winner at
the festival) and Willie
Mullins's novice staying
chasers **Boston Bob** and
Back In Focus.

☞ Gold Cup fancy **Sir Des
Champs** and **Quevega**,
who goes for a fifth win
at the festival in the
Mares' Hurdle, will be
bidding to maintain Robin
Des Champs' strong
Cheltenham record – six
winners from 14 runners
(43%). The sire also has
Un Atout among Willie
Mullins's strong team of
novice hurdlers

☞ Oscar has a fine festival
record with eight winners
from 78 runners (10%)
and his progeny excel at
a wide range of distances
(four winners at 2m-2m5f
and four winners at
3m-plus). The sire has a
strong battalion for this
year's festival including
Rock On Ruby, who
returns to defend the
Champion Hurdle crown,
World Hurdle favourite
Oscar Whisky and
leading Albert Bartlett
fancy **At Fishers Cross**.

☞ Presenting has sired
ten festival winners from
106 runners (9%), with
eight of those scoring
over 3m or further.
That is encouraging for
Gold Cup hopes **First
Lieutenant** and **China
Rock** (below) if they go
for that race instead of
the Ryanair Chase and for
Ballycasey if he lines up
in the Albert Bartlett.

Inside the stables

The champion trainers discuss their main hopes, plus an in-depth look at the challenge from Ireland and the major British training centres

A new beginning

Paul Nicholls discusses the young stars he hopes can put him back on top at the festival

Dodging Bullets Supreme Novices' Hurdle He won his two races at Cheltenham earlier in the season and ran really well in the Christmas Hurdle at Kempton. He might be the forgotten horse in the race as he is rated 156 over hurdles and that should be good enough to make him competitive. His previous course experience will stand him in good stead.

Fago Arkle Chase He was unlucky to fall at Warwick, where he knuckled over on landing two out, but he's none the worse for that and is a high-class novice chaser, as he showed at Newbury on his first start in Britain. He's also in the Jewson, but we're favouring the Arkle as the pace of that race will suit him.

Zarkandar Champion Hurdle I've been very pleased with him this season as everything has gone to plan, which is more than can be said of the past when niggling problems interrupted things. He still seems progressive but, looking at the race realistically, he will need a career-best to win. He's nothing if not game and was not beaten that far last year when we had to rush him a bit.

Sire Collonges National Hunt Chase His Cheltenham options are ground-dependent as I don't think he wants soft conditions and he could well end up in the four-miler. He stays and jumps well, as he showed when winning well at the course in October. He simply kept galloping that day, so the longer test should suit.

Aaim To Prosper Neptune Novices' Hurdle He's also entered in the Albert Bartlett and stays well, so which race he goes for will be decided closer to the day. He essentially needs good ground, as he showed when winning the Cesarewitch on the Flat, but he has not yet encountered that over hurdles. He joined us a bit late in life but has done little wrong in his runs over hurdles.

Rocky Creek RSA Chase Rocky Creek is a lovely horse for the future and if he runs at the festival it will be in the RSA Chase rather than the four-miler, for which he's also entered. His overall form this season is good but I think he has got a bit more maturing to do before he is the finished article.

Unioniste RSA Chase If the ground was testing we might consider running him in the Jewson but this race has been the plan and we're sticking to it at the moment. He'll come on a ton for his Newbury win, where things did not pan out as he has always idled in front and did so again. He ideally needs a true-run affair with plenty of horses giving him a tow into the race, as he showed when winning at Cheltenham in December.

Sanctuaire Champion Chase He will run in the race only if it cuts up

- Manor Farm Stables, Ditcheat, Somerset
- British champion trainer 2005-06, 2006-07, 2007-08, 2008-09, 2009-10, 2010-11, 2011-12
- Festival winners 32 (19 in chases, 13 over hurdles)
- Top festival trainer six times (1999, 2004, 2006, 2007, 2008, 2009)
- Last five festivals (earliest first): 3/5/2/3/2
- Has had at least one winner at each of the past ten festivals, winning the trainer award at five of them
- Only two of his six leading trainer awards were achieved without winning the Cheltenham Gold Cup
- Has not had a chase winner since Kauto Star's second Gold Cup in 2009 and has returned a level-stakes loss on all chase runners at the festival for eight years in a row
- His best handicap races are the County Hurdle (three winners) and the Grand Annual Chase (two winners)

and the ground is good as he has lots of other options later in the spring.

Wonderful Charm Coral Cup He had a breathing operation after winning the Persian War at Chepstow in October. He also has an entry in the World Hurdle but the weather has really held us up with him and we've not been able to give him more experience, so this race is likely to be the plan. I think he is very good and we expect a decent run.

Saphir Du Rheu Fred Winter Hurdle He won well at Taunton in the mud and still seems to be on the upgrade. He should appreciate better ground if we ever get any.

Sam Winner Pertemps Final He has had problems in the past but qualified for the Pertemps Final at Sandown on his comeback run. The

Irish Saint (right) is closely matched with Far West on their home work

Vital statistics

The festival by numbers

Eight of the nine Champion Bumper runners that started 3-1 or less have been beaten

20-1

The SP of both Nicky Henderson winners of the Grand Annual since the race was renamed in honour of his father Johnny in 2005 – Greenhope in 2006 and Bellvano (below) last year. Be wary of shorter-priced Henderson runners – he has had three beaten favourites in the past five years

Nicky Henderson has had at least two Grade 1 winners at each of the past four festivals

bad weather then made us go for a bumper for jumpers race at Kempton, which he won. I don't think three miles will present a problem for him and there is every chance he will go well in the race.

Far West Triumph Hurdle He's been a revelation in winning his four novice hurdles since joining the yard. He has been to Cheltenham twice and won, so he must have a leading chance in the race that has been the plan for him all season.

Irish Saint Triumph Hurdle There is not a lot between him and Far West on their home work. He has had only two tries for us, winning at Kempton and then finishing second at Cheltenham, where he might not have got the run of the race. He's a nice horse for the future.

The festival by numbers

7

Of the past 13 winners of the Byrne Group Plate, seven were French-breds – a 53 per cent-strike rate from 32 per cent of the runners

Philip Hobbs with Balthazar King (below) last year became the first British trainer in eight runnings to win the Cross Country

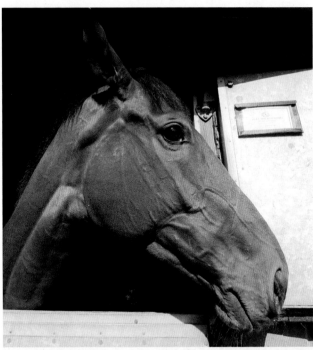

Tricky Trickster is being aimed at the Foxhunter

Dark Lover County Hurdle He could be joined by Prospect Wells and Pearl Swan but all three have other entries as well. Dark Lover has won twice at the course this season and is likely to go for this race as he was staying on again behind My Tent Or Yours in the Betfair Hurdle at Newbury and the fast pace in the County is just what he needs.

Silviniaco Conti Gold Cup He's a star and has won his last four chases. I've no doubt he'll improve no end from what he did when winning the Denman Chase at Newbury. He has done nothing but progress with every run. He almost mirrors what Kauto Star has done in the past and he went on to win the Gold Cup. He is a true professional who stays well and jumps well. Ruby [Walsh] is very keen on his chances but Gold Cups take an awful lot of winning. I would dearly love to make it five wins in the race with him.

Tricky Trickster Foxhunter He's had his problems to say the least as he broke some vertebrae in his neck when falling in the Midlands National two years ago and it was touch and go with him for a while. He seems back to himself now and won at Huntingdon on his comeback. We'll do our best to get him qualified for this race.

Salubrious Martin Pipe Hurdle He needs decent ground, as he showed when winning well at Musselburgh. Harry Derham rode him there and is likely to be in the saddle again.

THE ALL NEW
SPINCAST APP

Available on the
App Store

The **NEW** & **EXCLUSIVE**
SMALL STAKES - BIG WIN
mobile football betting app from BetVictor

Spin the reels to reveal selections in
Match Betting, Over/Under Total Goals & Anytime Goalscorer Markets
& let Spincast give you a price on all three outcomes.

Download your **FREE** Spincast app today

Going for gold

Willie Mullins shares his hopes and dreams for Sir Des Champs and the rest of his powerful team

Champagne Fever Supreme It was great to see him put a bad run at Naas behind him when winning at Leopardstown on Hennessy day and he did it the hard way. I suppose we shouldn't be surprised at that because throughout his career he has been nothing but brave. In terms of Cheltenham he could do anything. We know from winning last year's Champion Bumper that he could go two miles but we've never been worried about his staying ability, so he's in all of the novice hurdles.

Mozoltov Supreme He definitely travels and if people like him I wouldn't put them off because he could be as good as any of mine. We haven't seen him much of him this season just because the other horses were there and there was no point in them taking each other on. Besides, his work was always quite good. He's a good sort and jumps well going at speed, which would be a huge asset in a race like the Supreme if he ended up in that.

Pique Sous Supreme He won his maiden and we put him away before giving him a nice prep on the all-weather at Dundalk. The better the ground, the better his chance and he'll go to Cheltenham based on his performance in the Bumper last year as opposed to anything he has done over hurdles. He showed he liked the track and as long as it didn't come up very soft or heavy he'd be entitled to go back again.

Un Atout Supreme He goes straight to Cheltenham after missing the Deloitte and is in good form. At the moment the plan is the Supreme but he's the type who could definitely go a longer trip if he had to. In both his hurdle runs so far he has done nothing wrong and, being closely related to Sir Des Champs, you'd hope he'd take to Cheltenham as well as the other fellow.

Arvika Ligeonniere Arkle The Arkle is the plan for him. It was disappointing he fell so easily last time at Leopardstown and he will have to put that behind him. I'm sure he will – he's a classy horse who has won two Grade 1 novices this season. This looks a tough Arkle, though.

Hurricane Fly Champion Hurdle He summered well this time and we've been happy with him at every stage this season. He's in great form at home and we couldn't ask for more. Similarly on the track he has done everything we've asked of him and we're just looking forward to getting him there now and having a crack at regaining the Champion Hurdle.

Uncle Junior Cross Country It looks like Uncle Junior will be near the top of the weights for the Cross Country Chase and that won't make things easy. But he likes the track and the trip and always runs a good race there.

Quevega Mares' Hurdle She's in good form and it's all systems go for another crack at the Mares' Hurdle. As is well known now, she is

Mozoltov "could be as good as any of mine"

Vital statistics

The festival
by numbers

....

10

*Of the last 12 winners
of the JLT Specialty
Handicap Chase, ten
had finished in the first
three last time out
(six had won)*

8-1

*Synchronised (below)
last year was the
longest-priced Gold
Cup winner in the past
12 runnings. Every
winner in that period
has come from the first
three in the betting*

campaigned a little differently to others and like last year will be having her first run of the season at Cheltenham. But she's coming along fine and doing some nice work. We're happy with her.

Back In Focus National Hunt Chase He stays well and is all about jumping and stamina. To that end we're looking at the National Hunt Chase for him, to play to his assets. Ground-wise he seems to operate well in softer conditions.

Pont Alexandre Neptune He's in the Neptune and the Albert Bartlett

but you'd have to say he's likely to head down the Neptune route. Of course you don't know what's going to come around the corner, so we just have to make the best decision as late as we can. At Leopardstown this fellow was very good and he has done nothing wrong. He's only a five-year-old with very little experience, so what he has done has been on raw, natural talent.

Boston Bob RSA Chase His work picked up before Leopardstown and he showed great guts to win the PJ Moriarty Chase. He jumped very well that day and slowly but surely is returning to the form of last season. Options are open regarding the Jewson and the RSA Chase.

Clondaw Court Bumper The weather meant we couldn't get a run into him after his debut victory in November and it's probably too late now, so we'll go straight there.

Union Dues Bumper He has proved it and goes to Cheltenham. He goes on both types of ground and has won his winners' race, so you'd have no worries about him.

Aupcharlie Jewson It looks like the Jewson for him, although he is also in the Arkle. He jumps so well and is a fine, big chasing type, so it's no surprise he's a better chaser than hurdler. It's because of his fluent jumping that for now he's probably best kept to shorter trips.

Blood Cotil Triumph He disappointed at Leopardstown, having been good there at Christmas, but there's more to come from him. Whether he's handicapped on his first run or his second will determine whether the Fred Winter is an option.

Diakali Triumph He looked to be well beaten by Our Conor at Leopardstown, but if we can improve his jumping it could be all to play for if we go for the Triumph. He was very good two runs back and has plenty of talent.

Ballycasey Albert Bartlett He had the benefit of three point-to-point runs before he came to us and has put that experience to good use. From what we've seen in his bumper and over hurdles he's an out-and-out stayer, so the Albert Bartlett looks the one. On pedigree and on the way he runs, you'd hope there's more to come from him on better ground.

Inish Island Albert Bartlett He'll probably get an entry in the Coral Cup but he'd be more than entitled to head for the Albert Bartlett. He was very good at Clonmel last time but it's his run at Cheltenham in December that would have you thinking the novice route. He was just beaten by At Fishers Cross that day and that looks solid form in the context of that race.

Sir Des Champs Gold Cup I couldn't have been happier with his performance at Leopardstown, where he beat a horse many people were hailing as this, that and the other. That trial was good enough for me and I'm looking forward to getting him back to Cheltenham, where he's unbeaten in two runs.

BETVICTOR. BET QUICKER

SPORTS • LIVE • CASINO

Introducing the new iPhone App from BetVictor

Built for iPhone
Fast Navigation
Improved Racecards
Football Coupons
Live Streaming
In App Casino

Available on the **App Store**

Scan to download

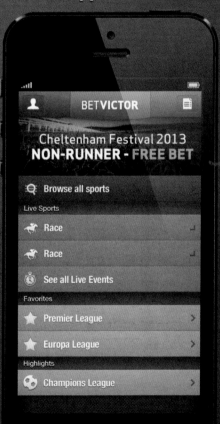

FOR OUR **BEST ODDS** TALK TO VICTOR

BET**VICTOR**
Online and mobile

🐎 In the past six
runnings of the
Pertemps Final, only
two horses carrying
11st or more have
made the first four.
Eight of the last nine
winners carried 10st
11lb or less

15%

The festival strike-rate
of David Pipe (below)
with handicap runners
carrying 10st 12lb or
less. Six of his seven
festival handicap
winners have been in
that category

DAVID PIPE

Have faith in Sir Des Champs

Johnny Ward expects golden glory to crown a fabulous week for Ireland's strong raiding party

The economy may be in deep recession but at the highest level on the racetrack it's boom time for Ireland. The raiding party features the Champion Hurdle favourite, the usual strong challenge for the novice hurdles and the Champion Bumper, the ever-reliable Quevega, handicap fancies galore and, as the potential icing on a fabulous festival, the best chance in the Gold Cup since War Of Attrition won in 2006.

The memory of big-race disappointments at the 2012 festival is still fresh, but hope rises anew. Surely this year will be different.

GOLD CUP The feeling as they crossed the line in last year's Gold Cup was that the 2013 renewal would be up for grabs. The sad death of Synchronised opened up the race further and Long Run, even in winning the King George, did not exactly challenge the notion that he is pretty beatable.

Sir Des Champs was generally cut to 4-1 for the Gold Cup after his Hennessy win in February, yet arguably he did only what he was entitled to. Having been ridden more prominently than in the Lexus, he seemed to enjoy jumping out of the better ground and was always likely to do Flemenstar for stamina.

Everything about Sir Des Champs asks for a bet on him for the Gold Cup. Firstly, he was a high-class novice last year who easily beat Champion Court in the Jewson. That he travelled so strongly in the Jewson, having won the Martin Pipe on his only other start at Cheltenham, suggests he thrives at the track. Furthermore, he is trained by a genius in Willie Mullins and he can be expected to peak on Gold Cup day. Lastly, he stays well and is a sound jumper in the main. Given that he has had only ten starts since coming to Ireland, he ought to have it in him to find more improvement.

Davy Russell said, sweat still on his brow after riding a canny race in the Hennessy: "I've never lost faith in this horse." Come March 15, given who trains him and his colours, a rare level of Irish – and British – faith in Sir Des Champs is expected.

CHAMPION HURDLE My ante-post fancy for this race was Darlan and his death in early February robbed the race of arguably its most fascinating contender. At the time of writing, another JP McManus horse in My Tent Or Yours is no longer than 6-1 with a run, yet it is envisaged he will go for the Supreme Novices' Hurdle.

This is not the strongest crop of Champion Hurdle contenders. Rock On Ruby, who stayed so stoutly to score in 2012, appeared to be beaten when Darlan fell fatally at Doncaster. He can be expected to peak at Cheltenham but a three-and-three-quarter-length win over Overturn is hardly sensational Grade 1 hurdling form, particularly as **Hurricane Fly** never looked happy that day.

All season, Willie Mullins has reiterated that 'The Fly' is in a better

Rebel Fitz is an outsider to watch in the Champion Hurdle

place than he was last term. Like so many Montjeus, he has his kinks and anyone who has ever seen him in a parade ring will tell you as much. What is perhaps less known than it should be is that he spent far longer in the ring at Cheltenham in 2012 than he did in 2011, when connections went to every conceivable length to ensure he would not get worked up in the preliminaries.

Mullins, moreover, insists Hurricane Fly does not need deep ground,

'He's timing it just right'

Rodger Sweeney, trainer of Salsify
(Foxhunter) "He's coming along nicely and is timing it just right. Hopefully he'll come on another bit from his Leopardstown win" *Form figures of 172U1111F11 in hunter chases from February onwards*

Liz Doyle, trainer of Le Vent D'Antan (below)
(Bumper) "A better race would suit him and a little better ground. Everything he's done since he arrived in the yard has been exceptional. He works as well as Cheltenian" *Al Ferof and 2011 Champion Bumper winner Cheltenian are two of the stars who started in bumpers with Doyle*

Solwhit will be interesting in the World Hurdle if he gets the green light

which he really thrives on. I am not entirely convinced he is less than a 2-1 chance but on overall form he probably is the one to beat.

An Irish challenger at longer odds worth some consideration is last year's Galway Handicap Hurdle winner **Rebel Fitz**. Remember, he was sent off 4-6 to beat a field that included Thousand Stars and Captain Cee Bee when he last ran at Thurles in October. It would be surprising if that 11-length defeat represented his best form and he has plenty of class.

CHAMPION CHASE Sprinter Sacre simply takes the breath away. It is hard to think of another chaser who has tanked so powerfully into a fence and, even if Cheltenham might not be a track that plays entirely to his strengths, he looks a class apart.

Sizing Europe lost his crown last season and, a year older, looks to have no more than place claims if Sprinter Sacre stands up. Arguably he would be more at home over the Ryanair trip and the odds suggest he would have a better chance in that race, but don't forget he is an electric jumper with a tremendous record at Cheltenham and over two miles.

If there is a chink in Sprinter Sacre – and admittedly it's impossible

What they say

'He has run well there twice before'

Colm Murphy, trainer of Glam Gerry (below) *(Byrne Group Plate)* "He got stopped at the bypassed fence when he was getting into a nice position at Leopardstown but ran on well to finish fifth and I was delighted with the run. He's been around Cheltenham twice and run well there twice. He was third in the Byrne Plate last year and we'd be hoping for a nice run but we're under no illusions about the task" *Has recorded highest two RPRs at Cheltenham*

Tony Martin, trainer of Golantilla *(Bumper)* "I'm absolutely delighted to get a horse of his calibre into the yard. I had a horse of mine running against him when he won at Cork and I must say he looked really good" *Won by 13 lengths at Cork on only bumper start*

to see one – Sizing Europe is the most likely one to benefit if he lines up here.

WORLD HURDLE All of a sudden, with the injury to Big Buck's, Ireland might be able to snare a race that has proved elusive since Dorans Pride triumphed 18 years ago. It is not easy to predict what will run, however.

Solwhit, who seems to have retained plenty of his ability, has always given the impression that three miles was worth trying. Understandably, trainer Charles Byrnes is taking it softly with him and may decide Cheltenham is not in the nine-year-old's interest at this stage.

Bog Warrior has reverted to hurdling to great effect in recent months and proved he gets three miles when easily beating Zaidpour in the Galmoy at Gowran Park. That form indicates he may have an edge over Monksland, whose Leopardstown victory at Christmas suggested he was worth a shot at the World Hurdle too.

If all three take their chance, Ireland would probably have in the region of a 50-50 chance of taking the stayers' hurdling crown.

Ballycasey looks a solid Albert Bartlett candidate

NOVICE HURDLES Willie Mullins has a handful of smart novices – several of them owned by Rich Ricci – and his task when it comes to Cheltenham, partly, will be to keep them apart. **Ballycasey** looks an Albert Bartlett candidate through and through, while **Pont Alexandre** would probably be fine in that race or the Neptune. All three races are open to Champagne Fever and, if as seems likely, he runs in the Supreme, his chance of a Cheltenham win will arguably be compromised because of Ricci's strength and depth.

Pont Alexandre is hugely likeable and he screams 'Irish banker' to a great many punters here. Considering he had run just once in France, the level of market support for him to beat Don Cossack in a Grade 1 on his Irish debut was remarkable, particularly as he is said to be a relatively average worker. He bolted up then and was even more impressive subsequently at Leopardstown in really demanding conditions. He looks too classy for the likes of The New One and should score in the Neptune.

The Paul Nolan-trained **Defy Logic** produced a scintillating effort on his only hurdling start, which he won by 34 lengths, and is an outsider with plenty going for him. He does not need to improve a great deal on ratings to run a big race in the Neptune or Albert Bartlett.

My Tent Or Yours' awesome performance at Newbury off 149 entitles him to be favourite for the Supreme but **Jezki** will carry major Irish hopes. The probability of better ground improving him, given how dominant he has been on the Irish two-mile hurdling scene, suggests bright prospects at the festival. All the more fascinating is that JP McManus now owns him and, with Tony McCoy highly likely to ride

Race	Wins	2nd/ 3rd	Runners	Profit/ loss	Winner's SP
Record of Irish runners in past ten years					
Supreme Novices'	5	5	64	8	3-1, 7-2, 40-1, 17-2, 12-1
Arkle Chase	2	3	37	-21	8-1, 6-1
JLT Specialty Chase	2	1	15	1	7-1, 7-1
Champion Hurdle	5	6	54	8	33-1, 7-2, 7-4, 16-1, 11-4
Cross Country Chase	7	14	61	-5	4-1, 7-2, 5-2, 4-1, 7-2, 25-1, 13-2
Mares' Hurdle	4	3	22	-13.1	2-1,6-4, 5-6,4-7
Pulteney Nov Hcp Chase	1	6	24	-14	9-1
National Hunt Chase	2	9	47	0	40-1, 5-1
Neptune Novices' Hurdle	5	9	50	-14	6-1, 17-2, 7-1, 5-2, 7-1
RSA Chase	4	6	35	5.25	25-1, 9-4, 10-1
Champion Chase	5	7	29	14.3	7-4, 6-4, 16-1, 10-1, 10-1
Coral Cup	4	6	50	9	4-1, 11-1, 14-1, 16-1
Fred Winter H'cap Hurdle	2	5	47	-16	20-1, 9-1
Champion Bumper	7	10	103	-18.5	7-1, 7-2, 33-1, 11-2, 12-1, 9-2, 16-1
Jewson Novices' Chase	2	1	5	4	4-1, 3-1
Pertemps Final H'cap Hurdle	2	8	46	16	10-1, 50-1
Ryanair Chase	0	5	23	-23	
World Hurdle	0	8	34	-34	
Byrne Group Plate H'cap Chase	0	4	25	-25	
Kim Muir H'cap Chase	0	7	38	-38	
Triumph Hurdle	0	7	56	-56	
County Hurdle	6	6	63	66	10-1, 12-1, 50-1, 20-1, 10-1, 20-1
Albert Bartlett Nov Hurdle	2	5	41	2	8-1, 33-1
Gold Cup	2	4	24	-10.5	4-1, 15-2
Foxhunter Chase	3	9	48	11.5	20-1, 33-1, 7-2
Martin Pipe H'cap Hurdle	1	2	8	-2.5	9-2
Grand Annual H'cap Chase	2	5	32	-15.5	7-1, 15-2
Total	**75**	**161**	**1081**	**-161**	

My Tent Or Yours, Jezki will be some ride for whoever gets the call.

Our Conor is clearly the top Irish hope for the Triumph Hurdle, having bolted up in the Grade 1 on Hennessy day. He was fast enough to win over seven furlongs on the Flat last year, yet stays well and basically seems to have everything going for him. Ireland's Triumph record is lamentable but Our Conor appeals plenty in an open renewal.

NOVICE CHASES Willie Mullins has a good bunch of novice chasers, without having the same 'wow' factor as the hurdlers. The Graham Wylie-owned **Boston Bob** and **Back In Focus** are both possibles for the RSA Chase, while **Aupcharlie** and **Vesper Bell** are novices with other targets.

Aupcharlie, perhaps curiously for a chaser beaten on his last two outings, is to be greatly respected regardless of what race he goes for. The Jewson and two and a half miles around Cheltenham, where he has run well before, could be just what he wants. He likes decent ground and is an excellent jumper. He merits a bet.

Mullins has **Arvika Ligeonniere**, generally a sound jumper, in the Arkle and the Tony Martin-trained **Beneficient** has a shot after winning the Irish version, albeit in somewhat fortunate circumstances. We must concede, however, likely defeat to a one-time Irish horse: Simonsig.

'This is the one they have to worry about'

Nicky Henderson, trainer of Oscar Whisky
(World Hurdle) "We ran in the Cleeve Hurdle to answer a question and no one can say he didn't stay. He might be better suited by better ground and we'll be able to ride him closer now we know the trip isn't a problem. If it's good ground you'll probably see him running in the World Hurdle" *More than half of his hurdle runs have been at Cheltenham, with form figures of 41311512*

Nick Williams, trainer of Reve De Sivola
(World Hurdle) "His win at Ascot was the best three-mile performance without Big Buck's. He needs three miles and he doesn't have to have soft ground, although he wouldn't want it very quick. He runs his race every time and is just so tough and genuine" *Only Big Buck's has beaten him in three starts over hurdles at 3m-plus*

Nicky Henderson, trainer of Rolling Star
(Triumph) "He's a lovely horse, great temperament, great attitude. He's always looked like a nice horse. I don't think he'd mind better ground; it won't hurt him" *Three of the last four Triumph winners had previously raced in France*

David Bridgwater, trainer of The Giant Bolster *(Gold Cup)*
"This is the one they all have to worry about. I guarantee we've missed more work because we're so high up in the Cotswolds. I'm chuffed to bits with him and so excited" *112 in completed runs over fences at Cheltenham but form figures at the track also include FUU*

Captain fantastic

The Racing Post's regional correspondents with their picks from around the training centres

LAMBOURN In recent weeks I've been asked the same two questions about this year's Cheltenham Festival, *writes Rodney Masters.* Can Nicky Henderson surpass last season's record-breaking achievement of seven winners? And what's the best-value bet from Seven Barrows?

All evidence would suggest Henderson is marshalling the strongest strike force of his 35-year training career, although that does not necessarily generate more winners, particularly with Willie Mullins lining up a similar army of elite troops. Such is the awesome power of Henderson's challenge, however, that anything less than three winners is likely to be viewed as an underachievement.

As for the value bet from our region, it must be the 5-1 available about **Captain Conan** *(above)* in the Jewson, provided of course that, as expected, Dynaste is routed to the RSA Chase. Captain Conan is held

Watch every UK & Irish horse race
LIVE on your mobile with
our live stream from ATR & RUK

Plus **LIVE** racing from Dubai &
South Africa now available*

in such regard at Seven Barrows – and in particular by long-serving head lad Corky Browne, the best judge I know – that it would have been a case of black armbands issued for everyone had he not won at Cheltenham on his chasing debut. There was never a worry – jumping skilfully throughout, he won with ease – and he has since followed up with two Grade 1 wins at Sandown.

Some onlookers were nit-picking after Barry Geraghty had to ask Captain Conan for a supreme effort to come from off the pace to overhaul Third Intention, who looked to have got away from them, close home when stepped up to 2m4f for the first time in the Scilly Isles. There was plenty of experiment in the mix with him that day, primarily over whether he'd stay. As Geraghty explained afterwards, they did learn from the mission. Apart from ending doubt over his stamina, the main factor was he appreciates being ridden up with the pace, in preference to being dropped out.

Accordingly, we can be confident of a more positive ride over the same trip in the Jewson and it will be a surprise if he is ever out of the first five there, unless of course there is a frenetic gallop. There appears to be no flaw in Captain Conan. He certainly does not lack speed, and

What they say

'This one has got extraordinary gears'

Barry Geraghty, rider of Captain Conan (*Jewson*) "He just lacked a bit of race fitness at Sandown. I don't think the ground was an issue. He's a big horse who wants a lot of work. I would say two and a half miles is perfect for him" *Hasn't won in three starts on faster ground than soft*

Nicky Henderson, trainer of My Tent Or Yours (*Supreme*) "The Betfair Hurdle was an extraordinarily run race. There was no pace in the race and you'd expect an awful lot of horses to come there, but this one has got extraordinary gears. I'd swear he's better on better ground" *The five-length winning margin in the Betfair was the biggest in 11 years*

Pick of the bunch
from Lambourn

Captain Conan Flawless. Jumps, stays and expected to outclass opposition in Jewson

Coneygree Game and reliable. Good each-way shot for the Albert Bartlett

Henderson yankee Captain Conan, Bobs Worth, Rolling Star, Oscar Whisky

Henderson accumulator Captain Conan, Simonsig, Sprinter Sacre, Bobs Worth, My Tent Or Yours

but for Simonsig's presence he would have been equally at home in the Racing Post Arkle Chase.

Like Captain Conan, there is no deficiency in Simonsig, although the same must be said of the latter's chief Arkle opponent, Overturn, who had the pace to finish second in last season's Champion Hurdle and has been fault-free over fences. As a result, I would back Simonsig only if he went odds-against because his current price is too short.

It will be fascinating to see how first-time cheekpieces galvanise Long Run in the Betfred Gold Cup as he attempts to regain his title. He pulled out everything to win a second King George VI Chase in dire conditions at Kempton and the concern would be that the effort bottomed him. I much prefer the chance of stable companion **Bobs Worth**, who comes into the race fresh, albeit by accident rather than design after a below-par tracheal wash ruled him out of the Argento Chase on trials day at Cheltenham.

A slog in the mud there would have been a negative and, although some may question this, it is a positive that he has not raced since winning Newbury's Hennessy Gold Cup on the first day of December. He was soon over his little hiccup with the trachea and Henderson

Nigel Twiston-Davies, trainer of The New One *(Neptune)* "He's a complete machine. He really could be the best one we've ever had. He seems to have so much speed and staying power" *Beat My Tent Or Yours in Champion Bumper at Aintree last season*

Philip Hobbs, trainer of Captain Chris *(Gold Cup)* "It's very likely he'll go for the Gold Cup, possibly the Ryanair. Overall at Cheltenham he has had four runs – two wins, a second and a disaster last time. Although he has an inclination to go right it is not necessarily going to stop him winning" *Yet to win in five starts beyond 2m4½f*

Harry Fry, trainer of Rock On Ruby *(Champion Hurdle)* "He has improved and is much bigger and stronger. He's a real tough horse. He will keep galloping and keep finding all day" *Form figures of 12213 at Cheltenham*

Jonjo O'Neill, trainer of Taquin Du Seuil *(Neptune)* "He's got enough experience, jumps well and does everything right. He's only run on really soft ground but works well on good ground at home and I don't envisage any problems on that score" *Only defeat in four starts over hurdles was against My Tent Or Yours*

Jeremy Scott, trainer of Melodic Rendezvous *(Supreme)* "He's improving with each race, which is amazing as I always thought he needed good ground but he keeps winning on soft and heavy. He has a lot of pace and it's most likely he will end up in the Supreme." *RPR has risen with each run over hurdles (122, 133, 146, 155)*

knows all the secrets of how to get him ready at home.

Bobs Worth won the Hennessy without being hard pressed, yet the form is as robust as it comes. Runner-up Tidal Bay went on to win the Grade 1 Lexus Chase, where he beat First Lieutenant – who was third at Newbury – and the minor places at Leopardstown were filled by Flemenstar and Sir Des Champs. Bobs Worth is unbeaten in four visits to Cheltenham and is on a festival hat-trick after his wins in the Albert Bartlett Novices' Hurdle and the RSA Chase.

My Tent Or Yours will take plenty of beating if he takes his chance in the William Hill Supreme Novices' Hurdle but the same will apply if connections decide to supplement six days beforehand for the Stan James Champion Hurdle. He has the gears and class to win in the best of company, but it is not, probably most sensibly, J P McManus's strategy to pitch a novice into a championship for seniors.

If connections opt for the easier option, **Grandouet** must be the one for the Champion Hurdle. It is worth remembering that at this stage last season, until injury intervened, he was considered by many within the stable as their leading hope.

The Champion Hurdle picture remains more than a shade confused because if the ground came up testing there is every prospect of Oscar Whisky being diverted from the Ladbrokes World Hurdle, while such conditions would not see Grandouet at his best.

Cash And Go, who was surprisingly backed to beat My Tent Or Yours in the Betfair, has an entry but it would be no surprise if attention was switched to the Vincent O'Brien County Handicap Hurdle. Any of the available 16-1 with a non-runner, no bet clause would be tempting, although he needs to improve his jumping.

Henderson will field his usual strong team for his father's memorial race, the Johnny Henderson Grand Annual Chase, and one of particular interest, provided the ground is no worse than good to soft, will be **Tanks For That**, who was runner-up to stable companion Bellvano in the race last season. He shaped with promise on his latest start when fourth in the Game Spirit at Newbury, where the ground was unsuitably testing.

The 16-1 on offer about the Mark Bradstock-trained **Coneygree** represents decent each-way value in the Albert Bartlett, especially when taking into account his two Grade 2 wins at the course this winter. It cannot be said his bubble was burst by the subsequent defeat, also at the course, behind At Fishers Cross and The New One because they are the best three-mile novices around. Coneygree is as game and reliable as they come and he should make the frame.

WEST COUNTRY The Stan James Champion Hurdle had not been a happy hunting ground for West Country horses in the recent past until **Rock On Ruby** changed all that last March by bringing the hurdler's crown back to the area for the first time in nine years, *writes Andrew King.*

Then officially trained by Paul Nicholls, the eight-year-old is now running in the name of Harry Fry, who oversaw last year's success in his role as the champion trainer's assistant, and confidence is high that a repeat victory is on the cards.

He has been trained all year specifically to peak in the big race and

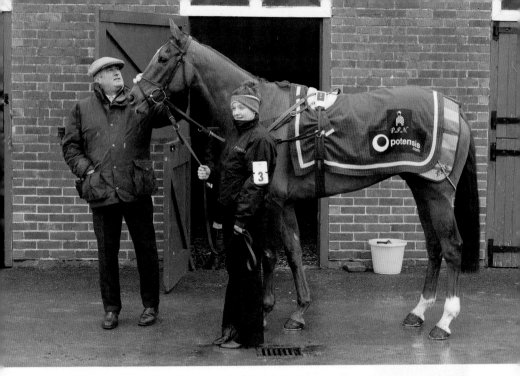

he looked on the burly side when making his comeback in December with third place behind Zarkandar at Cheltenham, where the gluey ground did not help his cause.

On better ground at Doncaster in February, Rock On Ruby looked an altogether different proposition as he won the race that unfortunately saw Darlan take a fatal last-hurdle fall. The key to Rock On Ruby is decent ground and connections are hopeful conditions at Cheltenham will be in his favour. If they are, he will take all the beating again.

Silviniaco Conti carries the area's hopes in the Betfred Cheltenham Gold Cup, having passed every examination this term with flying colours. There is a question mark hanging over his effectiveness at Cheltenham, as his only previous visit ended in defeat by Menorah over hurdles, but that was more than three years ago and the Paul Nicholls team are confident he is a bigger, better and stronger proposition now. They have no worries in that respect.

Just like 12 months ago, David Pipe approaches the festival with the short-priced RSA Chase favourite. Grands Crus let his supporters down last March, but the word from Pond House is that **Dynaste** is a more robust type. He has done nothing wrong in three runs over fences, winning comfortably at Cheltenham, Newbury and Kempton, and he will take all the beating.

In recent years the Ladbrokes World Hurdle was the area's banker with Big Buck's and now it is down to **Reve De Sivola** to carry the baton in his absence. He has a big chance of securing glory for Nick Williams.

On the novice hurdle front it seems the West's best chance lies with Jeremy Scott's **Melodic Rendezvous**, who is in the William Hill Supreme Novices' Hurdle and the Neptune Investment Management Novices' Hurdle over an extra half a mile.

Silviniaco Conti is expected to banish doubts about his effectiveness at Cheltenham

Donald McCain, trainer of Overturn (Arkle) "He can be spectacular over a fence and otherwise he's neat, which is how you want him. He finished second in a Champion Hurdle. Why should I be afraid of anyone?" *Trying to become the first nine-year-old to win the Arkle since Danish Flight in 1988*

Raymond Anderson Green, owner of Rival D'Estruval (NH Chase) "He goes exceptionally well fresh. Everything about him suggests he'll stay and he acts on any ground" *Form figures of 22211 after a layoff of at least two months*

Donald McCain, trainer of Our Mick (JLT Specialty) "The plan is to head for the race he was third in last year. You have to think he could go close off his current mark granted a clear round" *Form figures of 5311133 in completed chases*

Pick of the bunch
from the North

Kashmir Peak Solid each-way chance of giving his stable another Triumph

Rival D'Estruval Smart novice who has been aimed at the National Hunt Chase all season

Overturn Top-flight hurdler who has taken so well to chasing. Exciting prospect for the Arkle

Ifandbutwhynot Interesting outsider for the County Hurdle. Still on the upgrade and will be ideally suited by the strong gallop

Viva Colonia Up in grade for the Grand Annual but travels and jumps well and should get in the frame

The ground will decide where he goes, but he has the pace for the two-miler on softish ground and stays well enough to be a real threat in the longer race.

Nicholls's best chance of landing the JCB Triumph Hurdle for a third time is **Far West** but the champion trainer will also be represented by Irish Saint, Sametegal and possibly Caid Du Berlais.

Far West is unbeaten since moving to Somerset and two of his victories have been at Cheltenham, albeit on testing ground. It is hoped he will be just as effective if things dry out.

NORTH John Quinn won the Triumph Hurdle last year with Countrywide Flame and he has another good shot this time with the unexposed **Kashmir Peak**, who is one of the north's best chances at the 2013 festival, *writes Colin Russell.*

A good-looking sort who is straightforward at home, according to Quinn, Kashmir Peak showed fair form for Ger Lyons on the Flat in Ireland and has made up into a better hurdler. He was impressive when beating some ordinary performers on his debut at Market Rasen and really caught the eye next time at Doncaster when he came from off the pace to beat the Paul Nicholls-trained Sametegal by a length.

Admittedly he was receiving 3lb from the runner-up that day, and the pair were at level weights when they met in the John Smith's Scottish Triumph Hurdle, where unfortunately Kashmir Peak unseated his rider before the race had begun in earnest.

Despite that unfortunate experience, Kashmir Peak remains on course for Cheltenham, where the stiff uphill finish is expected to be ideal for him.

Quinn has a useful second string for the Triumph in Hidden Justice, who impressed when winning on his Wetherby debut and following up at Catterick.

Countrywide Flame heads for the Champion Hurdle, having developed into a top-class performer this term by winning the Fighting Fifth Hurdle at Newcastle and finishing a good second to Rock On Ruby at Doncaster. Quinn is hopeful of a good run as he feels a strongly run race and the stiff Cheltenham track will suit the five-year-old far better than Doncaster or Kempton, where he finished well beaten behind the ill-fated Darlan in the Christmas Hurdle.

The other northern challenger for the Champion Hurdle is last season's Supreme Novices' Hurdle winner Cinders And Ashes from the Donald McCain yard. He has been a shade disappointing this season and was behind Countrywide Flame at Newcastle and Kempton. The ground was testing on both occasions, however, and McCain reckons he'll be much better on good ground.

McCain appears to have better chances at the meeting and the spearhead of his challenge is **Overturn**. Last year's Champion Hurdle runner-up is three from three over fences and should prove the major threat to Simonsig in the Racing Post Arkle Chase.

Another McCain runner to command plenty of respect is **Peddlers Cross**, who has an excellent festival record over hurdles, having won the Neptune in 2010 and been runner-up to Hurricane Fly in the Champion the following year.

Overturn can win his exciting Arkle clash with Simonsig

He now goes for the Ladbrokes World Hurdle and, although he wasn't particularly impressive when winning at Musselburgh on his hurdles comeback, he jumped brilliantly that day and left the impression he will be seen to much better advantage in the World Hurdle.

Although he's had a stack of novice hurdle winners this season, McCain doesn't have a potential star among them for the festival, but two others from his yard worth noting are Real Milan, who could go for the RSA Chase, and Son Of Flicka, who has finished second and first at the last two festivals.

Son Of Flicka, who needs good ground, landed a gamble in the Coral Cup last year and that handicap is his objective again. Another live northern contender is Mike Smith's Orsippus, who was third in the race two years ago.

After his battling win in the Argento Chase, the Malcolm Jefferson-trained **Cape Tribulation** is no forlorn hope for the Gold Cup. Admittedly last year's Pertemps Hurdle winner has a bit to find with a few of his rivals, but he has a good Cheltenham record and is still improving.

The National Hunt Chase has long been the target for Pauline's Robson's **Rival D'Estruval**, who has won two out of three over fences this term. He hasn't run since early December but is considered to be at his best when fresh and on decent ground.

The Brian Ellison-trained **Viva Colonia**, who has taken well to fences this term, is firmly on course for the Grand Annual Handicap Chase and the strong-travelling **Ifandbutwhynot**, trained by David O'Meara, should be ideally suited by the big field and strong gallop in the County Hurdle.

Vital statistics

Record of horses wearing headgear

Supreme Nov Hurdle
0 wins-9 runs; £9 loss to £1 stake

Arkle Chase
0-12 (-£12)

JLT Specialty Chase
2-37 (-£14)

Champion Hurdle
2-24 (+£14.50)

Cross Country
0-26 (-£26)

Mares' Hurdle
0-10 (-£10)

Pulteney Chase
0-25 (-£25)

National Hunt Chase
2-43 (+£1)

Neptune Hurdle
0-9 (-£9)

RSA Chase
0-8 (-£8)

Champion Chase
0-9 (-£9)

Coral Cup
1-45 (-£33)

Fred Winter Hurdle
2-40 (+£11)

Champion Bumper
0-3 (-£3)

Jewson Chase
0-2 (-£2)

Pertemps Final
2-56 (-£18)

Ryanair Chase
1-11 (-£6)

World Hurdle
0-31 (-£31)

Byrne Group Plate
0-29 (-£29)

Kim Muir
1-57 (-£52.70)

Triumph Hurdle
2-25 (-£14)

County Hurdle
0-37 (-£37)

Albert Bartlett
1-10 (0)

Gold Cup
0-23 (-£23)

Foxhunter
2-44 (+£11)

Martin Pipe
0-18 (-£18)

Grand Annual
1-28 (-£11)

Statistics from 2003 to 2012 (not including tongue straps)

The key trials

Form Book editor Graham Dench runs the rule over the big winter action

Conti upwardly mobile

Graham Dench says it would be a mistake to underestimate Paul Nicholls's rising star

GOLD CUP It is unheard of in modern times for a horse to win the Gold Cup with only one previous run that season, but that is not putting off backers of Bobs Worth, who has been ante-post favourite ever since his win in the Hennessy Gold Cup at Newbury.

Bobs Worth looked a thorough professional when winning that ultra-competitive handicap off a mark of 160 on just his fifth start over fences and four Cheltenham wins from four tries, including festival wins in the Albert Bartlett and the RSA Chase, leave no doubt he is a top-class operator who is equally at home on an undulating track with a stiff uphill finish.

However, missing Cheltenham's Argento Chase following a below-par tracheal wash has left him short of top-level match practice and it is not as if his form puts him head and shoulders clear of the rest. Far from it, as he was getting 6lb from three-and-a-quarter-length runner-up Tidal Bay in the Hennessy, which puts that form into perspective.

No horse will go into the Gold Cup with greater top-level experience than Bobs Worth's stablemate Long Run, who looked set for a long reign at the top after he followed a first King George win, when he had only just turned six, with a comprehensive defeat of Denman in the 2011 Gold Cup.

The Long Run we marvelled at then would probably make short work of the current crop, but two years on his profile is far less convincing. His third behind the ill-fated Synchronised and 50-1 chance The Giant Bolster in a sub-standard 2012 Gold Cup is still too raw a memory for many punters, and his dramatic last-strides defeat of Captain Chris for a second win in the King George – admittedly in desperate ground – was nowhere near persuasive enough.

He has work to do if he is to turn the tables on the upwardly mobile Silviniaco Conti on Betfair Chase form at Haydock. Please don't blame the jockey, though. We have no right to expect an amateur to be a match for Tony McCoy or Ruby Walsh, but he was plenty good enough when Long Run was good enough.

Silviniaco Conti is the type who might easily be underestimated, because there is nothing flashy about him. A former high-class novice hurdler, he is the sort who goes about his business quietly and efficiently and keeps on delivering, just like Bobs Worth, and three wins from three starts in his second season over fences underline what a good crop of novices they were last season. He was reportedly by no means fully wound up when a comprehensive winner from The Giant Bolster in the Betfair Denman Chase at Newbury and the runner-up, though himself held up by the weather, will do well to reverse placings on 4lb worse terms.

The Gigginstown Stud pair both merit respect, but Sir Des Champs' improvement seems to have levelled off and First Lieutenant has no more than place prospects on all known form. Sir Des Champs heads

Vital statistics

Races with the 'festival factor'

Paddy Power Gold Cup
Cheltenham,
November 17, 2012
2m4½f, soft

1	**Al Ferof** 7 11-8	R Walsh 8-1
2	**Walkon** 7 10-6	R Thornton 7-1
3	**Nadiya De La Vega** 6 10-8	AP McCoy 12-1
4	**Casey Top** 9 9-9	M Enright 40-1

Trainer: Paul Nicholls
Distances: 3l, 12l, 6l
18 ran

Festival pointer Four of the first five Ryanair winners came out of this race (and the other was a former Paddy Power winner) but it has not had the same influence in recent years, although Long Run was third before his Gold Cup win in 2011. Six festival winners have come out of this race in the past ten years

Betfair Chase
Haydock,
November 24, 2012
3m, soft

1	**Silviniaco Conti** 6 11-7	R Walsh 7-4
2	**Long Run** 6 11-7	S Waley-Cohen 11-8f
3	**The Giant Bolster** 7 11-7	T Scudamore 15-2

Trainer: Paul Nicholls
Distances: 2½l, ½l. 5 ran

Festival pointer This race has featured the Gold Cup winner three times out of seven, although only Kauto Star (2006-07) has won both in the same season. Every Betfair winner has gone on to run in the Gold Cup, with finishing positions of 012P3PP. Three festival winners in seven years

to Cheltenham on the back of a first Grade 1 win of the season in Leopardstown's Hennessy Gold Cup, but a hard-fought defeat of a non-staying and off-colour Flemenstar does not represent Gold Cup-winning form. What could make a huge difference to him is better ground. Both of his festival wins have been on good going and he could be a very different proposition if it dries out.

Verdict Silviniaco Conti is preferred to Bobs Worth on value grounds, but don't be surprised if Sir Des Champs improves past them all if the ground dries out.

CHAMPION HURDLE

Hurricane Fly *(below)* was a lacklustre third behind Rock On Ruby when a strong fancy for last year's Stan James Champion Hurdle, but that sole blip in his last 12 starts is not too hard to excuse following a troubled campaign during which he had appeared just once in public.

While that defeat is likely to strike a cautionary note among those who might otherwise regard him as a banker, there is considerably more substance to his preparatory runs this time and he is very much the one to beat again.

Three Grade 1 wins in the current season have taken his career total at that level to 14 and, while the ill-fated Go Native still had every chance of beating him when tipping up at the last in Punchestown's Morgiana Hurdle, subsequent Leopardstown defeats of Unaccompanied and Thousand Stars in the Istabraq Hurdle and of Thousand Stars and Binocular in the Irish Champion Hurdle have been thoroughly convincing. Indeed he travelled, jumped and quickened as well as ever in the last-named.

Not that it is likely to be easy for him. Peddlers Cross made a race of it in the 2011 Champion Hurdle and he will face worthy opposition once again, not least from Rock On Ruby, who was not given the credit he deserved when beating Overturn 12 months ago and might easily be underestimated once again.He had unsuitably testing ground to contend with when only third behind Zarkandar and Grandouet in a hot little International Hurdle and then had his recent Doncaster success in another intriguing affair overshadowed by the fatal fall of Darlan. Cheltenham will suit him better than Doncaster and he should be much sharper for that race.

Zarkandar, whose fifth in last year's Champion Hurdle was his first defeat over hurdles, enjoyed a fitness advantage and a 4lb allowance from both when beating Grandouet and Rock On Ruby in the International, so he is theoretically no certainty to confirm the placings, but Paul Nicholls insists he is a different horse this season and his win

Vital statistics

Sportingbet Tingle Creek Chase
Sandown, December 8, 2012
2m, soft

1 **Sprinter Sacre** 6 11-7
B Geraghty 4-11f

2 **Kumbeshwar** 5 11-7
W Hutchinson 25-1

3 **Sanctuaire** 6 11-7
R Walsh 11-4

Trainer: Nicky Henderson
Distances: 15l, 4½l
7 ran

Festival pointer The key guide to the Champion Chase. Although only four of the 15 to try have won both races since the Tingle Creek became a Grade 1, the Champion Chase winner had run in the Tingle Creek in six of the past ten years
Seven festival winners in the past ten years

....

Paul Stewart Ironspine Charity Challenge Gold Cup
Cheltenham, December 15, 2012
2m5f, heavy

1 **Unioniste** 4 9-9
H Derham 15-2

2 **Walkon** 7 10-12
R Thornton 7-2f

3 **Golden Chieftain** 7 10-2
D Crosse 20-1

Trainer: Paul Nicholls
Distances: 11l, 6l
14 ran

Festival pointer Salut Flo was last of the 12 finishers in this race last season (on his return from a long layoff) before landing the Byrne Group Plate on his next start. Three of the eight Ryanair Chase winners had run in this race, although the last was Taranis in 2007. None of the festival scorers to come out of this race in the past ten years had won here
Six festival winners in the past ten years

in the Kingwell at Wincanton was achieved without too much fuss.

Like Hurricane Fly, Zarkandar goes to post demonstrably at the top of his game, whereas Grandouet, who remains a horse with untapped potential, will have a question mark over him after missing the Wincanton race with a reportedly minor leg issue.

Cinders And Ashes looked a potential champion when beating Darlan in the Supreme Novices' but has yet to fulfil that promise. However, he could leave this season's form well behind if the ground dries out, especially with the likely bigger field and stronger pace playing to his strengths.

One other who would have to be of interest if supplemented is the Betfair Hurdle winner My Tent Or Yours, who would be a worthy substitute for Darlan and more appealing than owner JP McManus's former Champion Hurdle winner Binocular. The form of his hugely impressive Newbury win off 149 puts him within touching distance of championship level and the hint ought to be taken if he runs here, as the Supreme Novices' looks there for the taking.

Verdict Hurricane Fly is a strong fancy again, with last year's winner Rock On Ruby the main danger. Take the hint, however, if My Tent Or Yours is supplemented.

....

CHAMPION CHASE AND RYANAIR CHASE

There is no better trial for the Queen Mother Champion Chase than the Racing Post Arkle Chase and few have won the novice race in better style than Sprinter Sacre, who has gone on to extend a stunning unbeaten run over fences to seven.

A hugely impressive winner from Cue Card and Menorah in the Arkle, Sprinter Sacre has been so utterly flawless again this season in the Tingle Creek Chase at Sandown and in a Victor Chandler Chase transferred from Ascot to Cheltenham that it is inconceivable any of the horses he beat in either race will turn the tables.

He looks a near certainty to follow in the footsteps of the likes of Azertyuiop, Moscow Flyer, Voy Por Ustedes and Sizing Europe, who all won the Arkle and Queen Mother in consecutive seasons.

One would have to respect stablemate Finian's Rainbow, if it dried out, as last year's Queen Mother winner, and also Sizing Europe, who was a shade unlucky in second on that occasion and won it the year before, but Finian's Rainbow was most disappointing again in the Ascot Chase on his return from a break and both have as an alternative the Ryanair Chase, which might well turn out one of the highlights of the festival.

It is impossible to tell exactly who will be lining up for the Ryanair, and at the time of writing the favourite Cue Card, who won the Ascot Chase, is not even certain to run as connections are tempted to have another crack at Sprinter Sacre. This, however, is a race that simply gets better by the year.

It is a shame Flemenstar will not be taking part, but a cracking affair is in prospect nevertheless, for it is not inconceivable that we might see Sizing Europe, who is unbeaten in four starts at the intermediate trip and still unexposed, and Finian's Rainbow taking on last year's winner Riverside Theatre and exciting second-season chasers Champion Court and Cue Card, who were both non-stayers in the King George.

Riverside Theatre owed last year's success to an extraordinary ride

Rock On Ruby is the main danger to Hurricane Fly

from Barry Geraghty and he has not looked the same horse since. He baffled connections in the King George and has it to prove all over again now.

Cue Card's runaway win at Exeter on his reappearance was one of the chasing performances of the season and his King George fifth, a place behind last year's Jewson second Champion Court, who looked the winner turning in, can be forgiven following early mistakes. He looked very good again in the Ascot Chase, even allowing for the blunder made by runner-up Captain Chris when upsides two out, and let us not forget he ran Sprinter Sacre to seven lengths in the Arkle. No horse has got anywhere near as close since.

Verdict Sprinter Sacre is impossible to oppose in the Queen Mother Champion Chase. Cue Card will be a strong fancy if confirmed for the Ryanair.

WORLD HURDLE The Ladbrokes World Hurdle will not be the same without four-time winner Big Buck's, but it might be even better.

Although only a shade of odds-on for his last three wins in the race, Big Buck's would almost certainly have been significantly shorter this time but for injury, having won in a canter from Reve De Sivola at Newbury on Hennessy day. Since he was ruled out for the remainder of the season, the staying hurdle division has taken on a whole new complexion, and no fewer than 61 entries were made for a race that 12 months earlier received a mere 34.

It is a measure of the superiority of Big Buck's over the rest that Reve De Sivola, beaten out of sight at Newbury, is likely to be vying for favouritism in the World Hurdle with Oscar Whisky, who 12 months ago could finish only fifth when widely regarded as the only credible alternative to the favourite.

Vital statistics

William Hill.com Christmas Hurdle
Kempton,
December 26, 2012
2m, heavy

1 **Darlan** 5 11-7
AP McCoy 3-1

2 **Raya Star** 6 11-7
R Thornton 8-1

3 **Dodging Bullets** 4 11-7
R Walsh 8-1

Trainer: Nicky Henderson
Distances: 4½l, 2¾l
7 ran

Festival pointer The last to do the Christmas/ Champion Hurdle double was Kribensis in 1989-90 but last season's five-runner field featured three of the first four in the Champion (runner-up Rock On Ruby became the fourth beaten horse from the past 11 runnings to land the Champion)
Five festival winners in the past ten years

....

Lexus Chase
Leopardstown,
December 28, 2012
3m, soft

1 **Tidal Bay** 11 11-10
R Walsh 9-2

2 **First Lieutenant** 7 11-10
B Cooper 14-1

3 **Flemenstar** 7 11-10
A Lynch 5-4f

Trainer: Paul Nicholls
Distances: hd, ½l. 9 ran

Festival pointer Four of the past nine runnings have featured that season's Gold Cup winner and three were British raiders who won here (Best Mate, Denman and Synchronised). The only Irish-trained Gold Cup winner to come out of this race was War Of Attrition, runner-up before his Cheltenham triumph in 2006
Four festival winners in the past ten years

Vital statistics

**Rewards4racing
Cleeve Hurdle**
Cheltenham,
January 26, 2013
3m, heavy

1 **Reve De Sivola**
8 11-8
R Johnson 15-8f

2 **Oscar Whisky**
8 11-8
B Geraghty 2-1

3 **Kentford Grey Lady**
7 10-7
D Elsworth 11-1

Trainer: Nick Williams
Distances: nk, 6l
10 ran

*Festival pointer
Principally a World Hurdle
trial (four of the past six
winners did the double)
but has been used to prep
successfully for a variety
of races – the Champion
Hurdle, National Hunt
Chase and JLT Specialty
Chase (twice in the past
three years). Eight festival
winners in the past ten years*
....

Boylesports.com Hurdle
Leopardstown,
January 26, 2013
2m, heavy

1 **Abbey Lane** 8 10-8
E Mullins 16-1

2 **Rocky Wednesday**
6 10-0
R Colgan 33-1

3 **Ted Veale** 6 10-13
D Russell 9-2f

4 **Joxer** 6 11-5
B Cooper 25-1

Trainer: Willie Mullins
Distances: 2½l, 4¾l
28 ran

*Festival pointer Four
of the six Irish-trained
County Hurdle winners in
the past decade had run
in this race (only Final
Approach, in 2011, won
both) – one of the other
two ran in the Betfair
Hurdle at Newbury.
Xenophon followed up
victory here by taking the
Coral Cup in 2003
Five festival winners in the
past ten years*

Unless Quevega is rerouted from the Mares' Hurdle – unlikely, since a fifth straight win in that race appears a virtual formality – it looks as if Reve De Sivola and Oscar Whisky will be the two to concentrate on. They finished clear of five more World Hurdle entries when fighting out a cracking finish to the Cleeve Hurdle, over the World Hurdle course and distance on heavy ground late in January.

Reve De Sivola, who spent two seasons over fences after his second to Peddlers Cross at the festival as a novice in 2010, won the Cleeve by a neck, but Oscar Whisky at least proved this time that he got the trip and it was interesting to hear Barry Geraghty report that he did so without at any stage having felt quite the horse who has carried him to a host of stylish wins over shorter trips.

If Oscar Whisky ran Reve De Sivola close without being 100 per cent, as might well be the case, he will have a fine chance of reversing placings, but judged strictly on their form at 3m Reve De Sivola has the more convincing profile, having the previous month thrashed last year's World Hurdle third Smad Place and good yardstick Trustan Times in Ascot's Long Walk Hurdle.

Former Champion Hurdle runner-up Peddlers Cross made harder work than one would have liked when winning at Musselburgh but continues to work like a top-class horse by all accounts and still has his fans, although arguably more persuasive cases can be made for three Irish challengers.

Monksland was successful from Zaidpour and So Young in a Grade 2 at Leopardstown on his first start at 3m, while Solwhit, who has won five Grade 1s over 2m in Ireland despite being a contemporary of the brilliant Hurricane Fly, might now be ready to step up to 3m. Bog Warrior has yet to travel out of Ireland but would have a squeak on his win in the Galmoy Hurdle, which was his first try at the trip.

Verdict Like Big Buck's before him, Reve De Sivola never totally convinced as a chaser but has really come into his own since being reinvented as a staying hurdler. Drying ground would temper confidence but on good to soft or softer he should be hard to beat.
....

NOVICE CHASES The Racing Post Arkle Chase looks another belter and might not be the walk in the park for Simonsig that the betting suggests.

There is no question last year's Neptune winner is a tremendously exciting prospect over fences, but a 49-length thumping of a far inferior rival in a two-finisher chase at Ascot, followed six days later by a similarly easy defeat of an admittedly smarter rival in another small field at Kempton, hardly constitute a classic preparation for a task as demanding as this one. Comparisons with Sprinter Sacre are inevitable and he is the likeliest winner, but he faces classy opposition and is no good thing.

Most years one would expect a Champion Hurdle runner-up who has taken as well to fences as Overturn has to be a pretty warm favourite for the Arkle, but that is far from the case.

The extraordinarily versatile Overturn has not put a foot wrong in three all-the-way wins over fences and if he attacks Cheltenham with the same enthusiasm as he has attacked flatter tracks he could put the jumping of even his classiest rivals under pressure. Underestimate him at your peril.

Arvika Ligeonniere and Fago, the other market principals, look classy too, but both will go to post with recent falls to their names. That is far from ideal, even though they were soft, novicey falls and neither had done much wrong beforehand.

The RSA Chase is a little more open, but Dynaste looks a thoroughly worthy favourite. He might be at shorter odds too but for the memory of stable companion Grands Crus, who went to post a year ago with near identical credentials but finished a disappointing fourth. Dynaste, just like Grands Crus, was a high-class staying hurdler and is unbeaten in novice chases at Cheltenham, Newbury and Kempton. The form of all three races has worked out well and the impressive Grade 1 Feltham success at Kempton was as good a performance as we have seen from a staying novice all season. Hopefully he will prove a stronger stayer than Grands Crus, in which case he will be hard to beat.

Unioniste, only third in Dynaste's Cheltenham novice, went on to beat Walkon and other classy handicappers in a hot race at Cheltenham in December and can be rated better than the bare form when remote Feltham runner-up Hadrian's Approach ran him close at Newbury on his latest start. A solid stayer who jumps well and handles Cheltenham well, he looks the one to take advantage if Dynaste is either below form or switched to the shorter Jewson.

Last year's Albert Bartlett runner-up Boston Bob is the main Irish challenger according to the ante-post lists, but his chase form is so far not a patch on Dynaste's. In fairness he has not raced over 3m yet over fences and the stiffer test should bring significant improvement.

All of the leading contenders for the Jewson also have entries in either the Arkle or the RSA, but while this race still has only Grade 2 status it is hardly a poor relation.

Captain Conan might have been going for the Arkle if Nicky Henderson did not have Simonsig for that race, but the Jewson looks the right race for him, even though confidence was shaken somewhat when he was all out to land odds of 1-2 on his first try at the trip at Sandown. He will need to do better than that to win the Jewson but remains the likeliest winner unless Dynaste or Fago is switched from one of the other races.

Verdict Overturn looks good value against Simonsig and, if successful, he is one punters would kick themselves for missing. It is hard to fault the case for Dynaste in the RSA Chase.

NOVICE HURDLES

NOVICE HURDLES My Tent Or Yours must be an outstanding novice to have shown such overwhelming superiority over seasoned handicappers off 149 in Newbury's Betfair Hurdle, especially as they did not go fast enough for him, and the inevitable big field and strong pace should show him to even better advantage in the Supreme Novices' Hurdle. He is a massive talent and, on paper, a banker if running here, but JP McManus also owns the principal Irish hope Jezki, so it would not be too surprising if he was supplemented for the Champion Hurdle.

Grade 1 defeats of Champagne Fever and Waaheb at Fairyhouse and Leopardstown mark Jezki down as a high-class novice, yet he is from a good-ground family and could well be even better on drier going.

Vital statistics

BHP Insurance Irish Champion Hurdle
Leopardstown, January 27, 2013
2m, soft

1 **Hurricane Fly**
9 11-10
R Walsh 1-6f

2 **Thousand Stars**
9 11-10
P Townend 9-1

3 **Binocular**
9 11-10
AP McCoy 11-2

Trainer: Willie Mullins
Distances: 5l, nose
5 ran

Festival pointer The most important hurdle race in Ireland before the festival, with six of the eight Irish-trained winners in the past 14 runnings of the Champion Hurdle having run here (five won)
Three festival winners in the past ten years

....

Dr PJ Moriarty Novice Chase
Leopardstown, February 9, 2013
2m5f, soft

1 **Boston Bob**
8 11-10
P Townend 6-4f

2 **Texas Jack**
7 11-10
P Carberry 9-2

3 **Lord Windermere**
7 11-10
R McNamara 4-1

Trainer: Willie Mullins
Distances: nose, ½l
6 ran

Festival pointer This has emerged as an excellent guide in recent years, with three of the last four RSA Chase winners having run here (two won, the other was second), as well as an Arkle winner who finished second here
Four festival winners in the past ten years

Deloitte Novice Hurdle
Leopardstown,
February 9, 2013
2m2f, soft

1 **Champagne Fever**
  6 11-10
  P Townend 2-1f

2 **Bright New Dawn**
  6 11-10
  D Russell 11-2

3 **Wingtips**
  5 11-9
  B Cooper 14-1

Trainer: Willie Mullins
Distances: 1¾l, 13l
8 ran

Festival pointer This race produced a festival winner each year from 2002 to 2004 but none since. Two winners in those years dropped back in trip to land the Supreme, while a runner-up stepped up to win the Neptune (and two of them subsequently went on to take the Champion Hurdle too). Two festival winners in the past ten years

Hennessy Gold Cup
Leopardstown,
February 9, 2013
3m, soft

1 **Sir Des Champs**
  7 11-10
  D Russell 11-8

2 **Flemenstar**
  8 11-10
  A Lynch 4-5f

3 **Joncol**
  10 11-10
  R Power 33-1

Trainer: Willie Mullins
Distances: 1¾l, 23l
4 ran

Festival pointer No festival winners in the past ten years, although four have placed in the Gold Cup after running in this race. Since the race's inception in 1987, only Jodami (1993) and Imperial Call (1996) have won this race and the Gold Cup in the same year

His trainer Jessica Harrington was making very positive noises indeed until My Tent Or Yours muddied the waters.

Champagne Fever is a candidate in his own right, having won the Champion Bumper as well as the Punchestown Grade 1 bumper (from Melodic Rendezvous) last spring and added a third major prize at the expense of Bright New Dawn with an all-the-way win in the Deloitte Novice Hurdle at Leopardstown. Willie Mullins also has Un Atout and Mozoltov here.

Melodic Rendezvous has rattled up successive hurdles wins at Cheltenham, Sandown (Grade 1 Tolworth Hurdle) and Exeter. There is a suspicion that previously unbeaten runner-up Puffin Billy was not at his best at Exeter, but even so Melodic Rendezvous looks really smart and his finishing kick is a potent weapon.

Dodging Bullets, who ran so well in the Triumph last year and again when third behind Darlan in Kempton's Christmas Hurdle, is another worthy of a deal of respect.

Unlike so many others, Dodging Bullets has only one entry, whereas Melodic Rendezvous is also in the Neptune Investment Management Novices' Hurdle and would be interesting there against Pont Alexandre and company.

Pont Alexandre won a Grade 1 at Navan in December on his first run in Ireland and followed up with another all-the-way win in a Grade 2 at Leopardstown. Both were over the Neptune distance and he gets the trip well. He clearly has pace too and Willie Mullins thinks the world of him.

Vital statistics

Betfair Hurdle
Newbury,
February 9, 2013
2m½f, soft

1 **My Tent Or Yours**
 6 11-2
 AP McCoy 5-1f

2 **Cotton Mill**
 6 10-9
 J Quinlan 9-1

3 **Swing Bowler**
 6 10-1
 T Murphy 8-1

4 **Dark Lover**
 8 10-12
 R Mahon 16-1

Trainer: Nicky Henderson
Distances: 5l, 1¼l
21 ran

Festival pointer This
has produced at least one
festival winner in six of
the past nine runnings.
The last two years have
been exceptions but in
both years also-rans in this
race went on to take two
seconds and a third at the
festival. In the past three
years, three novices with
finishing positions here
of F11 have gone for the
Supreme, finishing 252
Six festival winners in the
past ten years

The New One is clearly not short of speed and Sam Twiston-Davies admits he used it too soon against At Fishers Cross at Cheltenham in January. He beat My Tent Or Yours in the Aintree bumper last April and had impressed in his first three novice hurdles.

Taquin Du Seuil met his only defeat when giving weight to My Tent Or Yours over an inadequate 2m at Ascot and is another worthy contender.

At Fishers Cross is a possible for the Neptune but is already proven over 3m at Cheltenham and, what's more, in handicap company. He seems more likely to run in the longer Albert Bartlett and with a BHA mark of 152 he sets a high standard, although Gevrey Chambertin, also proven in handicap company, is not far behind on 145 and Mullins will fancy his chances again with Ballycasey, whose two comfortable wins have been gained in less taxing company.

Twice in the last three years the winner of the JCB Triumph Hurdle had not even been sighted in Britain until Kempton at the end of February, so this is a race in which to tread warily.

Our Conor looked good when beating the highly rated Diakali in the Spring Juvenile at Leopardstown and Rolling Star made an excellent impression when beating Irish Saint on his British debut at Cheltenham. However, Far West *(above)* has always been Paul Nicholls's Triumph horse ahead of Irish Saint and is preferred, following four good wins from four starts for the stable.

Verdict My Tent Or Yours looks banker material in the Supreme and Pont Alexandre is preferred to The New One in the Neptune. At Fishers Cross is a strong fancy for the Albert Bartlett.

Betfair Ascot Chase
Ascot, February 16, 2013
2m5½f, soft

1 **Cue Card** 7 11-7
 J Tizzard 15-8f

2 **Captain Chris** 9 11-7
 R Johnson 11-4

3 **Ghizao** 9 11-7
 R Walsh 12-1

Trainer: Colin Tizzard
Distances: 6l, 1½l
6 ran

Festival pointer A good
guide to the Ryanair, with
three winners having
prepped here. In the past
five years, first-three
finishers from this race
have finished 131256 in
the Ryanair
Three festival winners in the
past ten years

Trainer analysis

Kevin Morley pinpoints the key trainer trends and the jockey-trainer combinations to follow as the top stables chase the big trophies

Paul Nicholls
Festival winners **32** *Last five years* **3/5/2/3/2**

Nicholls took the British jumps trainers' title for the seventh consecutive season in 2012 but a bug in his Ditcheat stable in February meant he was not his usual dominant self at the Cheltenham Festival with only two winners – the lowest total of his title-winning years.

Although one of those winners was Rock On Ruby, who gave Nicholls a first Champion Hurdle success, he was not a 'Ditcheat horse' as he was prepared at Seaborough by Nicholls's assistant Harry Fry. Big Buck's, with his fourth World Hurdle, was the only winner from the main Nicholls yard.

Neither of those winners will represent Nicholls this year. Fry now trains Rock On Ruby in his own name, while Big Buck's is absent for the rest of the season with a tendon injury.

Punters will have noted Rock On Ruby and Big Buck's have another significant factor in common: they are part of Nicholls's shift towards hurdling success at the festival. Hurdlers have provided Nicholls with all seven of his victories at the last three festivals, with Kauto Star's 2009 Gold Cup his last success over fences.

With Kauto Star, Denman and Master Minded all retired, Nicholls needs to find his next big star over fences and he has yet to develop a chaser rated in the 180s despite the evident promise of Silviniaco Conti, Sanctuaire and Al Ferof (the latter is another festival absentee this year through injury).

While Nicholls could have chase winners lower down the ladder, of course, he doesn't have the gilt-edged chances in the big chases that used to be the bedrock of his festival team and once again he looks better placed to land a Grade 1 over hurdles this year.

Rock On Ruby may no longer be running in Nicholls's name but he still has **Zarkandar** for the Champion Hurdle. The six-year-old reportedly suffered a troubled preparation when fifth in the race last year and that is his only defeat in completed starts over hurdles. He has been in great form this season and should go close in this year's renewal.

Zarkandar won the Triumph two years ago and Nicholls has another first-rate chance in that race this year with **Far West**, twice a winner over course and distance. Nicholls has had two winners (Celestial Halo in 2008 was the other) and two fourths in the past four Triumphs where he has fielded a runner, which makes Far West a solid each-way shot.

Nicholls-trained festival winners

1999 Flagship Uberalles (Arkle), Call Equiname (Champion Chase), See More Business (Gold Cup)
2003 Azertyuiop (Arkle)
2004 Azertyuiop (Champion Chase), Earthmover (Foxhunter), St Pirran (Grand Annual), Sporazene (County)
2005 Sleeping Night (Foxhunter), Thisthatandtother (Ryanair)
2006 Noland (Supreme), Star De Mohaison (RSA), Desert Quest (County)
2007 Denman (RSA), Kauto Star (Gold Cup), Andreas (Grand Annual), Taranis (Ryanair)
2008 Master Minded (Champion Chase), Denman (Gold Cup), Celestial Halo (Triumph)
2009 Master Minded (Champion Chase), Chapoturgeon (Jewson), Big Buck's (World Hurdle), American Trilogy (County), Kauto Star (Gold Cup)
2010 Sanctuaire (Fred Winter), Big Buck's (World Hurdle)
2011 Al Ferof (Supreme), Big Buck's (World Hurdle), Zarkandar (Triumph)
2012 Rock On Ruby (Champion Hurdle), Big Buck's (World Hurdle)

		Hurdles Handicap		Hurdles Non-handicap		Chases Handicap		Chases Non-handicap		Bumper			Overall		
Nicholls's Cheltenham record Festival	2008	0/5	0% -5	1/7	14% -1	0/10	0% -10	2/11	18% -3.75	0/1	0%	-1	3/34	8%	-20.75
	2009	1/5	20% 16	1/6	17% 1	1/9	11% 0	2/13	15% -8.89	0/2	0%	-2	5/35	15%	6.11
	2010	1/6	17% -1	1/6	17% -4.17	0/9	0% -9	0/9	0% -9	0/1	0%	-1	2/31	7%	-24.17
	2011	0/5	0% -5	3/7	43% 13.41	0/4	0% -4	0/12	0% -12	0/0	0%	0	3/28	11%	-7.59
	2012	0/6	0% -6	2/11	18% 2.83	0/4	0% -4	0/9	0% -9	0/0	0%	0	2/30	7%	-16.17
	Total	2/27	7% -1	8/37	22% 12.07	1/36	3% -27	4/54	7% -42.64	0/4	0%	-4	15/158	9%	-62.57
Season	08/09	7/34	21%	16.71		7/46	15%	-22.27		0/5	0%	-5	14/85	16%	-10.56
	09/10	3/33	9%	-20.17		8/45	18%	-7.83		1/3	33%	1.5	12/81	15%	-26.5
	10/11	8/45	18%	-8.77		7/50	14%	-6.74		1/2	50%	1.75	16/97	16%	-13.67
	11/12	10/52	19%	3.5		4/43	9%	-29.29		0/1	0%	-1	14/96	15%	-26.79
	12/13	7/23	30%	-1.54		5/24	21%	10.25		1/2	50%	0.63	13/49	27%	9.33
	Total	35/187	19%	-10.27		31/208	15%	-55.88		3/13	23%	-2.12	69/408	17%	-68.19

This year's principal Nicholls contenders

Black Thunder *(Pertemps)*, Dark Lover *(County)*, Dildar *(County)*, Dodging Bullets *(Supreme)*, Edgardo Sol *(County)*, Fago *(Arkle)*, Far West *(Triumph)*, Ghizao *(Byrne Plate)*, Hinterland *(Grand Annual)*, Lac Fontana *(Triumph)*, Mr Mole *(County)*, Prospect Wells *(County)*, Ptit Zig *(Fred Winter)*, Rocky Creek *(NH Chase)*, Rolling Aces *(Byrne Plate)*, Saint Roque *(Martin Pipe)*, Sametegal *(Fred Winter)*, Sam Winner *(Pertemps)*, Saphir Du Rheu *(Fred Winter)*, Sidney Melbourne *(Martin Pipe)*, Silviniaco Conti *(Gold Cup)*, Tricky Trickster *(Foxhunter)*, Ulck Du Lin *(Grand Annual)*, Unioniste *(RSA)*, Wonderful Charm *(Coral Cup)*, Zarkandar *(Champion Hurdle)*

This year's principal Henderson contenders

Alexandre Six *(Fred Winter)*, Binocular *(Champion Hurdle)*, Bobs Worth *(Gold Cup)*, Captain Conan *(Jewson)*, Cash And Go *(County)*, Finian's Rainbow *(Champion Chase)*, Grandouet *(Champion Hurdle)*, Hadrian's Approach *(RSA)*, Kid Cassidy *(Grand Annual)*, Long Run *(Gold Cup)*, Molotof *(Byrne Plate)*, My Tent Or Yours *(Supreme)*, Oscara Dara *(Coral Cup)*, Oscar Nominee *(Martin Pipe)*, Oscar Whisky *(World Hurdle)*, River Maigue *(Supreme)*, Riverside Theatre *(Ryanair)*, Rolling Star *(Triumph)*, Simonsig *(Arkle)*, Sprinter Sacre *(Champion Chase)*, Une Artiste *(Mares' Hurdle)*, Utopie Des Bordes *(Mares' Hurdle)*, Vasco Du Ronceray *(Fred Winter)*

🖋 *After each horse's name is the race that is their nominated target or for which they are shortest in the betting*

Dodging Bullets, fourth in the Triumph last year, had his novice status still intact for this season and looks a live each-way contender in the Supreme as he seems likely to be suited by a solid pace in a big field. As well as two wins over hurdles at Cheltenham this season, he was a creditable third in the Christmas Hurdle and few novices turn up at the festival with that level of experience.

On the chasing front **Silviniaco Conti** appears to be Nicholls's best hope at the top level in an open-looking Gold Cup. The seven-year-old lowered Long Run's colours in Haydock's Betfair Chase in November and, although he has yet to prove his effectiveness at Cheltenham, he hs improved with every run in an unbeaten campaign.

By far Nicholls's best performance over fences at last year's festival came in the four-mile National Hunt Chase when Harry The Viking finished a gallant runner-up. **Rocky Creek** is an ideal type for this year's race judged on his last three victories in staying novice chases and looks one of the trainer's best chances if gets the go-ahead.

In the handicaps, look especially for Nicholls's runners at around two miles who are young, fancied (five of his seven handicap winners have been 8-1 or lower) and off a mark in the mid-130s or below.

Nicky Henderson
Festival winners **46** *Last five years* **0/3/3/2/7**

Last year Henderson became the leading trainer in the history of the Cheltenham Festival – and in some style. He not only overtook Fulke Walwyn's record of 40 winners but roared past with seven winners in 2012 – itself a record at a single festival – to a new mark of 46.

The half-century could be reached this year as he has the strongest team on paper once again. Bankers come in the shape of the awesome **Sprinter Sacre** in the Queen Mother Champion Chase and **Simonsig** in the Arkle Chase and he holds a strong hand in the Gold Cup (**Bobs Worth** and **Long Run**) and Champion Hurdle (**Grandouet**). It's common for those who have run well at previous festivals to do so again and it bodes well that all of them have won or placed at Cheltenham in recent years.

With **Oscar Whisky** (World Hurdle), **Rolling Star** (Triumph), **Captain Conan** (Jewson), **My Tent Or Yours** and **River Maigue** (both Supreme) among his other strong contenders for Grade 1 glory, it's easy to see Henderson enjoying another fabulous festival in the top-level contests.

Henderson's record is particularly strong in the Champion Hurdle and the four Grade 1 novice hurdles, with six winners and 23 per cent of the first three finishers in those races in the past four years. His runners are especially worthy of respect in the Champion Hurdle, Supreme Novices' Hurdle and Triumph Hurdle.

Handicaps hadn't been a great source of success at recent festivals until last year when things took a turn for the better with two winners – one over hurdles (Une Artiste in the Fred Winter) and the other over fences (Bellvano in the Grand Annual).

Surprisingly for a trainer of Henderson's standing, his festival handicap winners often reward backers at massive prices. Bellvano

Rolling Star could give Nicky Henderson a sixth Triumph

Henderson-trained festival winners

1985 First Bout (Triumph), See You Then (Champion), The Tsarevich (Byrne Plate) **1986** See You Then (Champion Hurdle), River Ceiriog (Supreme), The Tsarevich (Byrne Plate) **1987** Alone Success (Triumph), See You Then (Champion Hurdle) **1989** Rustle (World Hurdle) **1990** Master Bob (Kim Muir), Brown Windsor (Cathcart) **1991** Remittance Man (Arkle) **1992** Flown (Supreme), Remittance Man (Champion Chase) **1993** Travado (Arkle), Thumbs Up (County) **1994** Raymylette (Cathcart) **1997** Barna Boy (County) **1999** Katarino (Triumph), Stormyfairweather (Cathcart) **2000** Tiutchev (Arkle), Stormyfairweather (Cathcart), Bacchanal (World Hurdle), Marlborough (JLT) **2002** The Bushkeeper (Kim Muir) **2005** Liberthine (Byrne Plate), Juveigneur (Kim Muir), Trabolgan (RSA) **2006** Non So (Byrne Plate), Fondmort (Ryanair), Greenhope (Grand Annual) **2009** Punjabi (Champion Hurdle), Zaynar (Triumph), Andytown (Martin Pipe) **2010** Binocular (Champion Hurdle), Spirit River (Coral Cup), Soldatino (Triumph) **2011** Long Run (Gold Cup), Bobs Worth (Albert Bartlett) **2012** Sprinter Sacre (Arkle), Simonsig (Neptune), Bobs Worth (RSA), Finian's Rainbow (Champion Chase), Une Artiste (Fred Winter), Riverside Theatre (Ryanair), Bellvano (Grand Annual)

and Une Artiste went in at 20-1 and 40-1 respectively, meaning that all eight of his handicap winners since 2005 have obliged at 12-1 or bigger. Punters shouldn't be deterred by big odds on one of his handicappers.

Seven of those last eight handicap winners were rated from 127 to 138 (the other was 141) and the low-to-mid-130s is a good place to look for Henderson handicap winners – plenty of unexposed types lurk down there, which helps explain why they can pop up at big prices.

Henderson generally has a great strike-rate in bumpers throughout the season, but the Champion Bumper appears to be low on the list of his priorities as he has not had a runner in the race for three of the last four years. His strongest candidate would be **Oscar Hoof** but he appears to be more of a long-term project.

Henderson's Cheltenham record — Festival

		Hurdles Handicap			Hurdles Non-handicap			Chases Handicap			Chases Non-handicap			Bumper			Overall		
	2008	0/2	0%	-2	0/9	0%	-9	0/7	0%	-7	0/1	0%	-1	0/1	0%	-1	0/20	0%	-20
	2009	1/12	8%	14	2/10	20%	19.5	0/7	0%	0	0/3	0%	-3	0/0	0%	0	3/32	9%	23.5
	2010	1/12	8%	3	2/10	20%	7	0/8	0%	-8	0/8	0%	-8	0/0	0%	0	3/38	8%	-6
	2011	0/12	0%	-12	1/11	9%	-8.13	0/9	0%	-9	1/10	10%	-5.5	0/1	0%	-1	2/43	5%	-35.63
	2012	1/8	13%	33	1/7	14%	-4	1/13	8%	8	4/9	44%	7.73	0/0	0%	0	5/37	14%	44.73
	Total	3/46	7%	36	6/47	13%	5.37	1/44	2%	-16	5/31	16%	-9.77	0/2	0%	-2	13/170	8%	6.6

Season

		Hurdles			Chases			Bumper			Overall		
	08/09	7/47	15%	16.71	0/15	0%	-15	1/7	14%	-4.63	8/69	12%	14.13
	09/10	9/39	23%	-20.17	3/26	12%	-13.67	1/4	25%	1	13/69	19%	11.53
	10/11	9/51	18%	-8.77	2/39	5%	-30.17	1/6	17%	-1	12/96	13%	-38.29
	11/12	8/38	21%	26.03	9/35	26%	24.73	1/1	100%	2	18/74	24%	52.76
	12/13	2/18	11%	13.3	3/13	23%	1.3	0/0	0%	0	5/31	16%	-12
	Total	35/193	18%	0.5	17/128	13%	-32.81	4/18	22%	-2.63	56/339	17%	28.13

Abbey Lane (Coral Cup),
Arvika Ligeonniere
(Arkle), **Aupcharlie**
(Jewson), Back In Focus
(RSA), Ballycasey (Albert
Bartlett), Boston Bob
(RSA), Boxer Georg
(Cross Country), Call Me
Bubbles (Fred Winter),
Call The Police (Byrne
Plate), Champagne Fever
(Supreme), Clondaw
Court (Bumper), Darroun
(Pertemps), Diakali
(Triumph), Dogora (Fred
Winter), Drive Time (Coral
Cup), Fatcatinthehat (Fred
Winter), Hurricane Fly
(Champion Hurdle), Inish
Island (Pertemps), Irish
Saint (Triumph), Midnight
Game (Coral Cup), Pique
Sous (Supreme), Pont
Alexandre (Neptune),
Quevega (Mares' Hurdle),
Simenon (Coral Cup),
Sir Des Champs (Gold
Cup), Tarla (Mares'
Hurdle), Tennis Cap
(Coral Cup),Twinlight
(Grand Annual), Un Atout
(Supreme), Uncle Junior
(below) (Cross Country),
Union Dues (Bumper),
Vesper Bell (NH Chase),
Wonderful Charm (Coral
Cup), Zuzka (Mares'
Hurdle)

Willie Mullins

Festival winners **24** *Last five years* **2/3/2/4/3**

Over the past five years Mullins has established himself as one of the giants of the festival with 14 winners in that period – only one fewer than Nicky Henderson and Paul Nicholls.

Last year the perennial Irish champion trainer sent 35 runners to Cheltenham – his biggest festival team – and went home with three winners. While that was short of his personal-best four winners in 2011, it was a reasonable effort considering he had short-priced favourites Hurricane Fly and Boston Bob beaten in the Champion Hurdle and Albert Bartlett Novices' Hurdle respectively.

As a general rule, despite those setbacks, it is worth following the money with Mullins runners. Eight of his 11 winners at the past four festivals were sent off favourite and the record of Mullins-trained favourites in that period is 511110113013P12.

Two of last year's winners came as little surprise. Quevega dotted up in the Mares' Hurdle for the fourth consecutive year and Champagne Fever re-established Mullins as the king of the Champion Bumper, giving him a seventh victory in 20 runnings.

Chase successes are rarer for Mullins, but his other winner last year was over fences with impressive Jewson Novices' Chase scorer Sir Des Champs. It is notable that this new race is on the Mullins radar because his other three chase winners at the festival all came in the RSA Chase – from now on, Mullins runners look worthy of respect in both races.

Boston Bob looks a solid contender for this year's RSA and Mullins's strong team for the novice chases is augmented by **Aupcharlie** and **Arvika Ligeonniere**.

Another notable factor with Mullins's winners at the festival is that most have been in their first season at whatever speciality – bumpers, novice hurdles or novice chases. This year's leading novice hurdle contenders are **Un Atout** and **Champagne Fever** (Supreme), **Pont Alexandre** (Neptune), **Ballycasey** (Albert Bartlett) and **Blood Cotil** (Triumph).

The main weakness in his record remains the fact that Hurricane Fly in the 2011 Champion Hurdle is his only winner in one of the major feature races.

Hurricane Fly was third at 4-6 when defending his crown last year but on form he has a fine chance of regaining it this time. Sir Des Champs is Mullins's best chance of a first Gold Cup since the days of

		Hurdles Handicap			Hurdles Non-handicap			Chases Handicap			Chases Non-handicap			Bumper			Overall		
Mullins's Cheltenham record	**Festival**	2008	0/0	0%	-3	1/5	20%	3	0/0	0%	0	0/2	0%	-2	1/4	25%	9	2/11	18%	10
		2009	0/1	0%	-1	2/9	22%	-2.5	0/0	0%	0	1/3	33%	0.25	0/8	0%	-8	3/21	14%	-11.25
		2010	1/7	14%	14	1/9	11%	-6.5	0/2	0%	-2	0/8	0%	-8	0/3	0%	-3	2/29	7%	-5.5
		2011	2/6	33%	10.5	2/9	22%	-3.42	0/1	0%	-1	0/7	0%	-7	2/2	0%	-2	4/25	16%	-2.92
		2012	0/3	0%	-3	1/18	6%	-16.43	0/3	0%	-3	1/9	11%	-5	1/2	50%	15	3/35	9%	-12.43
		Total	3/17	18%	17.5	7/50	14%	-25.85	0/6	0%	-6	2/29	7%	-21.75	2/19	11%	11	14/121	12%	-22.1
	Season	08/09		2/10	20%			-3.5		1/3	33%			0.25		0/8	0%	-8	3/21	14%	-11.25
		09/10		2/16	13%			7.5		0/12	0%			-12		0/3	0%	-3	2/31	6%	-7.5
		10/11		4/15	17%			7.08		0/8	0%			-8		0/2	0%	-2	4/25	16%	-2.92
		11/12		2/24	8%			-13.93		2/15	13%			-5.5		1/4	25%	13	5/43	12%	-6.43
		12/13		0/2	0%			-2		1/4	25%			1.5		0/0	0%	0	1/6	17%	-0.5
		Total		10/67	15%			-4.85		4/42	10%			-23.75		1/17	6%	0	15/126	12%	-28.6

*Triumph hope
Blood Cotil is part
of a strong team of
young hurdlers*

Florida Pearl, who came up short three times in the blue riband event, but still that doubt remains over Mullins's record in the main features.

Mullins's Champion Bumper raids are legendary, although it has become more difficult to win in recent years owing to increased competition. One notable factor with his last two winners (Champagne Fever last year and Cousin Vinny in 2008) is that neither was his most fancied runner. His son Patrick was on board both winners, so perhaps the jockey booking is a more crucial guide then the betting.

The stable's two early contenders for this year's contest were **Clondaw Court** and **Union Dues**, although the late closing date for entries makes this a difficult race to assess until running and riding plans become clear.

Mullins has opened a new front at the festival in the past three years with his successes in handicaps, all over hurdles. Although he wasn't successful in that sphere last year, he has had three winners from 17 runners in handicap hurdles since 2010 for a profit of £21.50 to a £1 stake. His two County Hurdle winners had run in the Boylesports. com Handicap Hurdle at Leopardstown, which makes Abbey Lane an obvious leading contender.

Abbey Lane won this year's Boylesports off a mark of 124 – Final Approach was 123 when he won the Boylesports before following up in the County off 139.

Mullins-trained festival winners

1995 Tourist Attraction (Supreme)

1996 Wither Or Which (Bumper)

1997 Florida Pearl (Bumper)

1998 Alexander Banquet (Bumper), Florida Pearl (RSA)

2000 Joe Cullen (Bumper)

2002 Scolardy (Triumph

2004 Rule Supreme (RSA)

2005 Missed That (Bumper)

2007 Ebaziyan (Supreme)

2008 Cousin Vinny (Bumper), Fiveforthree(Neptune)

2009 Quevega (Mares' Hurdle), Mikael D'Haguenet (Neptune), Cooldine (RSA)

2010 Quevega (Mares' Hurdle), Thousand Stars (County)

2011 Hurricane Fly (Champion Hurdle), Quevega (Mares' Hurdle), Final Approach (County), Sir Des Champs (Martin Pipe)

2012 Quevega (Mares' Hurdle), Champagne Fever (Bumper), Sir Des Champs (Jewson)

Jonjo O'Neill

Festival winners **21** *Last five years* **1/1/1/1/3**

1991 Danny Connors (Pertemps)

1995 Front Line (NH Chase)

2000 Master Tern (County)

2002 Rith Dubh (NH Chase)

2003 Inching Closer (Pertemps), Sudden Shock (NH Chase), Spectroscope (Triumph)

2004 Creon (Pertemps), Native Emperor (NH Chase), Iris's Gift (World Hurdle)

2006 Black Jack Ketchum (Albert Bartlett)

2007 Butler's Cabin (NH Chase), Wichita Lineman (Albert Bartlett), Drombeag (Foxhunter)

2008 Albertas Run (RSA)

2009 Wichita Lineman (JLT)

2010 Albertas Run (Ryanair)

2011 Albertas Run (Ryanair)

2012 Alfie Sherrin (JLT), Sunnyhillboy (Kim Muir), Synchronised (Gold Cup)

Main contenders at this year's festival

Alfie Sherrin *(JLT)*, Cloudy Copper *(Albert Bartlett)*, Galaxy Rock *(Kim Muir)*, Get Me Out Of Here *(Coral Cup)*, Holywell *(Pertemps)*, It's A Gimme *(Coral Cup)*, Lost Glory *(Byrne Plate)*, Merry King *(NH Chase)*, Mister Hyde *(Kim Muir)*, Mr Watson *(County)*, Shutthefrontdoor *(Pertemps)*, Taquin Du Seuil *(Neptune)*

Quality ruled over quantity for O'Neill last year when he had just nine runners – his smallest team since 2000 – but enjoyed his best festival yet with three winners and two seconds, including Gold Cup success with Synchronised.

That cemented O'Neill's status as one of the most consistent trainers at Cheltenham in March. He has scored at least one winner at each of the past seven festivals – a sequence bettered by Paul Nicholls but matched by no-one else, not even Nicky Henderson.

O'Neill's record reveals a strong leaning towards staying races (17 of his 21 festival winners have been over at least three miles) and recently towards chases (just one of his ten winners since 2007 was over hurdles). Last year's three winners followed those patterns, all in chases over 3m-plus. Two of those were in handicaps, but it is the non-handicap chases where he has been most profitable to follow (he has had at least one winner in that category – and a level-stake profit – in five of the past six years).

He has an outstanding record in the National Hunt Chase, with five wins, and has a good candidate this year in **Merry King**. The six-year-old's form this season over 2m4f-3m has worked out well and he shapes as if he will appreciate the step up to four miles.

O'Neill has enjoyed recent success in the JLT Specialty Handicap Chase, with Alfie Sherrin's win last year adding to Wichita Lineman's last-gasp victory in 2009. **Alfie Sherrin** features high in the ante-post lists for this year's renewal and is certainly in the right hands for a repeat bid.

Over hurdles O'Neill has won the Pertemps Final three times and the Albert Bartlett twice (both over three miles). One of his Albert Bartlett winners (Wichita Lineman in 2007) landed the Challow Hurdle at Newbury en route to the festival and **Taquin Du Seuil** could bid for the same double following his impressive nine-length win in the Challow, although the betting suggests the Neptune is the target. **Cloudy Copper** could represent O'Neill in the Albert Bartlett.

O'Neill also has one of the festival's unluckiest horses in **Get Me Out Of Here** – a runner-up at each of the past three festivals. He could go for the Coral Cup again or even try his luck over three miles in the World Hurdle. Given O'Neill's ability to train a horse to stay further, another bold festival show is on the cards.

		Hurdles Handicap			Hurdles Non-handicap			Chases Handicap			Chases Non-handicap			Bumper			Overall		
O'Neill's Cheltenham record Festival	2008	0/1	0%	-1	0/2	0%	-2	0/4	0%	-4	1/5	20%	0	0/0	0%	0	1/12	8%	-7
	2009	0/6	0%	-6	0/0	0%	0	1/7	14%	-1	0/4	0%	-4	0/0	0%	0	1/17	6%	-11
	2010	0/7	0%	-7	0/2	0%	-2	0/6	0%	-6	1/2	50%	13	0/0	0%	0	1/17	6%	-2
	2011	0/4	0%	-4	0/0	0%	0	0/5	0%	-5	1/3	33%	4	0/0	0%	0	1/12	8%	-5
	2012	0/4	0%	-4	0/0	0%	0	2/3	67%	19.5	1/2	50%	7	0/0	0%	0	3/9	33%	22.5
	Total	**0/22**	**0%**	**-22**	**0/4**	**0%**	**-4**	**3/25**	**12%**	**3.5**	**4/16**	**25%**	**20**	**0/0**	**0%**	**0**	**7/67**	**10%**	**-2.5**
Season	08/09	1/18	6%	-5				1/20	5%	-14				0/2	0%	-2	2/40	5%	-19
	09/10	0/19	0%	-19				3/19	16%	13				0/1	0%	-1	3/39	8%	-7
	10/11	0/15	0%	-15				3/23	13%	-10.38				0/3	0%	-3	3/41	7%	-28.38
	11/12	1/8	13%	15				4/14	29%	27.5				0/1	0%	-1	5/23	22%	41.5
	12/13	1/7	14%	-3.25				0/8	0%	-8				0/0	0%	0	1/15	7%	-11.25
	Total	**3/67**	**4%**	**-25.25**				**11/84**	**13%**	**8.13**				**0/7**	**0%**	**-7**	**14/158**	**9%**	**-25.25**

Philip Hobbs
Festival winners **16** *Last five years* **0/0/2/2/1**

Hobbs has performed reasonably well at recent festivals with a total of five winners in the past three years. He has never had more than two winners at a single festival but has got on the scoreboard at nine of the last 12 festivals.

Balthazar King in the Cross Country Chase was the yard's sole winner from 13 runners last year, having been heavily backed on the day, and he must have a good chance of a repeat success in this specialists' race. The nine-year-old will have to defy a higher rating this time but being suited by the track's unique nature is arguably more important than a handicap mark and he performed well again over course and distance when runner-up at the November meeting.

The usual suspects in the Diana Whateley colours – **Captain Chris**, **Menorah** and possibly **Wishfull Thinking** – look set to be Hobbs's main hopes in the Grade 1 races. Captain Chris, the 2011 Arkle winner, was fourth in last year's Ryanair, finishing powerfully after looking likely to drop out at one stage. The impression that a longer trip would suit him appeared to be confirmed by his gallant second in this season's King George VI Chase and the Gold Cup is the aim this year.

Menorah is set to be the Hobbs/Whateley representative in the Ryanair and he merits respect on his Cheltenham record of three wins from six outings, plus third place in last year's Arkle and fifth in the 2011 Champion Hurdle. He came back to form in the rearranged Peterborough Chase at Kempton over Christmas, which was his second victory in as many starts over fences at trips close to the Ryanair distance of 2m5f.

Another interesting contender is **Colour Squadron**, who is owned by JP McManus. The seven-year-old is likely to be aimed at the Pulteney Novices' Handicap Chase and he has a similar profile to Copper Bleu, who won the race for Hobbs in 2010. It hasn't quite gone to plan for Colour Squadron in two novice chases and some have crabbed his jumping, but the same criticism was levelled at Copper Bleu, also beaten on his first two starts over fences, before his victory on the big day.

Hobbs-trained festival winners

1990 Moody Man (County)
1996 Kibreet (Grand Annual)
2000 What's Up Boys (Coral Cup)
2002 Rooster Booster (County), Flagship Uberalles (Champion Chase)
2003 Rooster Booster (Champion Hurdle), One Knight (RSA)
2004 Monkerhostin (Coral Cup), Made In Japan (Triumph)
2006 Detroit City (Triumph)
2007 Massini's Maguire (Neptune)
2010 Menorah (Supreme), Copper Bleu (Jewson)
2011 Captain Chris (Arkle), Cheltenian (Bumper)
2012 Balthazar King (Cross Country)

Main contenders at this year's festival

Balthazar King (*Cross Country*), **Bold Henry** (*Pulteney*), **Captain Chris** (*Gold Cup*), **Colour Squadron** (*Pulteney*), **Fair Along** (left) (*Pertemps*), **Menorah** (*Ryanair*), **The Skyfarmer** (*Bumper*)

		Hurdles Handicap			Hurdles Non-handicap			Chases Handicap			Chases Non-handicap			Bumper			Overall		
Hobbs's Cheltenham record	Festival	2008	0/5	0%	-5	0/1	0%	-1	0/5	0%	-5	0/3	0%	-3	0/2	0%	-2	0/16	0%	-16
		2009	0/7	0%	-7	0/3	0%	-3	0/5	0%	-5	0/3	0%	-3	0/0	0%	0	0/18	0%	-18
		2010	0/7	0%	-7	1/2	50%	11	1/10	10%	3	0/1	0%	-1	0/2	0%	-2	2/21	10%	5
		2011	0/6	0%	-6	0/3	0%	-3	0/5	0%	-5	1/3	33%	4	1/1	100%	14	2/18	11%	4
		2012	0/4	0%	-4	0/2	0%	-2	1/2	50%	4.5	0/4	0%	-4	0/1	0%	-1	1/13	8%	-6.5
		Total	0/29	0%	-29	1/11	9%	2	2/27	7%	-7.5	1/14	7%	-7	1/6	17%	9	5/86	6%	-31.5
	Season	08/09	4/31	13%	1				5/26	19%	9				1/2	50%	2.5	10/59	17%	13.5
		09/10	3/28	11%	-2.5				2/34	6%	-19.5				1/4	25%	17	6/66	9%	-5
		10/11	3/30	10%	-11.75				5/33	15%	-7.5				1/4	25%	11	9/67	13%	-8.25
		11/12	2/26	8%	-19.2				5/28	18%	-7.84				0/1	0%	-1	7/55	13%	-28.04
		12/13	0/13	0%	-13				2/10	20%	1.73				0/0	0%	0	2/23	9%	-11.27
		Total	12/128	9%	-44.45				19/131	15%	-24.11				3/11	27%	29.5	34/270	13%	-59.06

1992 Tipping Tim (JLT)

1993 Gaelstrom (Neptune), Young Hustler (RSA)

1994 Arctic Kinsman (Supreme)

1998 Upgrade (Triumph)

2000 Rubhahunish (Pertemps)

2004 Fundamentalist (Neptune)

2008 Ballyfitz (Pertemps)

2009 Tricky Trickster (NH Chase), Imperial Commander (Ryanair)

2010 Imperial Commander (Gold Cup), Baby Run (Foxhunter), Pigeon Island (Grand Annual)

Main contenders at this year's festival

African Gold *(Albert Bartlett)*, Astracad (right) *(Grand Annual)*, **Imperial Commander** *(Gold Cup)*, **Little Josh** *(Byrne Plate)*, **Master Of The Sea** *(Coral Cup)*, **Same Difference** *(Pulteney)* **The Cockney Mackem** *(Byrne Plate)*, **The New One** *(Neptune)*, **Tour Des Champs** *(NH Chase)*

Nigel Twiston-Davies
Festival winners **13** *Last five years* **1/2/3/0/0**

Twiston-Davies has not had a winner at the past two festivals, although he was most unlucky in 2011 when Baby Run unseated two out in the Foxhunter and last year it is fair to say he didn't have any strong fancies.

It is only three years since the Naunton trainer had his best festival with three winners, including Gold Cup success for Imperial Commander. The 12-year-old was missing from the team last year but his comeback second in the Argento Chase, after a 22-month layoff, has set him up for a bid to regain the crown. At his best he would have every chance of doing so, but it's asking a lot from a veteran who has overcome injury.

Twiston-Davies's best performer at last year's festival was **The New One**, who finished an excellent sixth in the Champion Bumper and went on to beat My Tent Or Yours (now a leading Supreme fancy) in the Aintree version. The son of King's Theatre has been fulfilling that promise in novice hurdles this season and rates one of the leading contenders for the Neptune.

The yard also has a live outsider for the Albert Bartlett in **African Gold**, another son of King's Theatre. The Pertemps Final is a possible alternative.

With top-level candidates thin on the ground, Twiston-Davies will be hoping for some big performances from his handicappers. The one to catch the eye in this area is **Astracad**, who was taken off his feet when a staying-on seventh in last year's Grand Annual. Better suited by further, he looks ready for another crack.

		Hurdles Handicap			Hurdles Non-handicap			Chases Handicap			Chases Non-handicap			Bumper			Overall		
Festival	2008	1/2	50%	17	0/3	0%	-3	0/9	0%	-9	0/4	0%	-4	0/0	0%	0	1/18	6%	1
	2009	0/2	0%	-2	0/4	0%	-4	0/7	0%	-7	2/6	33%	13	0/0	0%	0	2/19	11%	0
	2010	0/4	0%	-4	0/3	0%	-3	1/4	25%	13	2/10	20%	3.5	0/0	0%	0	3/21	14%	9.5
	2011	0/3	0%	-3	0/5	0%	-5	0/4	0%	-4	0/4	0%	-4	0/2	0%	-2	0/18	0%	-18
	2012	0/3	0%	-3	0/2	0%	-2	0/7	0%	-7	0/1	0%	-1	0/1	0%	-1	0/14	0%	-14
	Total	1/14	7%	5	0/17	0%	-17	1/31	3%	-14	4/25	16%	7.5	0/3	0%	-3	6/90	7%	-21.5
Season	08/09	3/29	10%	28				5/49	10%	-16				0/1	0%	-1	8/79	10%	10
	09/10	4/33	12%	99				5/51	10%	-5.77				0/4	0%	-4	9/88	10%	89.23
	10/11	3/31	10%	-9.75				1/43	2%	-22				0/8	0%	-8	4/82	5%	-39.75
	11/12	0/20	0%	-20				3/37	8%	-19.75				1/3	33%	3.5	4/60	7%	-36.25
	12/13	3/13	23%	11				1/23	4%	-18.5				0/1	0%	-1	4/37	11%	-8.5
	Total	13/126	10%	108.25				15/203	7%	-82.02				1/17	6%	-10.5	29/346	8%	15.73

Twiston-Davies's Cheltenham record

Alan King
Festival winners **12** *Last five years* **3/1/0/1/0**

King-trained festival winners

2004 Fork Lightning (JLT)
2005 Penzance (Triumph)
2006 Voy Por Ustedes (Arkle), My Way De Solzen (World Hurdle)
2007 My Way De Solzen (Arkle), Katchit (Triumph), Voy Por Ustedes (Champion Chase)
2008 Katchit (Champion Hurdle), Old Benny (NH Chase), Nenuphar Collonges (Albert Bartlett)
2009 Oh Crick (Grand Annual)
2011 Bensalem (JLT)

Festival success has not come as easily to King as it did in the early years of his training career, with a blank from 16 runners last season leaving him with just two winners at the last four meetings, but the strength of his Barbury Castle stable still makes him a serious player.

That is particularly true in the juvenile hurdling division. Last year he had the beaten favourite in the Triumph and the Fred Winter but both gave a good account by finishing third. He has won the Triumph twice and had four placed runners, while he has gone close on several occasions without winning the Fred Winter (a runner-up and three thirds from his last ten runners in the juvenile handicap).

L'Unique has been his best juvenile this season and could be a live outsider for the Triumph, but she's likely to get a reasonable handicap mark and may be best aimed at the Fred Winter. King saddled the second, third and fifth in the Fred Winter in 2011, so it's clearly a race he's keen to win.

King seems to have place chances at best in the championship races this year with **Smad Place** in the World Hurdle possibly his brightest hope.

He also appears to be light on contenders for the novice races and increasingly he may have to look to the handicaps for festival success. Handicaps are usually a productive area for King – last season he ranked second only to Paul Nicholls for number of wins in British handicaps worth £20,000 or more – and it is a little surprising that only three of his Cheltenham winners have been in that category.

Two of those three winners (Fork Lightning and Oh Crick) were novice chasers who were on their way up the ladder and were able to exploit useful handicap marks, while the other (Bensalem) was coming back from a long absence. Perhaps King's relative lack of success in festival handicaps is due to his own competitiveness throughout the season, which means marks aren't protected, and the greater level of competition at Cheltenham in March.

Even so, King looks set to have several decent chances in handicaps this year. His best chance might be Bless The Wings in the Byrne Group Plate. Bensalem isn't a forlorn hope in his bid for a second JLT Specialty Handicap Chase win, while Godsmejudge is a novice who has already done well in a valuable handicap with his close second in the Betfred Classic Chase at Warwick in January.

Main contenders at this year's festival

Araldur *(Pertemps)*, Bensalem (below) *(JLT)*, Blessthewings *(Byrne Plate)*, Godsmejudge *(NH Chase)*, L'Unique *(Fred Winter)*, Medinas *(Coral Cup)*, Smad Place *(World Hurdle)*, Vendor *(Martin Pipe)*, Walkon *(Byrne Plate)*

		Hurdles Handicap			Hurdles Non-handicap			Chases Handicap			Chases Non-handicap			Bumper			Overall		
King's Cheltenham record — Festival	2008	0/3	0%	-3	2/7	29%	14	0/5	0%	-5	1/3	33%	7	0/0	0%	0	3/18	17%	13
	2009	0/10	0%	-10	0/6	0%	-6	1/5	20%	3	0/4	0%	-4	0/0	0%	0	1/25	4%	-17
	2010	0/8	0%	-8	0/6	0%	-6	0/4	0%	-4	0/3	0%	-3	0/0	0%	0	0/21	0%	-21
	2011	0/8	0%	-8	0/4	0%	-4	1/5	20%	1	0/2	0%	-2	0/1	0%	0	1/20	5%	-14
	2012	0/3	0%	-3	0/6	0%	-6	0/4	0%	-4	0/3	0%	-3	0/0	0%	0	0/16	0%	-16
	Total	**0/32**	**0%**	**-32**	**2/29**	**7%**	**-8**	**2/23**	**9%**	**-9**	**1/15**	**7%**	**-5**	**0/1**	**0%**	**-1**	**5/100**	**5%**	**-55**
King's Cheltenham record — Season	08/09	5/53	9%	-24.86				2/25	8%	-8				0/3	0%	-3	7/81	9%	-35.86
	09/10	0/32	0%	-32				0/15	0%	-15				0/6	0%	-6	0/53	0%	-53
	10/11	2/28	7%	-14				3/20	15%	13				1/4	25%	7	6/52	12%	6
	11/12	2/23	9%	-7.25				1/16	6%	-8.5				0/3	0%	-3	3/42	7%	-18.75
	12/13	0/11	0%	-11				0/7	0%	-7				0/0	0%	0	0/18	0%	-18
	Total	**9/147**	**6%**	**-89.11**				**6/83**	**7%**	**-25.5**				**1/16**	**6%**	**-5**	**16/246**	**7%**	**-119.61**

Murphy-trained festival winners

1996 Stop The Waller (Kim Muir), Paddy's Return (Triumph)
1998 French Holly (Neptune)
2006 You're Special (Kim Muir), Hot Weld (NH Chase)
2007 Joes Edge (JLT), L'Antartique (Pulteney)
2008 Naiad Du Misselot (Coral Cup)
2010 Poker De Sivola (NH Chase)
2011 Divers (Pulteney)

Main contenders at this year's festival

De Boitron (below) (Grand Annual), Divers (Byrne Plate)

Ferdy Murphy
Festival winners **10** *Last five years* **1/0/1/1/0**

Murphy has long been one of the best trainers at targeting the festival and, outside the trainers who usually figure in the top dozen of the prize-money table, he is the one who most regularly gets his name on the scoresheet at Cheltenham.

His blank in 2012 was only his second in the past six years, but in truth none of his seven runners looked like landing a blow. **Divers** was fourth in the Byrne Group Plate but that was as good as it got for Murphy last term and the 2011 Pulteney Novices' Handicap Chase winner is likely to be one of his leading lights again, most likely for another crack at the Plate.

Murphy usually fields a single-figure team and his habit of sending out winners at big odds means all his runners should be considered, particularly in long-distance chases. His followers have been rewarded by You're Special (33-1, 2006 Kim Muir), Hot Weld (33-1, 2006 NH Chase), Joes Edge (50-1, 2007 JLT Specialty Handicap Chase) and L'Antartique (20-1, 2007 Pulteney) – all of those were over fences and three were at 3m-plus. Only one of Murphy's ten festival winners came at a distance below 2m5f and six of the last seven were over fences.

As well as Divers, some other familiar names are likely to be in Murphy's team this year. **De Boitron** has been fourth and sixth in the past two runnings of the Grand Annual and has dropped to a lower mark now, while 2010 National Hunt Chase winner **Poker De Sivola** looks set to be on a handy weight in his bid to improve on his sixth place in the 2011 Cross Country Chase.

Going Wrong was Murphy's biggest disappointment in 2012 when fancied but well beaten in the Pulteney Novices' Handicap Chase. The Kim Muir , which Murphy won with Stop The Waller (1996) and You're Special (2006), might be the race for him this year.

None of the horses mentioned have set pulses racing with their displays this season but you cannot deny Murphy's ability to peak them when it matters and, if any of his string oblige, it will almost certainly be at a juicy price.

		Hurdles Handicap			Hurdles Non-handicap			Chases Handicap			Chases Non-handicaps			Bumper			Overall		
Murphy's Cheltenham record — Festival	2008	1/1	100%	7	0/1	0%	-1	0/4	0%	-4	0/1	0%	-1	0/0	0%	0	1/7	14%	1
	2009	0/1	0%	-1	0/0	0%	0	0/6	0%	-6	0/3	0%	-3	0/0	0%	0	0/10	0%	-10
	2010	0/1	0%	-1	0/1	0%	-1	0/5	0%	-5	1/3	33%	12	0/0	0%	0	1/10	10%	5
	2011	0/0	0%	0	0/0	0%	0	1/7	14%	4	0/1	0%	-1	0/0	0%	0	1/8	13%	3
	2012	0/0	0%	0	0/0	0%	0	0/6	0%	-6	0/1	0%	-1	0/0	0%	0	0/7	0%	-7
	Total	1/3	33%	5	0/2	0%	-2	1/28	4%	-17	1/9	11%	6	0/0	0%	0	3/42	7%	-8
Season	08/09	0/3	0%	-3				0/14	0%	-14				0/0	0%	0	0/17	0%	-17
	09/10	0/5	0%	-5				3/14	21%	10.5				0/0	0%	0	3/19	16%	5.5
	10/11	0/1	0%	-1				1/15	7%	-4				0/0	0%	0	1/16	7%	-5
	11/12	0/0	0%	0				0/12	0%	-12				0/0	0%	0	0/12	0%	-12
	12/13	0/0	0%	0				0/1	0%	-1				0/0	0%	0	0/1	0%	-1
	Total	0/9	0%	-9				4/56	7%	-20.5				0/0	0%	0	4/65	6%	-29.5

David Pipe
Festival winners **8** *Last five years* **2/0/2/2/1**

All but one of Pipe's festival winners have been in handicaps and he added to his tally last year when the strongly fancied Salut Flo galloped his rivals into submission in the Byrne Group Plate.

Fourth places last year in the JLT Specialty Handicap Chase, Pulteney Novices' Handicap Chase and the Fred Winter Juvenile Handicap Hurdle (two of which he has won in the past) emphasised how competitive the stable is in the handicaps. But Pipe does like to throw plenty of darts at the target – his total of 30 runners last year was exceeded only by Nicky Henderson and Willie Mullins and his tally of 21 in handicaps was matched only by Henderson.

The biggest blow for Pipe last year was the below-par performance of Grands Crus, who went off 6-5 favourite for the RSA Chase but faded into a well-beaten fourth. He has a similar candidate for this year's RSA in **Dynaste**, another French-bred grey in the same ownership. Like Grands Crus, Dynaste came up short behind Big Buck's in staying hurdles before a smooth transition to fences and he has won two of the novice chases Grands Crus landed last season, including the Grade 1 Feltham.

The RSA is something of a graveyard for favourites (only three of the last 13 have won) and the memory of Grands Crus' defeat may discourage many punters from backing Dynaste as he tries to give Pipe only his second Grade 1 victory at the festival.

As for the handicaps, Notus De La Tour is well treated on his hurdles form if he turns up in good shape for the Byrne Group Plate. Others to watch out for include The Package in the JLT Specialty Handicap Chase (twice placed in the race), Gevrey Chambertin if he skips the Albert Bartlett to go for the Coral Cup or Pertemps Final, and Katkeau in the conditionals' handicap hurdle named after Pipe's father.

Any Pipe representative in the Fred Winter is well worth noting – he has had a winner, two seconds and a fourth in five attempts at the race.

Pipe-trained festival winners

2007 Gaspara (Fred Winter)
2008 An Accordion (JLT), Our Vic (Ryanair)
2010 Buena Vista (Pertemps), Great Endeavour (Byrne Plate)
2011 Buena Vista (Pertemps), Junior (Kim Muir)
2012 Salut Flo (Byrne Plate)

Main contenders at this year's festival

Alderluck (*Kim Muir*), Amigo (*Pertemps*), **Buddy Bolero** (*NH Chase*), **Close House** (*Pertemps*), **Dynaste** (*RSA*), **Gevrey Chambertin** (*Pertemps*), **Goulanes** (*NH Chase*), **Grands Crus** (*Ryanair*), **His Excellency** (*Grand Annual*), **Katkeau** (*Martin Pipe*), **Kings Palace** (*Bumper*), **Notus De La Tour** (*Byrne Plate*), **Red Sherlock** (*Bumper*), **Salut Flo** (*Byrne Plate*), **Swing Bowler** (*County*), **Tanerko Emery** (*Coral Cup*), **The Package** (below) (*JLT*)

		Hurdles Handicap			Hurdles Non-handicap			Chases Handicap			Chases Non-handicap			Bumper			Overall		
Pipe's Cheltenham record	Festival	2008	0/10	0%	-10	0/4	0%	-4	1/6	17%	2	1/4	25%	1	0/2	0%	-2	2/26	7%	-13
		2009	0/16	0%	-16	0/7	0%	-7	0/6	0%	-6	0/3	0%	-3	0/0	0%	0	0/32	0%	-32
		2010	1/7	14%	10	0/3	0%	-3	1/9	11%	10	0/2	0%	-2	0/0	0%	0	2/21	10%	15
		2011	1/6	17%	15	0/3	0%	-3	1/9	11%	-4.67	0/4	0%	-4	0/1	0%	-1	2/23	9%	2.33
		2012	0/12	0%	-12	0/5	0%	-5	1/9	11%	-3.5	0/4	0%	-4	0/0	0%	0	1/30	3%	-24.5
		Total	2/51	4%	-13	0/22	0%	-22	4/39	10%	-2.17	1/17	6%	-12	0/3	0%	-3	6/90	7%	-52.17
	Season	08/09		1/47	2%		-39		1/23	14%	-13.5		0/0	0%	0	2/70	3%	-52.5
		09/10		3/26	12%		17.5		5/32	16%	7.69		0/0	0%	0	8/58	14%	25.19
		10/11		4/31	13%		20		1/31	3%	-26.67		0/1	0%	-1	5/63	8%	-7.67
		11/12		1/34	3%		-26.5		5/28	18%	6		0/0	0%	0	6/62	10%	-20.5
		12/13		1/13	8%		-5		5/18	28%	23.5		0/1	0%	-1	6/32	19%	17.5
		Total		10/151	7%		-33		17/132	13%	-2.97		0/2	0%	-2	27/285	9%	-37.97

Donald McCain

Festival winners **6** *Last five years* **1/0/2/0/2**

McCain-trained festival winners

2007 Cloudy Lane (Kim Muir)

2008 Whiteoak (Mares' Hurdle)

2010 Peddlers Cross (Neptune), Ballabriggs (Kim Muir)

2012 Cinders And Ashes (Supreme), Son Of Flicka (Coral Cup)

Main contenders at this year's festival

Cinders And Ashes (below) *(Champion Hurdle)*, **Cloudy Lane** *(Foxhunter)*, **Counsel** *(Fred Winter)*, **Desert Cry** *(Grand Annual)*, **Our Mick** *(JLT)*, **Overturn** *(Arkle)*, **Peddlers Cross** *(World Hurdle)*, **Real Milan** *(NH Chase)*, **She Ranks Me** *(Mares' Hurdle)*, **Son Of Flicka** *(Coral Cup)*, **Super Duty** *(Pulteney)*

McCain struck at his first festival in 2007 and since then has gone from strength to strength. He is the only British trainer who can compete with Paul Nicholls and Nicky Henderson overall on the numbers front and the rapid expansion of his string saw him send out a personal-best 19 runners at last year's meeting.

The Cheshire trainer walked away with two winners and the starting prices (10-1 Cinders and Ashes and 16-1 Son Of Flicka) meant that once again he returned a level-stake profit for his followers (as he has at each of the four festivals where he has got on the scoreboard).

McCain has yet to strike in one of the main four feature races but he has come close in the Champion Hurdle in the past two years with Peddlers Cross and Overturn both finishing runner-up. He will have another crack at the Champion Hurdle this year with 2012 Supreme hero **Cinders And Ashes**, while **Peddlers Cross**, ultimately a disappointment over fences last term, could chance his stamina in the World Hurdle.

However, all bar one of McCain's festival winners so far have come in handicaps and novice races and that's where he is most likely to strike again. On the novice front his best hope lies with **Overturn**, who looks the most credible challenger to Simonsig in the Arkle.

Son Of Flicka landed the biggest gamble of the meeting last year in the Coral Cup and, following some abject displays this season, it's interesting that his mark is now just 2lb higher. He's a festival specialist (having been a close second to Sir Des Champs in the 2011 Martin Pipe Handicap Hurdle) and will be worth watching to see if the money comes for him again.

The Kim Muir has been good for McCain, with two winners (Cloudy Lane in 2007 and Ballabriggs in 2010). Both were owned by Trevor Hemmings and this year **Wymott** may be the one to give a prominent showing in the yellow and green quartered colours. The nine-year-old hasn't been in the best form over the couple of seasons but he is well treated on his 2010-11 novice form and is another to watch out for in the market.

Tim Leslie is McCain's biggest patron and his colours are likely to be prominent with Overturn and Peddlers Cross. At a lower level, Leslie's **Dunowen Point** is a lightly raced handicap chaser who would make some appeal if he gets in the Grand Annual on a low weight.

		Hurdles Handicap			Hurdles Non-handicap			Chases Handicap			Chases Non-handicap			Bumper			Overall		
McCain's Cheltenham record — Festival	2008	0/2	0%	-2	1/1	100%	20	0/2	0%	-2	0/1	0%	-1	0/1	0%	-1	1/7	14%	14
	2009	0/1	0%	-1	0/1	0%	-1	0/1	0%	-1	0/0	0%	0	0/0	0%	0	0/3	0%	-3
	2010	0/4	0%	-4	1/1	100%	7	1/3	33%	7	0/2	0%	-2	0/0	0%	0	2/10	20%	8
	2011	0/3	0%	-3	0/5	0%	-5	0/4	0%	-3	0/2	0%	-2	0/1	0%	-1	0/15	0%	-15
	2012	1/7	14%	10	1/5	20%	6	0/3	0%	-3	0/4	0%	-4	0/0	0%	0	2/19	11%	9
	Total	1/17	6%	0	3/13	23%	27	1/13	8%	-2	0/9	0%	-9	0/2	0%	-2	5/54	9%	13
Season	08/09	0/8	0%	-8				0/2	0%	-2				0/1	0%	-1	0/11	0%	-11
	09/10	1/9	11%	-1				1/6	17%	4				0/0	0%	0	2/15	15%	3
	10/11	0/14	0%	-14				0/8	0%	-8				0/2	0%	-2	0/24	7%	-24
	11/12	2/24	8%	4				0/8	0%	-8				0/1	0%	-1	2/33	6%	-5
	12/13	0/4	0%	-4				1/3	33%	0.25				0/1	0%	-1	1/8	13%	-4.75
	Total	3/59	5%	-23				2/27	7%	-13.75				0/5	0%	-5	5/91	5%	-41.75

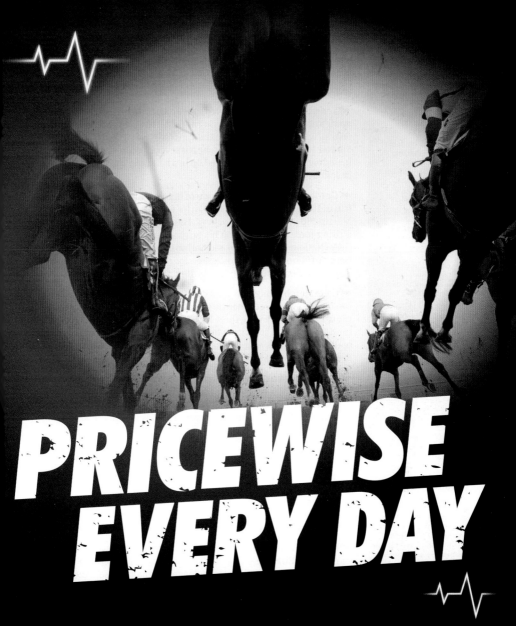

PRICEWISE EVERY DAY

DON'T MISS THE WORLD'S BEST TIPSTER EVERY DAY OF THE CHELTENHAM FESTIVAL

RACING POST
THE PULSE OF THE FESTIVAL

What they say

'It's exciting to have such a good horse'

Jessica Harrington, trainer of Jezki
(Supreme) "What particularly pleases me isn't that he remains unbeaten but the experience he has gained, as you can't go to the Cheltenham Festival with a horse who has only limited experience. It's exciting to have such a good horse to take to Cheltenham again. He will be a better horse on better ground" *Has won all four hurdle starts, although his only career defeats came on the two occasions he faced a field of more than 12*

Mouse Morris, trainer of Rule The World
(Neptune) "He's a big, raw bugger. Two and a half miles might be as far as he'd want to go around Cheltenham at the moment, although I've also entered him for the three-miler. I don't think the ground really matters to him but he might be a bit better on better ground" *Only defeat over hurdles was at 3m. Yet to race on ground without soft or heavy in description*

Rebecca Curtis, trainer of At Fishers Cross
(Albert Bartlett) "All of his form is on soft to heavy ground but that's not to say he won't go on better ground. He'll definitely run over three miles at the festival. He had a couple of problems that affected his jumping early in his career but we seem to have them sorted out now and he's progressing the right way" *Has won both starts at Cheltenham, both on heavy ground*

Williams on a roll

Five-time festival winner has her string in great form this season

Venetia Williams has enjoyed a resurgence this season and there is no sign of her momentum slowing as the festival approaches. Her five festival winners have been in handicaps (all have carried between 10st 5lb and 10st 11lb) and this year she has several progressive performers, including **Katenko**, who bolted up in a handicap chase at the course in January, and **Brick Red**.

Gordon Elliott placed with two of his nine runners last year, most frustratingly when Toner D'Oudairies was caught on the line in the Martin Pipe Conditional Jockeys' Handicap Hurdle, and is clearly a rising force after breaking his festival duck in 2011 with Chicago Grey (National Hunt Chase) and Carlito Brigante (Coral Cup). **Carlito Brigante** looks well handicapped for this year's Pulteney Novices' Handicap Chase judged on his hurdling form.

Colm Murphy is highly selective with his Cheltenham raiders and a big run is usually assured when he gives the green light. Of his 18 festival runners, three have won, three have finished second and six have been third. Some of his stars have been retired and handicaps look a more realistic target this time, but take note of any runners. **Glam Gerry** in the Byrne Group Plate could be his best chance.

Noel Meade has so much quality at his disposal that it's surprising his record doesn't read better than three winners from 117 runners since 2000. His best performer last year was **Monksland**, who was third in the Neptune, and the six-year-old looks his main hope again in an open World Hurdle.

Arthur Moore has to be respected with fancied runners in handicaps, particularly at the minimum trip. What A Charm's 2011 Fred Winter success added to the Grand Annual victories of Fadoudal Du Cochet (2002) and Tiger Cry (2008) – all at around two miles and at single-figure odds. **Free World** was 25-1 but still travelling reasonably well when he fell four out in last year's Grand Annual – he's likely to go for the race again and will almost certainly have a lower mark this time.

Henry de Bromhead has a tricky decision to make with his stable star **Sizing Europe** – take on Sprinter Sacre in the Queen Mother Champion Chase or switch to the longer Ryanair Chase? Another of the Alan Potts-owned Sizing horses, **Sizing Gold**, is an interesting prospect and wouldn't be the worst longshot in the Neptune or Albert Bartlett Novices' Hurdle, while **Sizing Australia** could be back for another crack at the Cross Country Chase, which he won in 2011.

Jessica Harrington had a disappointing festival last year with none of her five runners threatening, even though two were well fancied (Steps To Freedom in the Supreme and Citizenship in the County). That may well have been a blip as her record before last year was six winners from 38 since 2000. Her best hopes this year are **Jezki** (Supreme), **Oscars Well** (Arkle/Jewson) and **Bostons Angel** (Cross Country Chase).

🐎Enda Bolger won four of the first five runnings of the Cross Country Chase and has had the runner-up in three of the other four years, which makes him the trainer to watch even though the race has become increasingly competitive. **Arabella Boy**, who was travelling well when unseating his rider in a contest over the unique course in December, is the new star for Bolger.

🐎Mouse Morris didn't strike last year but two of his three runners were placed (First Lieutenant was runner-up in the RSA Chase and Four Commanders third in the National Hunt Chase). His three winners since 2002 (from 36 runners) were sent off at single-figure odds, so the market is a good guide. **First Lieutenant** (Gold Cup/Ryanair) and **Rule The World** (Neptune) are his leading hopes.

🐎Edward O'Grady may have lost his mantle as the festival's leading current Irish trainer to Willie Mullins but his raiders must still be respected. Of his four runners last year, two were placed at decent prices – **Catch Me** was 14-1 when runner-up in the Pertemps Final and Sailors Warn was third in the County Hurdle at 16-1. Catch Me appears to have been prepared for another crack at the Pertemps.

🐎John Ferguson has smart Flat-bred material to work with, giving him a better chance of hitting the target than most of the smaller jumps trainers. Of his four runners last year, **New Year's Eve** was a gallant second in the Champion Bumper and **Cotton Mill** would almost certainly have filled the same position behind Simonsig in the Neptune Novices' Hurdle but for jinking and unseating his rider two out. Neither should be written off for their respective targets this year, while **Population** would be interesting if he is aimed at one of the handicaps.

🐎Rebecca Curtis gained her first festival winner last term with the well-backed Teaforthree in the National Hunt Chase. A progressive trainer, she will have more arrows to fire at the target this year, most notably with **At Fishers Cross**. Originally a strong fancy for the Pertemps Final, he put himself firmly in the Albert Bartlett picture with a Grade 2 success at the course in January.

🐎Tim Vaughan has not found Cheltenham a happy hunting ground. Three of his 21 runners at the past four festivals have finished second but a more damning statistic is that none of his 77 runners at the course since the beginning of the 2007-08 campaign has obliged.

🐎Charlie Longsdon is a rising star but has yet to crack Cheltenham. He was nought from nine at the festival last year and just one of his 54 runners at the track over the past five seasons has been successful.

🐎Paul Webber seems unable to buy a festival victory as he is winless from 38 runners since 1999. **Cantlow** is prominent in the betting for the handicap chases but his trainer's record is off-putting.

Nicky Henderson last year had a record seven winners

Since Howard Johnson took the award at the first four-day festival in 2005, only Henderson, Paul Nicholls and Willie Mullins have won

More than half of the 2012 winners (14 out of 27) were trained by the festival's top four trainers (Henderson, Nicholls, Mullins and Jonjo O'Neill)

Mullins in 2011 is the only Irish trainer to have won the award outright (Edward O'Grady, who has shared the award three times, is the only other Irish-based trainer to have won since 1980)

Three winners has been the minimum winning total at each of the eight festivals since the meeting was expanded to four days

David Pipe has scored at five of his six festivals, meaning the stable started by his father Martin has missed out just twice in 23 years

Jockey-trainer pairings to note

Kevin Morley highlights the combinations that have been particularly profitable at the festival

Barry Geraghty/all Irish trainers (11 from 70, 16% strike-rate since 2000) It's usually indicative of a big run when Geraghty is released from his duties for Nicky Henderson. His rides for Irish trainers since 2000 have returned a 14.25pt profit and, while those rides are becoming rarer with Henderson possessing more firepower than ever, it's advisable to take note when the opportunity arises. Geraghty's mounts for Irish yards since taking the Seven Barrows job have yielded two winners from seven rides for a 13pt profit (form figures 163132P). He had no Irish-trained mounts last year but had two rides for John Ferguson – one of which was New Year's Eve, a heavily backed favourite and runner-up in the Champion Bumper. But let's not forget his record for his employer: last year Geraghty took his overall tally for Henderson to nine from 65 (14%/+9.10pt).

Conditionals/David Pipe (10% strike-rate since 2007, +20.50pt level stake) Pipe often puts his faith in conditional jockeys at the festival and has successfully done so four times from 42 attempts. Mob-handed attacks on the conditionals' handicap hurdle named after his father distort the figures unfavourably and, surprisingly, that is a race he has yet to win. However, the level-stakes profit shows the market often underestimates the ability of conditionals, whose claim can prove valuable in handicaps. Kieron Edgar, Tom Bellamy and Samuel Welton, who all claim the full 7lb, are names to watch this season.

Ruby Walsh/Willie Mullins (F619011143001FF0611300313150030P2 since 2008) Walsh has been the most successful jockey at recent festivals, which is hardly surprising given that he has the pick of runners trained by Paul Nicholls and Willie Mullins. His record for Mullins has been more profitable with nine winners from 33 rides since 2008 (27%/+5.40pt). The pair have struck four years running with Quevega *(below)* in the

Mares' Hurdle and really should have added to last year's tally with Boston Bob in the Albert Bartlett Novices' Hurdle.

Tony McCoy/Jonjo O'Neill (3U1PFFP12192192532018121 in non-handicaps since 2006) With six winners from 21 runners in level-weights races since 2006, the McCoy/O'Neill partnership is one of the most trustworthy at the meeting (added assurance for each-way punters is that another seven have been placed). They teamed up only twice in non-handicaps last year but had Gold Cup winner Synchronised and Ryanair runner-up Albertas Run.

Davy Russell/Gigginstown House Stud (0245F90191049R61417300P36 72P2180 since 2008) Gigginstown House Stud has become one of the biggest forces in jump racing and that has put retained rider Davy Russell among the elite. After one winner and three places from nine rides at the 2012 festival, Russell's record for Gigginstown now stands at five from 32 (16%/+17.50pt).

Richard Harding/Ferdy Murphy and Donald McCain (festival record 11F4610096) Harding has enjoyed more festival success than most amateurs and that's thanks to Ferdy Murphy and Donald McCain, who both like to target the amateur riders' races at the festival. Harding's record of three from ten when riding for the two trainers combined has returned a massive 68pt level-stake profit. His two winners for Murphy were 33-1 and McCain, who has used him for the last three festivals, put him up on 9-1 victor Ballabriggs in the 2010 Kim Muir.

Paul Carberry/all British-based trainers (5 from 27, 19% strike-rate since 1998) Being Noel Meade's stable jockey, Paul Carberry is unlikely to have a great festival strike-rate but concentrating on his rides for British-based trainers is a strategy that has reaped big rewards over the years. Since 1998 he has ridden a winner for five British trainers at SPs of 10-1, 16-1, 8-1, 14-1 and 20-1. Carberry is best known for employing exaggerated waiting tactics and did so spectacularly on Bellvano in last year's Grand Annual, but he can also ride more aggressively when necessary, as he showed on Unguided Missile in the 1998 JLT Specialty Handicap Chase and Looks Like Trouble in the 1999 RSA Chase. British trainers know they are getting a top-class jockey when they book him, and punters should also be keen to have him on their side.

Vital statistics

Leading jockeys at the festival

Festival award winners

2012 Barry Geraghty	5
2011 Ruby Walsh	5
2010 Ruby Walsh	3
2009 Ruby Walsh	7
2008 Ruby Walsh	3
2007 Robert Thornton	4
2006 Ruby Walsh	3
2005 Graham Lee	3
2004 Ruby Walsh	3
2003 Barry Geraghty	5

Total festival winners

Ruby Walsh	34
Tony McCoy	27
Barry Geraghty	25
Richard Johnson	18
Robert Thornton	16
Paul Carberry	12
Davy Russell	9
Timmy Murphy	8
Paddy Brennan	6
Jason Maguire	5

◄ *Barry Geraghty has got on the scoreboard at each of the past 11 festivals, winning the leading rider award twice*

◄ *Geraghty last year was a rarity among award winners in that all five victories came in Grade 1 races.*

◄ *Six of the previous ten award winners had a handicap scorer with an SP of 8-1 or lower*

◄ *Ruby Walsh is also on an 11-year winning run, with six awards*

◄ *Paul Nicholls has contributed to the leading rider's total eight times out of 13 since his first festival winner in 1999*

◄ *Tony McCoy was leading rider in 1997 and 1998 but hasn't won the award since. He has drawn a blank at just two of the 16 festivals since his first winner*

◄ *Richard Johnson has had a winner at ten of the past 14 festivals but has had only one winner since 2000 for a stable other than Philip Hobbs*

Tuesday, March 12
(Old Course)

🐎William Hill Supreme Novices' Hurdle

🐎Racing Post Arkle Chase

🐎JLT Specialty Handicap Chase

🐎Stan James Champion Hurdle

🐎Glenfarclas Cross Country Handicap Chase

🐎OLBG Mares' Hurdle

🐎Pulteney Land Investments Novices' Handicap Chase

1.30 William Hill Supreme Novices' Hurdle   C4/RUK
2m½f   Grade 1   £120,000

This revolves around My Tent Or Yours, who put up a sensational performance for a novice when running away with the Betfair Hurdle and has already run to a level that would have won just about any Supreme Novices' Hurdle since Golden Cygnet's in 1978. While that form entitles him to go off a short-priced favourite, it doesn't guarantee him success, and owner JP McManus has been thwarted lately with both Get Me Out Of Here and Darlan when coming here via the Betfair Hurdle. Nicky Henderson has an able second string in River Maigue, while McManus has an even stronger number two in Jezki, who is unbeaten in four novices in Ireland, the last two of them at Grade 1 level. Last year's Triumph Hurdle fourth Dodging Bullets also comes right into the reckoning, having picked up two novices before finishing a good third to Darlan in Kempton's Christmas Hurdle. Willie Mullins, who is so well represented in all of the festival novices, could run the unbeaten Un Atout as well as last year's Champion Bumper winner Champagne Fever.

My Tent Or Yours
6 b g; Trainer Nicky Henderson
Hurdles form 1211, best RPR 163
Left-handed 21, best RPR 163
Right-handed 11, best RPR 149

Decent bumper performer who has rapidly developed into one of the best, if not the best novice hurdler around. Has won three of his four hurdles starts and, given what he did before and afterwards, it remains a mystery how he got beat at Newbury in December, the second time he'd been beaten at odds-on at that track as he also lost a bumper there last March. He proved the track wasn't the problem when hacking up by five lengths from what looked a lofty enough mark of 149 in the ultra-competitive Betfair Hurdle in February. That prompted some very short prices for this race, with some bookmakers offering only 4-1 'with a run' for the Champion Hurdle, for which he'd have to be supplemented. Connections lost their main challenger for that prize when Darlan sadly died in a fall a few days before the Betfair Hurdle and owner JP McManus also has second favourite Jezki for this. As for his form claims for this, they will be obvious, although he has to prove he can do it in a faster-run race, which this will surely be. Indeed, the runners in the 3m½f handicap hurdle earlier on the Newbury card covered the first 2m½f in a time faster than the Betfair Hurdle was run.

Jezki
5 b g; Trainer Jessica Harrington
Hurdles form 1111, best RPR 149
Left-handed 111, best RPR 149
Right-handed 1, best RPR 149
Cheltenham form (bumper) 8
At the festival 14 Mar 2012: midfield, headway to chase leaders 4f out, ridden over 2f out, kept on same pace final furlong, 12l eighth to Champagne Fever in Champion Bumper

Decent bumper performer who could manage only a midfield finish in the Champion Bumper at last season's festival, but has really stepped up to the plate in his first season over hurdles. He reversed Cheltenham form with winner Champagne Fever when taking the Royal Bond at Fairyhouse in December and confirmed himself arguably Ireland's leading contender for this race when following up in the Future Champions Novice Hurdle at Leopardstown in December. Those two Grade 1s are the best Irish guides and there's little doubt Jezki is a potentially high-class hurdler, although according to Racing Post Ratings is tight in the market on what he has achieved so far. He certainly hasn't done anything wrong, seems to have a decent turn of pace and a fine attitude, so it would be foolish to ignore his claims. Scores pretty strongly as far as key trends are concerned, but so will most of the fancied runners. Better ground is expected to suit.

Melodic Rendezvous
7 ch g; Trainer Jeremy Scott
Hurdles form 2111, best RPR 155
Left-handed 1, best RPR 133
Right-handed 211, best RPR 155
Cheltenham form 1, best RPR 133

Beaten only by last year's Champion Bumper winner Champagne Fever (at Punchestown) in two bumpers last term and has made huge strides since getting turned over at short odds on his hurdles debut at Exeter. Punctured a few reputations when getting off the mark at Cheltenham in December in a race that has worked out well (third won by 29 lengths next time, fifth is now rated 139 after hacking up in a handicap hurdle at the trials meeting) and he followed it up with a commanding victory in the Grade 1 Tolworth Hurdle at Sandown. Trainer seems to think he may want better ground, but he clearly handles the mud very well, as he proved in his prep when slamming the previously unbeaten Puffin Billy by nine lengths at Exeter. Not sure that was the runner-up's true running as he may not have been suited by taking it up so early and was reported afterwards to have a foot problem, but Melodic Rendezvous was undeniably impressive. Also in the Neptune, but yet to race beyond 2m1f, which would give him an unlikely profile for that, and clearly has plenty of speed.

Un Atout
5 br g; Trainer Willie Mullins
Hurdles form 11 (both left-handed), best RPR 153

Looks like the No. 1 hope to give Willie Mullins a third success in this race following Tourist Attraction in 1995 and Ebaziyan in 2007. Both of those were outsiders, but this one won't be following a couple of bloodless successes over hurdles. Neither of those came in Graded company, however, and it's hard to put a figure on what he achieved in his latest wide-margin win on dreadful ground in a very slow time. Of course, there is no certainty this season that the ground will be any different come race time, but after his debut hurdles success his trainer said he was really a staying chaser in the making (has plenty of winning siblings over further) and it remains to be seen if he has the raw pace to deal with a race of this calibre at the festival.

River Maigue
6 b g; Trainer Nicky Henderson
Hurdles form 212, best RPR 137
Left-handed 2, best RPR 129
Right-handed 12, best RPR 137
Cheltenham form 2, best RPR 129

Lightly raced Nicky Henderson inmate who was a good second to Dodging Bullets in a steadily run Grade 2 novice on his hurdles

debut in November and made no mistake when slamming New Year's Eve by seven lengths at Kempton over Christmas. That looked good form at the time given New Year's Eve had finished second in last season's Champion Bumper, but he has since looked a weak finisher, getting turned over at odds of 2-7 at Ludlow on his next start. Beaten in his prep at Ascot in February but was giving weight to major Triumph Hurdle contender Far West, who was allowed to set his own pace and quicken from the front.

Dodging Bullets *(below, leading)*
5 b g; Trainer Paul Nicholls
Hurdles form 246113, best RPR 155
Left-handed 4611, best RPR 150
Right-handed 23, best RPR 155
Cheltenham form 411, best RPR 150
At the festival 16 Mar 2012: held up, headway approaching 3 out, strong challenge before last, not quicken run-in, kept on under pressure, but always held, finished fourth, beaten 4l by Countrywide Flame in Triumph Hurdle

One of the few near the front of the betting who doesn't qualify strongly on trends as he hasn't won at least 50 per cent of his hurdles starts and didn't win last time out. However, he does bring strong form credentials and not only those based on his third to the ill-fated Darlan in a slowly run Christmas Hurdle. He

was asked a big question by Paul Nicholls last term, but answered it well, finishing fourth in the Triumph Hurdle on only his second run. His novice status preserved, he set out on the Supreme route with two comfortable Cheltenham successes before stepping out of novice company at Kempton. Would not have been suited by the way that race was run, but clearly handles a strong pace and a big field and his trainer's record in 2m hurdles at the festival over the last ten years is just about the best around (eight wins, including this twice). Could run in the Dovecote, but Nicholls will be happy enough if he heads straight to Cheltenham, although that would put another black mark against him as far as trends are concerned (all recent winners ran within 45 days).

Champagne Fever
6 gr g; Trainer Willie Mullins
Hurdles form 1231, best RPR 150
Left-handed 31, best RPR 150
Right-handed 12, best RPR 150
Cheltenham form (bumper) 1, best RPR 142
At the festival 14 Mar 2012: Prominent, led after 1f, made rest, ridden when pressed over 1f out, kept on well and in control towards finish, won Champion Bumper by a length and a quarter from New Year's Eve

A 16-1 shot when winning last season's Champion Bumper despite being the chosen

mount of Patrick Mullins, and has since achieved a high level over hurdles without looking a superstar. Won easily on his debut at Cork but then found Jezki too speedy at Fairyhouse, although he arguably came out the best horse at the weights as he was conceding 3lb to the winner. Said to have had a lung infection when tailed off over 2m4f at Naas in January, a trip he should have had no problem in getting. After getting back on track in the Grade 1 Deloitte (2m2f) at Leopardstown in February he was confirmed as a runner in this race. Doesn't quite have the form of some of those ahead of him in the market, but the courage he showed in winning the Champion Bumper will stand him in good stead.

Chatterbox *(below)*
5 b g; Trainer Nicky Henderson
Hurdles form 11 (both left-handed), best RPR 117

Promsing youngster who seems to have surprised his trainer, but relatively lofty market position (as short as 14-1 in places) is rather silly and based on the beating of a hugely below-par My Tent Or Yours. Won again on Betfair Hurdle day to make it 2-2 but beat nothing of note and, according to Racing Post Ratings, has upwards of three stones to find (more on Topspeed). Trainer said at the time he thought he might be a bit weak for Cheltenham this year and, as his dam is a half-sister to My Will, staying will probably be his long-term game.

Pique Sous
6 gr g; Trainer Willie Mullins
Hurdles form (both right-handed) 21, best RPR 136
Cheltenham form (bumper) 3, best RPR 140
At the festival 14 Mar 2012: Midfield, headway over 6f out, ridden to challenge over 1f out, not quicken

entering final furlong, stayed on towards finish, finished third, beaten one and a half lengths, to Champagne Fever in Champion Bumper

Won three of his six bumper runs and was third in the big one at Cheltenham when the choice of Ruby Walsh. Won two of those bumpers on soft ground in the summer, but has been withdrawn on account of bad ground before and been restricted to just two runs over hurdles. He was second at Cork in August and two months later won a maiden at Thurles, where he beat nothing of note but did it easily. His next outing on the track came in an all-weather maiden in February, which suggests connections are keeping him fit just in case Cheltenham dries out in time for him to run, and he confirmed his wellbeing with another cosy success. Hard to know what to make of him but his position in a good bumper makes him potentially quite decent.

OTHERS TO CONSIDER

Rock Critic made it 2-2 over hurdles when beating Grand National favourite Seabass at Fairyhouse in February, but trainer Dermot Weld said afterwards he thought he was more of a Punchestown/Fairyhouse type of horse, so he is not guaranteed to travel. **Mozoltov** is also 2-2 over hurdles after beating Don Cossack in a Grade 2 at Punchestown, but the runner-up had arguably been found out the time before. **Waaheb** is promising but didn't do himself any favours when falling early on in the Deloitte. **Cause Of Causes** could look a big price if lining up on the day. The Ladbroke winner made no show at all in the Betfair Hurdle at Newbury but he needs a strong pace to get the best out of him. **Court Minstrel** travelled well considering he pulled hard in the Tolworth and he eventually paid the price. He's a good-ground horse who has the ability to run well off the guaranteed strong pace as long as it dries out. Looking at the exchange market, anything else with a form chance – The New One, Moscow Mannon – is likely to be running in another race or not at all.

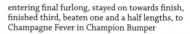

RACINGPOST.com
Snap up the value – compare odds and bet from our cards

Supreme Novices' Hurdle results and trends

FORM	WINNER	AGE & WGT	Adj RPR	SP	TRAINER	H.Runs	BEST RPR LAST 12 MONTHS (RUNS SINCE)
12 -2111	Cinders And Ashes D	5 11-7	152⁶	10-1	D McCain	4(19G)	won Aintree class 4 mdn hdl (2m1f) **(2)**
11 -F311	Al Ferof D	6 11-7	146⁻¹⁷	10-1	P Nicholls	4(15G)	won Newbury class 3 nov hdl (2m½f) **(0)**
10 11212	Menorah D, BF	5 11-7	160³	12-1	P Hobbs	4(18GS)	won Kempton class 2 nov hdl (2m) **(1)**
09 12121	Go Native D	6 11-7	153⁸	12-1	N Meade (IRE)	5(20GS)	won Punchestown Listed nov hdl (2m) **(2)**
08 1/711	Captain Cee Bee D	7 11-7	151⁻²	17-2	E Harty (IRE)	2(22GS)	won Punchestown hdl (2m) **(0)**
07 21	Ebaziyan D	6 11-7	121⁻⁴³	40-1	W Mullins (IRE)	2(22S)	2nd Cork mdn hdl (2m) **(1)**
06 -3111	Noland C, D	5 11-7	144⁻⁶	6-1	P Nicholls	4(20GS)	won Exeter Listed nov hdl (2m1f) **(0)**
05 1143	Arcalis D, BF	5 11-7	150⁻⁵	20-1	H Johnson	4(20G)	4th Christmas Hurdle Gd1 (2m) **(1)**
04 1-111	Brave Inca D	6 11-7	145⁻¹²	7-2F	C Murphy (IRE)	7(19G)	won Deloitte Hurdle Gd1 (2m2f) **(0)**
03 0-211	Back In Front C, D	6 11-8	155ᵀ	3-1F	E O'Grady (IRE)	3(19G)	won Limerick nov hdl (2m4f) **(0)**

WINS-RUNS: 4yo 0-8, 5yo 4-89, 6yo 5-73, 7yo 1-20, 8yo 0-3, 9yo 0-1 **FAVOURITES:** -£1.50

TRAINERS IN THIS RACE (w-pl-r): Paul Nicholls 2-1-12, Donald McCain 1-0-2, Noel Meade 1-1-9, Philip Hobbs 1-1-7, Willie Mullins 1-0-14, Alan King 0-1-5, Charlie Mann 0-0-1, Dermot Weld 0-0-4, Dessie Hughes 0-0-1, David Pipe 0-0-5, Evan Williams 0-0-2, Jonjo O'Neill 0-1-2, Mouse Morris 0-1-3, Jessica Harrington 0-0-3, Nicky Henderson 0-7-15, Nigel Twiston-Davies 0-0-5, Oliver Sherwood 0-0-1, Susan Nock 0-0-1, Tim Vaughan 0-0-1, Venetia Williams 0-0-2

FATE OF FAVOURITES: 1105325340 **POSITION OF WINNER IN MARKET:** 1102046436

Key trends

🏇Won at least 50 per cent of hurdle starts, 10/10

🏇Ran within the last 52 days, 10/10

🏇Rated within 12lb of RPR top-rated, 9/10

🏇Pre-race RPR of at least 137, 9/10

🏇Won last time out, 8/10

🏇Previously contested a Graded race, 7/10 (four won, three made the frame)

Other factors

🏇Ireland has won this 11 times in the past 22 years

🏇Two winners came via the Flat, where they had earned an RPR between 91 and 110, and neither of the two had won outside minor novice hurdle company. The other eight started their careers in bumpers, where they had earned an RPR of at least 110

🏇Two winners had previously run in the Champion Bumper (Back In Front was third in 2002 and Cinders And Ashes fifth in 2011)

🏇Montelado in 1993 is the only winner of the Bumper to follow up here. Four others have tried – Cork All Star (seventh), Cousin Vinny (fifth), Dunguib (third) and Cue Card (fourth)

🏇The last horse to win this after just one hurdle outing was Flown in 1992

🏇For many years, the shortest-priced Irish runner was often beaten by a compatriot. However, of the last six to win, four were the most fancied

Notes

2.05 Racing Post Arkle Chase C4/RUK
2m Grade 1 £150,000

Simonsig was favourite for the Racing Post Arkle Chase before he had even jumped a fence in public and he has barely been available at any better than evens since effortless wins at Ascot and Kempton either side of Christmas drew inevitable comparisons with his stablemate Sprinter Sacre, who was so impressive in this race last year. It would be disrespectful to Overturn to suggest it is a one-horse race, as last year's Champion Hurdle runner-up has looked just as exciting over fences as he was on the Flat and over hurdles. Paul Nicholls last won the Arkle with Azertyuiop ten years ago, but ex-French Fago impressed at Newbury on his debut for the champion trainer and was set to follow up when taking a soft fall at Warwick next time. Leading Irish challenger Arvika Ligeonniere also has to put a recent fall behind him, while connections of Oscars Well, who was sixth in the Champion Hurdle last year, have suggested he might wait for the Irish festivals.

Simonsig
7 gr g; Trainer Nicky Henderson
Chase form (both right-handed) 11, best RPR 167
Cheltenham form (hurdle) 1, best RPR 162
At the festival 14 Mar 2012 Held up in touch, hit 3rd, headway to take 3rd 3 out, closing on leader, travelling well and 1l down when left in 4l lead 2 out, quickened clear before last, pushed along run-in, easily, won Neptune by seven lengths from Felix Yonger

Big gossip horse at the start of last season and despite December defeat by Fingal Bay at Sandown he soon lived up to the hype. Connections had been considering the Supreme Novices' at the festival given his natural speed, but in the end he went for his original target, the Neptune, and hacked up by seven lengths from Felix Yonger, his task made easier when Cotton Mill, a length up at the time, ran out at the second-last. Few would have predicted anything other than a win for Simonsig, though, and he went on to dot up by 15 lengths at Aintree. Winner aside, it was probably an average Neptune, but he was in a league of his own. With Nicky Henderson so strong in the 2m hurdling division, any thought of a Champion Hurdle campaign was soon dispelled and Simonsig has so far done everything asked of him in impressive fashion. He had only an 82-rated rival to beat on his debut after his other three opponents had departed by halfway, but next time at Kempton he gave weight and a 35-length beating to the 148-rated four-year-old Hinterland. The runner-up has looked a soft finisher so far this term and was beaten at odds of 30-100 in a jumpers bumper by a 122-rated hurdler next time, so whether Simonsig has achieved as much as the figures suggest is open to question. He's going to go off a similar price to stablemate Sprinter Sacre last year but, having missed the Game Spirit owing to a slightly below-par trachea wash, he'll be going there with less experience than an average winner. Very little about him is average, though, and there's a fair chance he will frighten off a lot of the potential opposition despite his lack of experience.

Overturn
9 b g; Trainer Donald McCain
Chase form 111, best RPR 162
Left-handed 1, best RPR 161
Right-handed 11, best RPR 162
Cheltenham form (hurdles) 722, best RPR 167
At the festival 15 Mar 2011 Led to 4th, stayed pressing leaders, weakening on inner when hampered bend after 2 out, finished seventh in Champion Hurdle, beaten 16½l by Hurricane Fly

13 Mar 2012 Led, joined 2 out, headed soon after, kept on gamely under pressure run-in to maintain clear 2nd, but no impression on winner, finished second in Champion Hurdle, beaten 3¾l by Rock On Ruby

Quite deservedly one of the most popular horses in training, Donald McCain's nine-year-old has won a Northumberland Plate and been first and second in the Chester Cup on the Flat, and has won a Scottish Champion Hurdle,

Galway Hurdle, Fighting Fifth Hurdle and been second in a Champion Hurdle. Now, after three flawless chase sucesses (in the last two running not far off his previous hurdles best according to Racing Post Ratings), he can lay claim to being one of the most versatile racehorses of all time. There's no knocking what he has done over fences, as after being slightly hesitant at the first couple on his Sandown debut his jumping has been impeccable since. Two starts ago he thrashed the 142-rated Conquisto by an eased-down 25 lengths at Doncaster, while last time he was 29 lengths too good for Tetlami, who was rated 140 over hurdles. Hasn't seen another rival and in any other year would be a worthy favourite himself. The last winner aged as old as nine was Danish Flight in 1988, but it won't be age that stops Overturn winning.

Arvika Ligeonniere
8 b g; Trainer Willie Mullins
Chase form 111F, best RPR 156
Left-handed, 1F, best RPR 156
Right-handed 11, best RPR 156
Cheltenham form (hurdles) 4, best RPR 130
At the festival 19 Mar 2010 Held up, headway after 3 out, chased leader 2 out, lost 2nd between last 2, soon weakened, finished 4th in Albert Bartlett Novices' Hurdle, beaten 14l by Berties Dream

Promising novice hurdler a couple of seasons ago when he clearly didn't stay in the Albert Bartlett (finished fourth) but then missed just over two years through injury. Has returned even better, putting in a flawless round of jumping on his May debut at Punchestown and again when an easy all-the-way winner of a Grade 1 at Fairyhouse. Those two races were both over 2m4f, but he looked to have plenty of pace and proved the point when leading all the way in the Racing Post Novice Chase at Leopardstown over Christmas to beat former top-class hurdler Oscars Well by two and a half lengths. Was odds-on back at the same

track for the Irish Arkle the following month but surprisingly fell when holding a narrow advantage four out. It's hard to think he wouldn't have won given how tamely Oscars Well folded on the run-in. Connections may look to give him a confidence-booster before Cheltenham and he looks the best of the Irish if coming here (also in the Jewson).

Fago
5 b/br g; Trainer Paul Nicholls
Chase form (all left-handed) 22P31521F, best RPR 154

Five-year-old with more experience than most, having run seven times over fences in France before joining Paul Nicholls. Only won one of those seven but was runner-up in a Grade 1, to the now Nicky Henderson-trained filly he had earlier beaten, and improved on his first start in Britain, jumping soundly and winning with plenty in hand at Newbury. Was then sent for the often informative Kingmaker at Warwick but fell two out when looking to be going best of the front two. They had gone pretty hard, though, and it looked a tired fall (winner Majala stopped to a walk and was almost caught). Likely to take in another chase to wipe out the memories of that fall, but even at 10-1 looks to be priced on trainer rather than ability.

Captain Conan
6 b g; Trainer Nicky Henderson
Chase form 111, best RPR 152
Left-handed 1, best RPR 151
Right-handed 11, best RPR 152
Cheltenham form (chase) 1, best RPR 151

Good novice hurdler who missed Cheltenham last year but chased home his ill-fated stablemate Darlan in a Grade 2 at Aintree in April and has quickly made up into a useful novice chaser. Was a ready winner of his first two starts, beating Sire De Grugy at

Cheltenham and Hinterland in the Henry VIII at Sandown, but then needed some help from the runner-up when completing a Grade 1 double at the Esher track in February in the Scilly Isles. Captain Conan did not jump or travel as well as before and would not have won if Third Intention hadn't waited for him after the last. More likely to in the Jewson over 2m4f, but if that last run is as good as he is, he won't be winning. Fair chance the run was much needed, though.

Oscars Well
8 b/br g; Trainer Jessica Harrington
Chase form 1F122, best RPR 156
Left-handed 122, best RPR 156
Right-handed 1F, best RPR 152
Cheltenham form (hurdles) 46, best RPR 164
At the festival 16 Mar 2011: Took keen hold, raced in touch, headway to challenge 2 out, led soon after, 1 length lead and staying on when mistake and sprawled badly last, not recover, finished fourth, beaten 6¾l by First Lieutenant in Neptune

13 Mar 2012: Chased leaders, ridden 2 out, weakened before last, finished sixth, beaten eight lengths by Rock On Ruby in Champion Hurdle

Good hurdler who has had a bit of an up-and-down first season over fences. Looked like he'd develop into at least as good a chaser as over hurdles when putting in a flawless round of jumping on his debut at Punchestown but then fell heavily when odds-on for a Grade 2 next time. Back on track with an easy win at Navan afterwards and there was some suggestion he'd given easy winner Arvika Ligeonniere too much rope when second to that one in the Grade 1 Racing Post Novice Chase at Leopardstown over Christmas. However, when ridden closer to his rival in the Irish Arkle next time he folded after hitting the last when he should have had the race at his mercy with Arvika Ligeonniere having hit the deck. In truth, he looked beaten before the last, so he has questions to answer, although he will prefer stalking a stronger pace on better ground. Also in Jewson.

Benefficient (above)

7 ch g; Trainer Tony Martin
Chase form 21241, best RPR 153
Left-handed 2241, best RPR 153
Right-handed 1, best RPR 132
Cheltenham form (hurdle) 0, best RPR 116
At the festival 14 Mar 2012: Chased leaders, ridden 3 out, weakened rapidly 2 out, finished tenth, beaten 48 lengths by Simonsig in Neptune

Caused a massive shock when 50-1 winner of the Grade 1 Deloitte Novice Hurdle at Leopardstown last season and sprang another in the Irish Arkle this term at the same track when a 20-length scorer from Oscars Well as the 10-1 outsider of three. No-one knows if he'd have won had favourite Arvika Ligeonierre stood up, but he had the beating of the runner-up before that one made a mistake at the last. Stays a lot further than 2m (second to Harry Topper over 3m at Newbury in November) and is also in the Jewson, but tailed off in last season's Neptune and seems to need very bad ground.

OTHERS TO CONSIDER

Willie Mullins made stacks of entries and the most likely runners apart from Arvika Ligeonniere look to be **Twinlight** and **Aupcharlie**. Twinlight looked progressive enough when last seen in the autumn but is hardly an ante-post proposition having not run since and still needs to find plenty. Aupcharlie wouldn't be such a silly bet if lining up on the day. He has been beaten on his last two starts over 3m when looking all over the winner and he seems certain to drop back in trip at the festival. He appears more likely to contest the Jewson, however. **Majala** may well have been a sitting duck for Fago in the Kingmaker at Warwick, but it might not have been as clear-cut as it looked. He finished out on his feet, however, and will need to recover quickly. Trainer Tom George also has **Module**, who has looked decent on his last two starts but is probably Jewson-bound.

Arkle Chase results and trends

	FORM	WINNER	AGE & WGT	Adj RPR	SP	TRAINER	C.Runs	BEST RPR LAST 12 MONTHS (RUNS SINCE)
12	3-111	Sprinter Sacre D	6 11-7	179^T	8-11F	N Henderson	3$^{(6G)}$	won Newbury Gd2 ch (2m1f) (0)
11	22221	Captain Chris C, D	7 11-7	163^{-4}	6-1	P Hobbs	4$^{(10G)}$	2nd Sandown Gd1 nov ch (2m4½f) (1)
10	41111	Sizing Europe C, D	8 11-7	170^T	6-1	H De Bromhead (IRE)	4$^{(12GS)}$	won Leopardstown Gd1 nov ch (2m1f) (0)
09	-1222	Forpadydeplasterer D	7 11-7	160^{-6}	8-1	T Cooper (IRE)	4$^{(17GS)}$	2nd Gd1 Dr PJ Moriarty Nov Ch (2m5f) (0)
08	-1112	Tidal Bay C, BF	7 11-7	160^T	6-1	H Johnson	4$^{(14GS)}$	won Carlisle class 3 nov ch (2m4f) (2)
07	21211	My Way De Solzen C, D	7 11-7	161^{-1}	7-2	A King	5$^{(13S)}$	won Haydock Gd2 nov ch (2m4f) (0)
06	-1111	Voy Por Ustedes D	5 11-2	164^{-5}	15-2	A King	4$^{(14GS)}$	won Wincanton Gd2 nov ch (2m) (0)
05	-2213	Contraband C, D	7 11-7	161^T	7-1	M Pipe	4$^{(19G)}$	3rd Uttoxeter Gd2 nov ch (2m) (0)
04	3-151	Well Chief D	5 11-3	144^{-17}	9-1	M Pipe	1$^{(16G)}$	won Taunton class 4 nov ch (2m½f) (0)
03	5-111	Azertyuiop C D	6 11-8	165^{-1}	5-4F	P Nicholls	3$^{(9G)}$	won Wincanton class 3 nov ch (2m) (0)

WINS-RUNS: 5yo 2-20, 6yo 2-29, 7yo 5-51, 8yo 1-23, 9yo 0-5, 10yo 0-1, 12yo 0-1 **FAVOURITES:** -£6.02

TRAINERS IN THIS RACE (w-pl-r): Alan King 2-0-5, Nicky Henderson 1-3-8, Paul Nicholls 1-2-15, Colin Tizzard 0-1-1, David Pipe 0-0-2, Mouse Morris 0-0-1, Jessica Harrington 0-0-3, Nigel Twiston-Davies 0-0-1, Paul Webber 0-0-1, Tom Taaffe 0-1-1, Thomas Mullins 0-0-2, Tom George 0-0-1, Venetia Williams 0-0-2, Willie Mullins 0-0-7

FATE OF FAVOURITES: 1F0023F041 **POSITION OF WINNER IN MARKET:** 1525223341

Key trends

🐎SP no bigger than 9-1 (only one bigger than 16-1 at ante-post stage), 10/10

🐎Aged five to eight, 10/10

🐎Finished in the first two on all completed chase starts, 9/10 (exception finished no worse than third)

🐎Rated within 12lb of RPR top-rated, 9/10

🐎Pre-race RPR of at least 151, 9/10

🐎Three to five runs over fences, 9/10

🐎RPR hurdle rating of at least 153, 8/10

🐎Won novice chase over 2m to 2m1f, 7/10

Other factors

🐎Six had previously won a 2m-2m1f Graded chase (no race has proved a reliable guide)

🐎Eight winners had previously run at the festival, showing mixed form in a variety of hurdle races

🐎Three French-bred horses have scored and only three times has a French-bred not finished in the first three

🐎Only ten German-breds have run, but they include a winner, a second and a third

🐎There have been only two winning favourites in the past decade

Notes

2.40 JLT Specialty Handicap Chase   C4/RUK

3m½f   *Grade 3*   *£90,000*

The top handicap chase of the festival has strong stats concerning form (especially at Cheltenham), age, weight and market position.

Only two favourites have won since 1977 but the race usually goes to a fancied runner, with ten of the past 14 winners sent off at 10-1 or lower. Eight of the past ten winners were in the first five in the market and the only long-priced winners since 1999 were Chief Dan George (33-1 in 2010) and Joes Edge (50-1 in 2007). It is also notable they were the only winners in that period from the double-figure age band.

In fact, all the recent shocks were by older runners – the four winners at 20-1 or more in the past 20 years were aged ten or above. Younger winners tend to be well fancied – ten of the last 12 winners were aged seven, eight or nine, with nine of those ten younger winners sent off no bigger than 8-1.

Course form in the current season is worth noting and most winners have a previous good run at Cheltenham on their record – the only winner in the past ten years without any previous course form was the Irish-trained Dun Doire in 2006. Two of the past eight winners had run well in this race the year before.

Second-season chasers have traditionally done well and, after many years without a victory by a raw novice, there have been three novice winners in nine years with Wichita Lineman (2009) the highest-rated off 142.

Since 1983 no winner has had a mark above 150. Unguided Missile made all under 11st 10lb in 1998 when rated 149 in an uncompetitive renewal, but since then only one winner has carried more than 10st 12lb.

Paul Nicholls, whose established handi-cappers tend to be over-weighted by the time of the festival, has never won this race. Among his 11 losers in the past decade was a 5-1 joint-favourite and the closest he has come is third. His best chance is likely to be with a novice.

Nicky Henderson's runners are much more noteworthy. Although his last winner was Marlborough in 2000, five of his 12 runners since then have finished second or third.

The two Irish-trained winners had run to good effect in Britain in their successful season.

Cantlow (left) is a leading ante-post fancy for the JLT

JLT Specialty Handicap Chase results and trends

FORM	WINNER	AGE & WGT	OR	SP	TRAINER	C.Runs	BEST RPR LAST 12 MONTHS (RUNS SINCE)
12 -PF75	Alfie Sherrin (1oh) D	9 10-0	129^5	14-1	J O'Neill	6$^{(19G)}$	7th Kempton class 3 hcap ch (2m4½f) (0)
11 F2-52	Bensalem C, BF	8 11-2	143^T	5-1	A King	5$^{(19G)}$	fell Festival Handicap Chase (3m½f) (3)
10 -3701	Chief Dan George D	10 10-10	142^6	33-1	J Moffatt	9$^{(24GS)}$	won Doncaster class 2 hcap ch (3m) (0)
09 9-121	Wichita Lineman C, D	8 10-9	142^T	5-1F	J O'Neill	3$^{(21GS)}$	won Chepstow class 3 nov ch (3m) (0)
08 3-P61	An Accordion D	7 10-12	143^6	7-1	D Pipe	6$^{(14GS)}$	won Doncaster Listed hcap ch (3m) (0)
07 76-78	Joes Edge	10 10-6	130^8	50-1	F Murphy	17$^{(23GS)}$	13th Cheltenham Gold Cup (3m2½f) (4)
06 11111	Dun Doire D	7 10-9	129^9	7-1	T Martin (IRE)	9$^{(21GS)}$	won Gowran hcap ch (3m) (0)
05 03F43	Kelami D	7 10-2	133^9	8-1	F Doumen (FR)	19$^{(20G)}$	3rd Haydock Gd3 hcap ch (3m4½f) (0)
04 31U21	Fork Lightning C, D	8 10-5	136^4	7-1	A King	5$^{(11G)}$	2nd Kempton class 3 nov ch (3m) (1)
03 0-131	Youlneverwalkalone D	9 10-11	142^9	7-1	C Roche (IRE)	9$^{(18G)}$	won Thurles chase (3m) (2)

WINS-RUNS: 6yo 0-12, 7yo 3-28, 8yo 3-42, 9yo 2-48, 10yo 2-28, 11yo 0-19, 12yo 0-9, 13yo 0-3, 14yo 0-1 **FAVOURITES:** -£4.00

FATE OF FAVOURITES: 300P2312F0 **POSITION OF WINNER IN MARKET:** 3452031027

OR 121-133 4-3-44, **134-148** 6-24-123, **149-161** 0-3-23

Key trends

🐎 Aged seven to ten, 10/10

🐎 Carried no more than 11st 2lb, 10/10

🐎 Officially rated 129-143, 10/10

🐎 Won over at least 3m, 9/10

🐎 Finished first, second or third on either or both of last two starts, 8/10

🐎 Top-three finish last time out, 8/10

🐎 No more than nine runs over fences, 8/10

🐎 Ran no more than four times that season, 7/10

Other factors

🐎 Seven winners had run at a previous festival, four recording at least one top-four finish

🐎 Last year Alfie Sherrin was the first to win from out of the handicap since Maamur in 1996

🐎 Four winners had run well (two placing, one falling when going well and one sixth) in a handicap at Cheltenham earlier in the season. Bensalem, the 2011 winner, had run well in a Grade 2 hurdle

🐎 There have been two winning favourites in the past 30 years – Antonin in 1994 and Wichita Lineman in 2009

🐎 Three of the past seven winners had won a Class 1 handicap chase

🐎 Once seemingly an impossible task for novices, but three of the past nine winners have been first-season chasers

Notes

3.20 Stan James Champion Hurdle C4/RUK
⚞2m½f ⚞Grade 1 ⚞£400,000

The wet winter has given connections of some of the main challengers nightmares and we sadly lost a key contender when Darlan suffered a fatal fall in a trial put on by Doncaster specifically to compensate for the lost opportunities. Hurricane Fly has enjoyed an uninterrupted preparation in Ireland, unlike last season, and he has come through it unbeaten. Although he lost his aura of invincibility when only third to Rock On Ruby here a year ago he now has a great chance of becoming the first horse to regain his crown since Comedy Of Errors way back in 1975. Rock On Ruby appeared lucky to win the Doncaster race, but there was no fluke about last year's success here, even if the favourite was below form, and he merits every respect. Binocular is a third former Champion Hurdle winner due to line up – Punjabi might even be a fourth – but Zarkandar and Grandouet, first and second in Cheltenham's own trial, are much shorter in the ante-post lists.

....

Hurricane Fly
9 b g; Trainer Willie Mullins
Hurdles form 1121113111111131111, best RPR 173
Left-handed 1211111311, best RPR 173
Right-handed 111311111, best RPR 173
Cheltenham form 13, best RPR 171
At the festival 13 Mar 2012: held up in rear, headway 3 out, went 3rd 2 out and soon driven, kept on under pressure run-in but no impression on leading duo, finished third, beaten five and a half lengths by Rock On Ruby in Champion Hurdle

15 Mar 2011: Held up in touch, steady headway to track leaders 2 out and soon travelling well, driven to take slight lead last, ridden and edged right run-in, held on all out, won Champion Hurdle by a length and a quarter from Peddlers Cross
....

The outstanding 2m hurdler of his generation, having won 16 of his 19 starts, the last 14 in Grade 1 company. Won the 2011 Champion in a hard-fought battle with Peddlers Cross and, although restricted to only one run (easy success) before making his defence last term, was sent off at just 4-6 to sucessfully do so, but could manage only third to Rock On Ruby. Had to work hard to win at Punchestown the following month, giving some credence to the theory that he wasn't at his best last season, but seems right back on track now following three easy Grade 1 wins. That he has started at odds of 2-5, 1-5 and 1-6 for those contests and will be odds-against at Cheltenham gives some indication of what he has beaten (none of the next four in this year's betting) but you can only dispatch what is put in front of you

and he has done that with his usual panache. The question remains whether a strong-run 2m round Cheltenham really suits him as he was all out when beating Peddlers Cross and couldn't get to the front two last year. It has been suggested he was held up too far off the pace in a steadily run race last year, but Rock On Ruby's time has been beaten only once since the days of Istabraq (and by only 0.1sec) and Hurricane Fly was closer at the final hurdle than he was at the winning post. Still, he's fully entitled to be favourite in his bid to become the first horse to regain his title sine Comedy Of Errors in 1975 and just one Champion Hurdle crown doesn't really do him justice.
....

Grandouet
6 b/br g; Trainer Nicky Henderson
Hurdles form 33152113B1F112, best RPR 166
Left-handed 3315213B112, best RPR 166
Right-handed 11F, best RPR 146
Cheltenham form 2312, best RPR 166
At the festival 18 Mar 2011: Tracked leaders, challenging 2 out, led briefly approaching last, not quicken run-in, stayed on same pace final 100yds, finished third, beaten five lengths by Zarkandar in Triumph Hurdle
....

Decent juvenile two seasons ago, but a bit of a weak finisher and could manage only a five-length third to Zarkandar in the Triumph when seemingly not getting up the hill. However, emerged as a stronger horse last season and was second favourite for this race having

proved his ability to get up the hill with an impressive four-length success from Overturn in a strongly run International (Bula). Disaster then struck as he suffered an infection in a fetlock joint just three weeks before the festival and was ruled out of contention. Entitled to need his return from a year out in this season's International but looked as good as ever when a two-length second to Zarkandar, his 4lb concession to the winner making him the best horse at the weights. That said, Zarkandar was not suited by making his own running and is now 3-0 in meetings with Grandouet. Had another minor injury scare in February, but soft ground was given as the reason for him missing the Kingwell.

....

Zarkandar
6 b g; Trainer Paul Nicholls
Hurdles form 11115F111, best RPR 164
Left-handed 1115F1, best RPR 164
Right-handed 111, best RPR 163
Cheltenham form 151, best RPR 164
At the festival 13 Mar 2012 in touch, ridden after 3 out and soon outpaced, rallied but only 7th approaching last, stayed on strongly closing stages to take 5th last strides, beaten six and three-quarter lengths by Rock On Ruby in Champion Hurdle

18 Mar 2011: In touch, closed 2 out, led approaching last, ran on well run-in, always in control, won Triumph Hurdle by two and a quarter lengths from Unaccompanied

Arc winner Zarkava's half-brother had only three runs as a juvenile but proved the dominant force in the division, winning a red-hot Triumph in commanding fashion and following up at Aintree. Troubled by minor niggles the following season, he didn't return until February when becoming the first seasonal debutant to win the Betfair (formerly Totesport) Hurdle at Newbury. Didn't seem to run his race in the Champion Hurdle, though, as he was badly outpaced from three out only to storm up the hill when it was all over, causing many to believe he wanted a step up in trip, something he got in the Aintree Hurdle only to fall too far out to confirm it. Trainer Paul Nicholls was of the belief he never had him quite right last term, though, and Zarkandar returned looking a pacier sort when winning the Elite Hurdle under a big weight at Wincanton in November. He subsequently had to cut out most of his own running in the International (Bula) in December and looked a sitting duck for first Rock On Ruby and then Grandouet in the straight, but kept on pulling out more and was going away at the line. Only workmanlike in the end when completing his unbeaten build-up in the Kingwell, but the ground was heavy and trainer Paul Nicholls had left plenty to work on. Will surely run a much bigger race this year.

Rock On Ruby *(above, light green sleeves)*
8 b g; Trainer Harry Fry
Hurdles form 1223121331, best RPR 171
Left-handed 122311331, best RPR 171
Right-handed 1, best RPR 166
Cheltenham form 2213, best RPR 171
At the festival 13 Mar 2012 tracked leaders in 3rd,
went 2nd before 3 out, challenged 2 out, led soon after
and driven to assert, kept on under pressure run-in,
won going away in Champion Hurdle by three and
three-quarter lengths from Overturn

16 Mar 2011: In touch, good headway to chase leaders
2 out, ridden and 1 length down when left with 2
lengths lead last, stayed on well under pressure, caught
last stride, finished second, beaten a short head by First
Lieutenant in Neptune Hurdle

Something of a surprise winner of last season's
Champion Hurdle, but there was no fluke
about the victory as he was up with the pace
throughout and poured it on from three out
to win in the second-fastest time since 2000.
Was not so good in the Aintree Hurdle a month
later upped to 2m4f, but has never won at that
trip and post-Cheltenham flops are always
forgiveable. Harry Fry, who prepared him
last year when he was officially trained by
Paul Nicholls, did not bring him out until the
International at Cheltenham in December,
when he travelled like much the best horse
only to blow up between the last two and drop
eight lengths off Zarkandar at the line. Then
came his Cheltenham warm-up on a sad day
in February marred by the fatal last-flight fall
of Darlan. Most will have expected the strong-
travelling Darlan to have won from there but
Rock On Ruby had run into the teeth of a fierce
wind all the way up the straight and was still
giving generously, as he did in winning last
year's Champion Hurdle, when he pulled away
again after the last. He'll be better for the run
anyway and, as he'd have won the Neptune
if the race had been 100 yards shorter, he's
clearly a Cheltenham horse. Doesn't have the
blistering speed normally associated with a
top two-miler but is more in the mould of dual
winner Hardy Eustace and may well emulate
him.

Cinders And Ashes
6 b g; Trainer Donald McCain
Hurdles form 2111125, best RPR 151
Left-handed 11112, best RPR 151
Right-handed 25, best RPR 150
Cheltenham form 251, best RPR 151
At the festival 13 Mar 2012: Tracked leaders on
inner, mistake 4th, closed 2 out, ridden to lead and
mistake last, edged right but stayed on strongly flat,
won Supreme Novices' by one and a quarter lengths
from Darlan

16 Mar 2011: Prominent, progress to dispute lead over
3f out, headed and weakened well over 1f out, finished
fifth, beaten 16 lengths by Cheltenian in Champion
Bumper

With a fifth in the Champion Bumper and victory in last year's Supreme Novices' Hurdle to his name, he certainly has the right Cheltenham profile but otherwise doesn't seem to have much going for him this year. There's no doubt he was a good novice hurdler, but he hasn't stepped up to the plate this season, as he was hammered 12 lengths by Countrywide Flame in the Fighting Fifth at Newcastle and beaten a similar distance when only fifth of seven to Darlan in the Christmas Hurdle at Kempton. Both those defeats came on heavy ground, which he has won on in weaker company but is said not to like. However, his market position – 16-1 best at the time of writing – owes more to Donald McCain's belief that he'll be a different horse on better ground than his form, which suggests he has upwards of 20lb to find to be competitive. Falls down on a stack of trends, too, so hard to make a case for him being anything other than a very unlikely winner.

Binocular

9 b g; Trainer Nicky Henderson
Hurdles form 112111353113114321143, best RPR 172
Left-handed 21135134243, best RPR 172
Right-handed 1113111311, best RPR 172
Cheltenham form 2314, best RPR 172
At the festival 11 Mar 2008: In touch, tracked leaders 4th, challenged 2 out, slight lead soon after and still just ahead last, headed final 110yds but kept on well for 2nd, beaten two lengths by Captain Cee Bee in Supreme Novices' Hurdle

10 Mar 2009: Warm before start, well placed behind clear leaders, closed going to 3 out to track leading pair after and well ahead of rest, ridden to challenge last, not quicken soon after, kept on near finish, third, beaten a neck and a head, to Punjabi in Champion Hurdle

16 Mar 2010: Held up early, tracked leading quartet before 3rd, closed 5th, smooth progress 3 out to lead next, well in command last, ridden and ran on well, won Champion Hurdle by three and a half lengths from Khyber Kim

13 Mar 2012: Held up in rear, headway after 3 out, 6th and ridden 2 out, staying on one pace into 4th when mistake last, kept on again but no impression on leading trio, finished fourth, beaten six and a half lengths by Rock On Ruby in Champion Hurdle

Hugely talented performer at his best whose four Grade 1 successes are a poor return for one of his ability and indicative of the fact he's had a chequered history. Beaten fair and square as a four-year-old when second in the 2008 Supreme, he was reportedly undercooked when made 6-4 favourite for the following year's Champion as a five-year-old, but made no mistake the following year when travelling and jumping like a superstar and winning easily, despite having been backed at 1000 on Betfair a few weeks earlier when "ruled out for the season" with a muscle problem. Many thought he'd prove hard to beat for the next couple of seasons, but the wheels promptly fell off when he was well beaten at odds-on in the Fighting Fifth on his return in November 2010 and then made very hard work of beating clearly inferior opposition at Sandown the following February. Was still joint-favourite for that year's Champion but was a shock absentee at the 48-hour declaration stage when, on the advice of the BHA, he was not entered as medication used to treat an allergy was still in his system. He looked well on his way back last term, though, beating Rock On Ruby to land his second Christmas Hurdle and then slamming old rival Celestial Halo with all his old panache in the Kingwell. However, he had no answer to Rock On Ruby when fourth at Cheltenham and he managed only one run this term when sent to Ireland to take on Hurricane Fly at Leopardstown in January. Tony McCoy was given some stick for his tender handling there, but he'd never have won and his five-length third may be as good as he is now. Still, a Cheltenham Festival record of 2314 is not to be sneezed at.

Countrywide Flame (right)

5 b g; Trainer John Quinn
Hurdles form 11212312142, best RPR 161
Left-handed 121231212, best RPR 161
Right-handed 14, best RPR 154
Cheltenham form 1, best RPR 145
At the festival 16 Mar 2012: Tracked leaders until dropped into midfield after 2nd, pushed along and outpaced approaching 2 out, headway between last 2, led after last, ran on well when edged right and drew away towards finish, won Triumph Hurdle by three lengths from Hisaabaat

Heavily campaigned juvenile who answered almost every question in his first season and turned round Leopardstown Grade 1 form with Hisaabaat in a strongly run Triumph in March. Showed improved form on the Flat after that upped in trip, winning at 2m at Chester in September and then running a

game half-length second in the Cesarewitch the following month. Fitness was, therefore, not an issue when he returned over hurdles in the Fighting Fifth and ran clean away from Supreme winner Cinders And Ashes, scoring by 12 lengths. That impressed bookmakers enough to cut him to as short as 8-1 for the Champion, but he was on the drift after managing only an eight-and-a-half-length fourth to Darlan in the Christmas Hurdle. That race was run at a particularly slow gallop, though, and would not have suited, and he fared a bit better when three-lengths second to Rock On Ruby at Doncaster. Having cut out the early running, he was passed early in the home straight but was closing again at the line. Has a bit of quality about him and there's no doubt a strongly run contest would play to his strengths. Not without hope if he gets one.

OTHERS TO CONSIDER

My Tent Or Yours (*above*) was a hugely impressive winner of the Betfair Hurdle and will be prominent in the betting here if he gets the nod, but Tony McCoy didn't think it a good idea immediately after the race and the chances are he'll still take the novice route and run in the Supreme. Despite the visual impression of his Newbury success, he would certainly have enough to prove here as the Betfair Hurdle was incredibly slowly run. With the wet weather showing no signs of stopping in the weeks running up to the festival it's becoming ever more likely the meeting will be run on bad ground, but whether that would prompt connections of **Oscar Whisky** to have another rethink is doubtful. He went some way to proving his stamina at 3m in the Cleeve, so looks World Hurdle bound, but he'd take some pegging back in a heavy-ground Champion. **Cotton Mill** ran well enough when five-lengths second to My Tent Or Yours in the Betfair Hurdle but will need to come on a ton to be a threat.

Champion Hurdle results and trends

FORM	WINNER	AGE & WGT	Adj RPR	SP	TRAINER	H.Runs	BEST RPR LAST 12 MONTHS (RUNS SINCE)
12	23-12	**Rock On Ruby** C, D	7 11-10	170^{-7}	11-1	P Nicholls	6$^{(10G)}$	2nd Gd1 Christmas Hurdle (2m) (0)
11	1-111	**Hurricane Fly** D	7 11-10	172^{-2}	11-4F	W Mullins (IRE)	11$^{(11G)}$	won Gd1 Irish Champion Hurdle (2m) (0)
10	3-531	**Binocular** D	6 11-10	171^{-2}	9-1	N Henderson	10$^{(12GS)}$	won Sandown Listed hdl (2m½f) (0)
09	1-1F3	**Punjabi** D BF	6 11-10	168^{-8}	22-1	N Henderson	12$^{(23GS)}$	won Gd1 Punchestwn Champ Hdl (2m) (3)
08	-1321	**Katchit** CD	5 11-10	166^{-8}	10-1	A King	12$^{(15GS)}$	won Gd2 Kingwell Hurdle (2m) (0)
07	444-1	**Sublimity** D	7 11-10	146^{-31}	16-1	J Carr (IRE)	5$^{(10S)}$	4th Gd1 Supreme Nov Hdl (2m½f) (2)
06	11311	**Brave Inca** CD	8 11-10	172^{T}	7-4F	C Murphy (IRE)	20$^{(18GS)}$	won Gd1 Punchestwn Champ Hdl (2m) (4)
05	12331	**Hardy Eustace** CD	8 11-10	174^{T}	7-2J	D Hughes (IRE)	16$^{(14G)}$	won Gd1 Champion Hurdle (2m½f) (5)
04	-2722	**Hardy Eustace** C, D	7 11-10	154^{-26}	33-1	D Hughes (IRE)	10$^{(14G)}$	2nd Gowran Park Gd2 hdl (2m) (0)
03	-1111	**Rooster Booster** CD	9 12-0	170^{T}	9-2	P Hobbs	25$^{(17G)}$	won Gd3 Greatwood Hurdle (2m½f) (2)

WINS-RUNS: 5yo 1-28, 6yo 2-37, 7yo 4-32, 8yo 2-24, 9yo 1-9, 10yo 0-5, 11yo 0-5, 12yo 0-4 **FAVOURITES:** -£1.25

TRAINERS IN THIS RACE (w-pl-r): Nicky Henderson 2-5-13, Alan King 1-0-5, Paul Nicholls 1-1-8, Philip Hobbs 1-1-7, Willie Mullins 1-1-9, Charles Byrnes 0-0-1, Dermot Weld 0-0-1, David Pipe 0-1-3, Donald McCain 0-2-4, Emma Lavelle 0-0-3, John Quinn 0-0-1, Jessica Harrington 0-1-3, Nigel Twiston-Davies 0-1-2, Thomas Mullins 0-0-2, Venetia Williams 0-0-1

FATE OF FAVOURITES: 3211603013 **POSITION OF WINNER IN MARKET:** 2011659714

Key trends

🐎Ran within the past 51 days, 9/10

🐎Aged between six and nine, 9/10

🐎Ten to 25 runs over hurdles, 8/10

🐎Pre-race Racing Post Rating of at least 162, 8/10

🐎Topspeed of at least 152, 8/10

🐎Rated within 7lb of RPR top-rated, 8/10

🐎Had won either a Grade 1 hurdle or a Grade 3 handicap hurdle, 7/10

🐎Won a Grade 1 or 2 hurdle that season, 7/10

🐎Won last time out, 7/10

🐎Previous festival winner, 5/10

Other factors

🐎Only Hardy Eustace (2004) and Binocular (2010) had an unplaced effort in their form figures for that season.

🐎Katchit broke a long-standing trend when he became the first five-year-old to win since See You Then in 1985. In the intervening years 73 had failed.

🐎Rock On Ruby, Binocular, Punjabi, Sublimity and Hurricane Fly had not won at the festival, although the first-named trio had made the frame there. Make A Stand, Collier Bay, Alderbrook and Royal Gait are the only other winners in the past 20 years not to have won at Cheltenham

🐎Last season Rock On Ruby became only the fourth winner in the past 30 years who had not run since the turn of the year

🐎The last horse aged ten or more to win the Champion Hurdle was Sea Pigeon in both his winning years (1980 and 1981)

Notes

4.00 Glenfarclas Cross Country H'cap Chase C4/RUK
3m7f ♞£50,000

Philip Hobbs last year finally broke the Irish stranglehold on this race when Balthazar King became the first British-trained winner in eight runnings. Even so, British trainers have had 63 runners in this race with only that one winner and seven others making the frame.

Ireland dominated the first seven runnings of this specialist event, with chief exponent Enda Bolger leading the way with four of the first five winners. Although his grip has loosened, Bolger has had the runner-up in three of the four runnings he didn't win and his strong team is the starting point for punters, although Willie Mullins is a growing force.

Previous good form in this specialist discipline is important and the best guides are the two handicaps run over course and

distance in November and December (won by Uncle Junior and Outlaw Pete this season) and the PP Hogan Memorial Chase at Punchestown in February (won by Scotsirish).

The last three winners are the only ones who had not previously won a cross-country race at Cheltenham or Punchestown, yet all three had run well on the course (A New Story had been third in this race in 2008, Sizing Australia had form figures of 323 in the November and December races and Balthazar King had been going well when running out in the December race last season).

The market is usually a good guide, with seven of the eight winners having come from the first three in the betting and none of those sent off bigger than 13-2.

Cross Country results and trends

FORM		WINNER	AGE & WGT	OR	SP	TRAINER	C.Runs	BEST RPR LAST 12 MONTHS (RUNS SINCE)
12	15P00	**Balthazar King** c	8 10-9	139^{-3}	11-2	P Hobbs	13$^{(16GF)}$	won Cheltenham cl 2 hcap ch (3m½f) **(4)**
11	4-138	**Sizing Australia**	9 10-9	140^{-7}	13-2	H De Bromhead (IRE)	17$^{(15GF)}$	3rd Chelt cross-country ch (3m7f) **(0)**
10	70454	**A New Story** (4oh)	12 9-7	135^{-3}	25-1	M Hourigan (IRE)	48$^{(16G)}$	3rd Cork National hcap ch (3m4f) **(4)**
09	1-421	**Garde Champetre** CD	10 11-12	150^{-4}	7-2	E Bolger (IRE)	15$^{(16GS)}$	won Chelt cross-country ch (3m7f) **(0)**
08	9-9F1	**Garde Champetre**	9 10-13	129^{T}	4-1	E Bolger (IRE)	11$^{(16GS)}$	won Punchtwn cross-country ch (3m) **(0)**
07	-2341	**Heads Onthe Ground**	10 10-2	126^{-9}	5-2F	E Bolger (IRE)	14$^{(16S)}$	won Punchtwn cross-country ch (3m) **(0)**
06	5P-31	**Native Jack**	12 10-8	126^{T}	7-2J	P Rothwell (IRE)	16$^{(16GS)}$	won Punchtwn cross-country ch (3m) **(0)**
05	10114	**Spot Thedifference** CD	12 11-12	143^{-12}	4-1	E Bolger (IRE)	30$^{(16GS)}$	won Chelt cross-country ch (3m7f) **(0)**

WINS-RUNS: 6yo 0-1, 7yo 0-3, 8yo 1-18, 9yo 2-22, 10yo 2-28, 11yo 0-24, 12yo 3-18, 13yo 0-10, 14yo 0-3 **FAVOURITES:** -£2.25

FATE OF FAVOURITES: F116254P **POSITION OF WINNER IN MARKET:** 21122933

OR 117-131 3-10-59, **132-146** 4-11-57, **147-161** 1-3-11

Key trends

♞Won over at least 3m, 8/8

♞Trained in Ireland, 7/8

♞Officially rated 126-143, 7/8

♞Carried no more than 10st 13lb, 6/8 (two exceptions both topweight)

♞Won one of last two starts, 5/8 (four last time out)

♞Winner of a cross-country race at Cheltenham or Punchestown, 5/8 (two placed

and one carried out when set to place)

Other factors

♞JP McManus and Enda Bolger have teamed up for four of the winners

♞Three winners had taken the PP Hogan at Punchestown in February

♞In the eight runnings only eight British-trained runners have made the first four

♞Ireland has had a 1-2-3-4 three times

♞In 2009 Ireland had the first nine home

4.40 OLBG Mares;' Hurdle

RUK

2m4f *Grade 2* *£85,000*

Quevega *(below)* is already a record-breaker after four consecutive victories in this race and, in the absence of four-time World Hurdle winner Big Buck's, she can join the legendary Golden Miller as only the second horse to win the same Cheltenham Festival race five times. As usual, she will turn up here for her first run of the season and once again she'll be a first-day banker for Ireland, having scored at progressively shorter prices in the past four years (2-1, 6-4, 5-6 and 4-7). Her chief rivals are expected to be fellow Irish challenger Unaccompanied, a class act but yet to race beyond 2m1f (she was runner-up to Zarkandar in the 2011 Triumph over that distance), and last year's Fred Winter winner Une Artiste.

Mares' Hurdle results

	FORM	WINNER	AGE & WGT	Adj RPR	SP	TRAINER	H.Runs	BEST RPR LAST 12 MONTHS (RUNS SINCE)
12	1/1-1	**Quevega** CD	8 11-5	168^T	4-7F	W Mullins (IRE)	12$^{(19G)}$	won Gd1 Punchestown World Hdl (3m) **(0)**
11	3911-	**Quevega** CD	7 11-5	166^T	5-6F	W Mullins (IRE)	10$^{(14G)}$	won Gd2 Mares' Hurdle (2m4f) **(1)**
10	11-39	**Quevega** CD	6 11-5	168^T	6-4F	W Mullins (IRE)	8$^{(17G)}$	3rd Gd1 Punchestown Champ Hdl (2m) **(1)**
09	19-31	**Quevega** D	5 11-3	156^4	2-1F	W Mullins (IRE)	5$^{(21GS)}$	won Punchestown hdl (2m4f) **(0)**
08	23121	**Whiteoak**	5 11-0	139^{-23}	20-1	D McCain	5$^{(13GS)}$	won Ascot class 3 nov hdl (2m) **(0)**

WINS-RUNS: 4yo 0-3, 5yo 2-17, 6yo 1-28, 7yo 1-18, 8yo 1-11, 9yo 0-5, 10yo 0-2 **FAVOURITES:** £3.90

TRAINERS IN THIS RACE (w-pl-r): Willie Mullins 4-0-5, Donald McCain 1-0-3, Emma Lavelle 0-1-3, Nicky Henderson 0-2-7, Oliver Sherwood 0-0-1, Paul Webber 0-0-3

FATE OF FAVOURITES: 31111 **POSITION OF WINNER IN MARKET:** 71111

In its first six years this race was known as the Jewson and run on the New Course over 2m5f, but then it moved to the Old Course over half a furlong less and the last two winners carried the two biggest weights so far successful. Although the high-class Hunt Ball last year scored off the highest mark yet, five of the eight winners were officially rated 132-135. The ratings of winners may well stay in that range, as some of the better-class novices will run in what is now the Jewson on Thursday.

All eight winners had shown smart form and had finished first or second last time out. Six of the eight (although neither of the last two) had won no more than once. Another factor that makes assessment tricky for the handicapper is that the winners tend to stay below top grade to get a decent mark. Three winners had run at Exeter that season, while four had run at the previous year's festival. All eight winners arrived with a minimum of three runs over fences, with only the Irish-trained Finger Onthe Pulse not having won over fences.

Winners have been prominent in the betting, with seven sent off at odds between 9-2 and 12-1 (all those were in the first five in the market).

It is no surprise that the shrewd Ferdy Murphy (twice) and Philip Hobbs are on the roll of honour. Paul Nicholls won in 2009 with Chapoturgeon, who was in the right ratings band on a mark of 135, but many of his runners end up too high and he has had 12 beaten runners rated between 132 and 148, including three favourites.

Pulteney Chase results and trends

	FORM	WINNER	AGE & WGT	OR	SP	TRAINER	C.Runs	BEST RPR LAST 12 MONTHS (RUNS SINCE)
12	12111	**Hunt Ball** D	7 12-0	142-4	13-2F	K Burke	9(2OG)	won Kemp class 3 hcap ch (2m4½f) (0)
11	31591	**Divers** D	7 11-4	132-6	10-1	F Murphy	4(2OG)	won Muss class 3 nov ch (2m4f) (0)
10	-1321	**Copper Bleu**	8 11-1	139-3	12-1	P Hobbs	3(2OG)	won Exeter class 4 ch (2m1½f) (0)
09	9-F21	**Chapoturgeon**	5 10-11	135-2	8-1	P Nicholls	3(2OGS)	won Doncaster class 2 nov ch (2m½f) (0)
08	-3F22	**Finger Onthe Pulse** D	7 10-12	135-7	9-1	T Taaffe (IRE)	4(2OGS)	2nd Leopardstown Gd2 nov ch (2m5f) (0)
07	221F2	**L'Antartique** D	7 10-11	133-16	20-1	F Murphy	6(19GS)	won Bangor class 4 nov ch (2m4½f) (2)
06	6-221	**Reveillez** D	7 10-11	133-1	9-2F	J Fanshawe	3(18G)	2nd Exeter class 4 nov ch (2m3½f) (2)
05	FF212	**King Harald** (2oh) D	7 10-4	123T	9-1	M Bradstock	5(19G)	2nd Wetherby Gd2 nov ch (3m1f) (0)

WINS-RUNS: 5yo 1-15, 6yo 0-26, 7yo 6-65, 8yo 1-33, 9yo 0-13, 10yo 0-3, 11yo 0-1 **FAVOURITES:** £5.00

FATE OF FAVOURITES: P10F0051 **POSITION OF WINNER IN MARKET:** 21032541

OR 123-130 1-4-18, **131-140** 6-17-116, **141-148** 1-3-22

Key trends

🏇Top-two finish last time out, 8/8 (last four won on previous start)

🏇Carried no more than 11st 4lb, 7/8 (five between 10st 11lb and 11st 1lb)

🏇Finished in the first four all completed starts over fences, 7/8

🏇Officially rated 132-142, 7/8

🏇Won over at least 2m2f, 7/8

🏇No more than one win over fences, 6/8

🏇Aged seven, 6/8

Other factors

🏇Four winners had fallen at least once over fences

🏇Three winners had contested novice hurdles at the previous year's festival

🏇Three winners had hurdle RPRs of at least 144, three in the 120s and one in the 130s

🏇Two winners had been placed in Grade 2 novice chases

🏇Only one winner has started longer than 12-1 (outside first five in the market)

Wednesday, March 13
(Old Course)

- John Oaksey National Hunt Chase
- Neptune Investment Novices' Hurdle
- RSA Chase
- Sportingbet Queen Mother Champion Chase
- Coral Cup
- Fred Winter Juvenile Handicap Hurdle
- Weatherbys Champion Bumper

1.30 John Oaksey National Hunt Chase   C4/RUK

🏇 *4m*   🏇 *Amateur riders' novice chase*   🏇 *£85,000*

Boston Bob has been trading short ante-post for this race as well as the RSA Chase

Recent changes to the race conditions have made this more of a 4m RSA Chase in quality and that means the big yards have a greater chance of producing the winner. It is notable that the past two winners (Chicago Grey and Teaforthree) had the highest official rating in the field.

This is Jonjo O'Neill's best race at the festival with five wins, although he has not been successful in the five years since the race conditions were comprehensively revised – the closest he has come from five runners is fourth place with 4-1 favourite Can't Buy Time in 2009 and he didn't have a runner last year.

With more of an accent on quality, the race is starting to lose its reputation for producing big-priced winners. In the decade before the conditions changed, half of the winners were returned at 25-1 or bigger, whereas under the new conditions the biggest-priced winner has been 14-1 and the other three winners all came from the top five in the betting. Chicago Grey and Teaforthree in the past two years both went off 5-1 favourite.

All bar two of the winners since 1990 had been first or second in at least one of their latest two outings, with the exception achieving it three runs before this race. Five of the last ten winners had a good run at Cheltenham that season to their credit, while two more in that period had run well over 3m at the course in a previous season (finishing first or second).

Winning form over at least 3m is significant, but punters have to try to work out whether a chaser who is a bit one-paced at the end of 3m will relish the extra mile of this test. The difficulty of doing that explains why there have been only eight successful favourites since 1973, although there are signs that the class factor is starting to make this a more predictable betting heat.

Irish amateur riders have won this race seven times in the past 11 runnings, although there have been only two Irish-trained winners in that period. Irish riders have been used with particular success by O'Neill and Ferdy Murphy, who between them have won six of the past 11 runnings.

NH Chase results and trends

FORM	WINNER	AGE & WGT	Adj RPR	SP	TRAINER	C.Runs	BEST RPR LAST 12 MONTHS (RUNS SINCE)
12 321P1	Teaforthree	8 11-6	161^T	5-1F	R Curtis	5$^{(19G)}$	won Chepstow class 3 nov ch (3m) (2)
11 11F25	Chicago Grey C	8 11-6	163^T	5-1F	G Elliott (IRE)	9$^{(16G)}$	2nd Cheltenham class 2 nov ch (3m1½f) (1)
10 -2951	Poker De Sivola	7 11-6	145^{-8}	14-1	F Murphy	11$^{(18G)}$	2nd Kelso class 3 hcap ch (3m1f) (3)
09 42212	Tricky Trickster	6 11-11	140^{-18}	11-1	N Twiston-Davies	3$^{(19GS)}$	2nd Chelt class 2 nov hcap ch (2m5f) (0)
08 27322	Old Benny	7 11-7	135^{-18}	9-1	A King	3$^{(20GS)}$	2nd Newbury class 2 nov ch (3m) (0)
07 11430	Butler's Cabin C	7 12-0	131^{-20}	33-1	J O'Neill	7$^{(19GS)}$	won Aintree class 3 hcap ch (2m4f) (4)
06 15361	Hot Weld	7 11-11	113^{-32}	33-1	F Murphy	4$^{(22G)}$	3rd Wetherby class 4 nov ch (3m1f) (2)
05 -22F4	Another Rum	7 11-7	123^{-24}	40-1	I Duncan (IRE)	4$^{(20G)}$	4th Navan Gd3 nov ch (3m) (0)
04 -2212	Native Emperor C	8 11-11	142^{-1}	5-1J	J O'Neill	4$^{(22G)}$	2nd Wetherby Gd2 nov ch (3m1f) (0)
03 FF342	Sudden Shock	8 11-7	123^{-27}	25-1	J O'Neill	4$^{(24G)}$	2nd Kempton class 3 nov ch (3m) (0)

WINS-RUNS: 5yo 0-1, 6yo 1-29, 7yo 5-80, 8yo 4-51, 9yo 0-26, 10yo 0-7, 11yo 0-3, 12yo 0-2 **FAVOURITES:** £5.00

TRAINERS IN THIS RACE (w-pl-r): Jonjo O'Neill 3-1-17, Alan King 1-0-6, Gordon Elliott 1-0-2, Nigel Twiston-Davies 1-0-8, Rebecca Curtis 1-0-1, Tony Martin 0-1-1, Charles Byrnes 0-0-1, Charlie Longsdon 0-0-3, Charlie Mann 0-0-3, Colin Tizzard 0-0-4, Dessie Hughes 0-0-1, David Pipe 0-1-4, Donald McCain 0-0-5, Enda Bolger 0-0-2, Edward O'Grady 0-0-3, Evan Williams 0-0-1, Kim Bailey 0-0-1, Mouse Morris 0-1-3, Noel Meade 0-0-2, Paul Nicholls 0-1-10, Philip Hobbs 0-0-3, Seamus Mullins 0-0-1, Sue Smith 0-0-1, Tim Vaughan 0-1-2, Tom George 0-0-4, Venetia Williams 0-1-3, Willie Mullins 0-0-6

FATE OF FAVOURITES: 2153F54511 **POSITION OF WINNER IN MARKET:** 9100045711

Key trends

🏇Ran at least three times over fences, 10/10

🏇Finished first or second in a chase over at least 3m, 9/10

🏇Top five-finish last time out, 9/10 (exception unplaced in Class 1 chase)

🏇Aged six to eight, 9/10

🏇Had won over at least 3m (hurdles or chases), 9/10

🏇Finished first or second on either or both of last two starts, 8/10

Other factors

🏇Since a change in the conditions of the race nine years ago, all bar one winner had a hurdles RPR of at least 119

🏇Two winners had run and won in handicap company

🏇Three winners since 2002 have worn headgear, two of which were trained by Jonjo O'Neill

🏇The difference between the pre-race RPR and the winning RPR for the ten winners is between 1lb and 23lb

🏇Four winners started 25-1 or bigger

🏇The last two winners, Teaforthree and Chicago Grey, were outright favourites – the last to oblige before them was Keep Talking in 1992

🏇Paul Nicholls has never won this race despite strong representation

Notes

2.05 Neptune Investment Novices' Hurdle   C4/RUK
2m5f   Grade 1   £120,000

As the Neptune is run over an intermediate trip, it tends to be harder to know what might run here than in either of the other two novices, but Pont Alexandre is a good starting point, since it fits in for both trainer Willie Mullins and owner Rich Ricci, who each have good candidates for the other races. Punters had to sit up and take notice when Mullins said Pont Alexandre "looks to be one of the best novice hurdlers we've had, apart maybe from Hurricane Fly", and he looks a worthy favourite. Assuming At Fishers Cross runs in the Albert Bartlett, The New One, whom he beat at Cheltenham in January, and Taquin Du Seuil, who has been beaten over hurdles only by My Tent Or Yours, look the pick of the domestic defence, but Melodic Rendezvous would come right into the reckoning if running here rather than in the Supreme Novices' Hurdle.

Pont Alexandre
5 b g; Trainer Willie Mullins
Hurdles form (left-handed) 111, best RPR 156

Exciting five-year-old who could not have been any more impressive on his Irish debut when slamming Busty Brown by 13 lengths in a Navan Grade 1 and the winning margin would not have been much different if odds-on favourite Don Cossack (beaten again since) had not fallen at the last. Was again in a league of his own under a penalty in a Leopardstown Grade 2, cruising home by 11 lengths from the front. Like many horses coming into the festival his winning has been done in slow times on bad ground and it doesn't help that at the time of writing so few of his victims have run since, but his trainer, who has had two winners of this race since 2008 plus a second and a third, says he has loved him since he first saw him and "wanted him bought at any price". Seen as a staying chaser of the future, but stable selected for this race and warrants major respect.

The New One
5 b g; Trainer Nigel Twiston-Davies
Hurdles form (all left-handed) 1112, best RPR 154
Cheltenham form (all races) 1612, best RPR 154
At the festival 14 Mar 2012: Tracked leaders, ridden and outpaced 2f out, hung left over 1f out, rallied final 100yds, no impression on front 3, finished sixth, beaten six lengths by Champagne Fever in Champion Bumper

Finished sixth in the Champion Bumper at last season's festival but could be said to have won an even hotter version when bringing down the curtain on Grand National day with a one-and-a-quarter-length defeat of My Tent Or Yours. He found a lot more than the strong-travelling runner-up that day, suggesting a step up in trip would suit, and it certainly did as he proved a comfortable winner of his first three hurdles and briefly became favourite for this race after dotting up in the Leamington at Warwick. Eased slightly in the betting after a neck defeat at Cheltenham on trials day but was arguably even more impressive that day as he quickened clear on a part of the track jockeys normally avoid on heavy ground and was only reeled in by At Fishers Cross late on. If jockey Sam Twiston-Davies had the ride again he'd surely hold on to him a bit longer and would surely have won. Clearly has plenty of gears and looks easily the British No. 1 if running plans remain as they are.

Taquin Du Seuil
6 b/br g; Trainer Jonjo O'Neill
Hurdles form 1211, best RPR 150
Left-handed 11, best RPR 150
Right-handed 21, best RPR 139

Minor Flat winner in France who won his maiden hurdle easily but then couldn't live with the pace of My Tent Or Yours on his second hurdles start, before looking much happier upped in trip on two outings since. First won a small-field Grade 2 at Sandown in fine style and then repeated the dose when a heavily backed nine-length winner of the

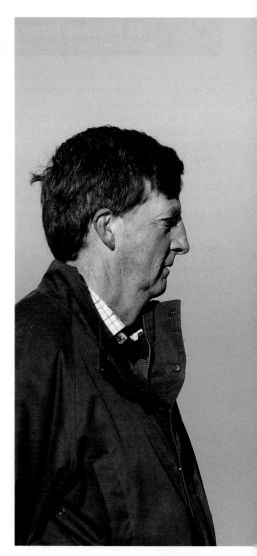

Melodic Rendezvous with Jeremy Scott, who could switch his star novice from the Supreme to the Neptune if the ground dries out

Grade 1 Challow at Newbury, where his main rival was pulled up after a mistake three out. As with Pont Alexandre, both wins came in bad ground in desperately slow times and few of his victims have run since. Still, Jonjo O'Neill called him "the best novice I've got" after Sandown and expects better ground to suit. Also in the Albert Bartlett, for which he's a slightly bigger price, although there are no hints from the exchanges.

Rule The World
6 b g; Trainer Mouse Morris
Hurdles form 1211, best RPR 150
Left-handed 11, best RPR 150
Right-handed 12, best RPR 137

Point winner who is progressing well and beat useful chaser Joncol on his third start one month after going down by only a head in a Grade 3 at Cork. His key line of form, though, is his surprise 16-length romp from Minsk in a Naas Grade 2 in January, with 1-4 favourite Champagne Fever beaten a long way in third. Champagne Fever was found to have a minor lung infection afterwards and returned a month later to dish out an even bigger beating to Minsk, so the jury is out on what he achieved, but Mouse Morris has a fine record and if he sends him over he'll be worthy of respect. Also in the Albert Bartlett, but exchange market seems pretty sure this is the preferred option.

Melodic Rendezvous
7 ch g; Trainer Jeremy Scott
Hurdles form 2111, best RPR 155
Left-handed 1, best RPR 133
Right-handed 211, best RPR 155
Cheltenham form 1, best RPR 133

Very promising and put a dent in Puffin Billy's reputation with an easy nine-length win on his final prep in February, although it later transpired the runner-up had finished lame. Dealt with in more detail in the Supreme section, as that is his more likely target, but may be switched if the ground dries out. Has the form to be a player if he does and should stay, but most winners of this race had already been tested over at least 2m4f.

Puffin Billy
5 b g; Trainer Oliver Sherwood
Hurdles form 112, best RPR 150
Left-handed 1, best RPR 130
Right-handed 12, best RPR 150

Reckoned by Oliver Sherwood to be his best horse since Large Action but couldn't live with the speed of Melodic Rendezvous at Exeter in February. Wasn't travelling that well from a long way out, however, and reportedly finished lame. Had earlier looked an extremely promising novice with victories at Newbury and Ascot, so it may be worth forgiving him that effort. Defeat has, according to Betfair at

least, made him far more likely to head here than the Supreme on Tuesday.

Defy Logic
6 ch g; Trainer Paul Nolan
Hurdles form (right-handed) 1, best RPR 146

The real unknown quantity of the party having won only his bumper in November and a maiden hurdle at Fairyhouse in early February. However, won the first by 35 lengths and the second by 34, which would have been about 20 had market rival Mad Brian not unseated at the last. Each time he took it up from the off and set a pace most of his rivals couldn't live with. Has never come off the bridle at home according to his trainer, who says "the way he gallops he just annihilates horses" and clearly holds him in the highest regard. Latest two runs in first-time blinkers and then first-time hood, which suggest he could be a bit highly strung, but exciting all the same. Also in the Albert Bartlett.

OTHERS TO CONSIDER

If the exchanges are right most of the other horses prominent in the ante-post market won't be running, so are dealt with elsewhere in the book where their participation is more likely. The most obvious left out here is **At Fishers Cross**, who beat second favourite The New One at Cheltenham on trials day. A strong stayer, he would clearly shake up the market if connections have a change of mind, but at the time of writing he was available at 40+ on Betfair, which puts into context the likelihood of a run as he's only 7-1 with some firms. The third in that race, **Coneygree**, is also likely to head for the Albert Bartlett. Willie Mullins's pair **Champagne Fever** and **Un Atout** have been confirmed as going for the Supreme, while **Gevrey Chambertin** was 100+ on Betfair and probably heading for the Albert Bartlett. **Two Rockers** won a weak Grade 2 over 3m at Haydock in February but wasn't entered in the Albert Bartlett, so will go here if anywhere, while last year's Bumper fourth **Moscow Mannon** would be interesting if all is right with him, but at the time of writing he hadn't been seen since his seasonal debut in December.

Neptune Novices' Hurdle results and trends

	FORM	WINNER	AGE & WGT	Adj RPR	SP	TRAINER	H.Runs	BEST RPR LAST 12 MONTHS (RUNS SINCE)
12	1121	Simonsig	6 11-7	160^T	2-1F	N Henderson	3$^{(17G)}$	2nd Sandown Gd2 nov hdl (2m4f) (1)
11	-4131	First Lieutenant	6 11-7	152^{-8}	7-1	M Morris (IRE)	4$^{(12G)}$	won Leopardstown Gd1 nov hdl (2m) (0)
10	111	Peddlers Cross	5 11-7	155^{-1}	7-1	D McCain	2$^{(17G)}$	won Haydock Gd2 nov hdl (2m½f) (0)
09	21111	Mikael D'Haguenet	5 11-7	160^{-4}	5-2F	W Mullins (IRE)	7$^{(14GS)}$	won Punchestown Gd2 nov hdl (2m) (0)
08	153-1	Fiveforthree	6 11-7	141^{-9}	7-1	W Mullins (IRE)	1$^{(15GS)}$	won Fairyhouse mdn hdl (2m) (0)
07	21U53	Massini's Maguire CD	6 11-7	145^{-8}	20-1	P Hobbs	9$^{(15GS)}$	won Cheltenham class 2 nov hdl (2m5f) (3)
06	1F221	Nicanor	5 11-7	147^{-17}	17-2	N Meade (IRE)	5$^{(17G)}$	won Leopardstown Gd3 nov hdl (2m4f) (0)
05	121	No Refuge D	5 11-7	152^T	17-2	H Johnson	3$^{(20G)}$	won Warwick Gd2 nov hdl (2m5f) (0)
04	12	Fundamentalist	6 11-7	147^{-17}	12-1	N Twiston-Davies	2$^{(15G)}$	2nd Haydock Gd2 nov hdl (2m7½f) (0)
03	-1d112	Hardy Eustace	6 11-7	156^{-11}	6-1	D Hughes (IRE)	4$^{(19G)}$	2nd Gd1 Deloitte Nov Hdl (2m2f) (0)

WINS-RUNS: 4yo 0-6, 5yo 4-53, 6yo 6-71, 7yo 0-28, 8yo 0-2, 9yo 0-1 **FAVOURITES:** -£3.50

TRAINERS IN THIS RACE (w-pl-r): Willie Mullins 2-3-11, Dessie Hughes 1-0-2, Donald McCain 1-0-2, Mouse Morris 1-1-5, Nicky Henderson 1-0-8, Nigel Twiston-Davies 1-0-8, Noel Meade 1-1-6, Philip Hobbs 1-1-6, Tony Martin 0-0-1, Alan King 0-1-6, Charlie Egerton 0-0-2, Charlie Longsdon 0-0-1, Charlie Mann 0-0-4, Dermot Weld 0-1-3, David Pipe 0-0-4, Evan Williams 0-0-1, Gary Moore 0-0-1, James Ewart 0-0-1, John Ferguson 0-0-1, Jonjo O'Neill 0-1-6, Mark Bradstock 0-0-1, Nick Williams 0-2-2, Paul Nicholls 0-2-6, Rebecca Curtis 0-0-1, Thomas Mullins 0-0-2

FATE OF FAVOURITES: 2252501331 **POSITION OF WINNER IN MARKET:** 3544841441

Key trends

🏇Aged five or six, 10/10

🏇Pre-race RPR of at least 145, 9/10

🏇Won at least 50 per cent of hurdle runs, 9/10

🏇Finished first or second on all completed starts over hurdles, 8/10

🏇Scored over at least 2m4f, 8/10

🏇Rated within 11lb of RPR top-rated, 8/10

🏇Started career in Irish points or bumpers, 8/10

🏇At least three runs over hurdles, 7/10

🏇Won a Graded hurdle, 6/10 (three of the exceptions were placed)

Other factors

🏇Only one winner had previously run at the festival (2008 winner Fiveforthree finished fifth in the Bumper the year before)

🏇Formerly a strong race for favourites but only two of the last ten winners were market leaders (Mikael D'Haguenet in 2009 and Simonsig in 2012)

Notes

2.40 RSA Chase
3m½f **Grade 1** **£150,000**

C4/RUK

A race that last year looked at the mercy of Grands Crus now revolves around his stablemate Dynaste and the similarities are uncanny. Both were classy staying hurdlers and both impressed at the same three tracks in their first three novice chases, on the last occasion in Grade 1 company in Kempton's Feltham Chase. And both are grey too. David Pipe must be praying the similarities end there, for Grands Crus finished only fourth and has not won since. Willie Mullins has two solid candidates in Boston Bob and Back In Focus, as does Paul Nicholls with Unioniste and Rocky Creek. Boston Bob was second in the Albert Bartlett a year ago, while Unioniste is unusual in that he has already won a top-class handicap chase at Cheltenham, and course experience like that might prove invaluable in such a demanding race.

Dynaste *(above with David Pipe)*
7 gr g; Trainer David Pipe
Chase form 111, best RPR 165
Left-handed 11, best RPR 162
Right-handed 1, best RPR 165
Cheltenham form (chase) 1, best RPR 156
At the festival 15 Mar 2012: Held up, effort from 3 out, ridden and close enough 2 out, soon weakened rapidly, tailed off, finished eighth, beaten 45 lengths by Big Buck's in World Hurdle

Good hurdler who won the big fixed brush race at Haydock in November 2011 and ran second to Big Buck's in the same season's Cleeve before flopping on good ground in the World Hurdle. Has made an impeccable start to chase career, winning three from three and beating good opposition each time. Had far too much speed for Fingal Bay and subsequent big handicap winner Unioniste on his debut over 2m4½f and was again in a league of his own when folowing up at Newbury. Saved his best for the Grade 1 Feltham at Kempton over Christmas, winning even more easily than stablemate Grands Crus had 12 months earlier. Winners of the Feltham have a long history of getting stuffed in the RSA, including recent short-priced defeats for Long Run and Grands Crus. Hard to put a finger on the reason why, though, especially as Long Run was able to win the King George and Gold Cup a year later. The opposition to Dynaste does not look as strong as last year and the only real worry with him would be the ground drying out as he has flopped on good ground both times he has raced on it and was once pulled out because of it. That prospect was looking ever more unlikely by the middle of February, however. Trainer says ground will dictate where he goes, with Jewson a possibility if it's testing, but hard to believe he'll take that route given the shape of the two races.

Boston Bob

8 b g; Trainer Willie Mullins
Chase form (both left-handed) 11, best RPR 146
At the festival 16 Mar 2012: Held up in touch, 4th halfway, went 2nd after 8th, niggled along after 3 out to get on terms next, pushed along to lead after last, hard ridden run-in and strongly pressed, kept on towards finish, finished second, beaten two lengths by Brindisi Breeze in Albert Bartlett

Good novice hurdler who looked a potentially top-class stayer early last season only to fail to make the expected improvement when upped to 3m at the festival. He certainly didn't run badly, finishing a two-length second to the ill-fated Brindisi Breeze, but never looked particularly happy through the race. That was his first effort on good ground, but trainer Willie Mullins seems to think he'd be better on a better surface. He certainly needs to be based on his two chase efforts so far, even though he is a Grade 1 winner. Had to work hard to get off the mark at odds of 1-5 first time at Navan and then really pulled it out of the fire in the Dr PJ Moriarty at Leopardstown in February, looking booked for fourth in the straight before powering home to get up late by a nose from Texas Jack. That form is some way short of what's required to give Dynaste a race (19lb according to Racing Post Ratings) and, while he looked for all the world that a step up to 3m would suit him better, his trainer, who admitted he wasn't sure Boston Bob was in the same form as last spring, was still leaning towards the Jewson after the race. Nothing is set in stone, though, and he remains much shorter for the RSA.

Unioniste

5 gr g; Trainer Paul Nicholls
Chase form (all left-handed) 11311, best RPR 153
Cheltenham form 31, best RPR 153

Won on his chase debut in France and has quickly developed into a useful performer for Paul Nicholls. Was particularly impressive when becoming the first four-year-old to land the Paul Stewart Gold Cup at Cheltenham in December and followed that up with a dour performance when winning in the mud at Newbury in February, although may have been fortunate as he bumped short-head runner-up Hadrian's Approach close home. Only chase defeat came when readily outpaced by Dynaste over 2m4½f at Cheltenham in November, so hopes of a reverse rest on different trip, although the winner is equally at home over further. Only one five-year-old has won in the history of this contest, but only nine have tried in the last 20 runnings and form figures of 323PF17F3 suggest they have punched well above their weight. One of the fallers would have been placed at worst and the winner, Star De Mohaison, was trained by Nicholls.

Back In Focus

8 ch g; Trainer Willie Mullins
Chase form 111, best RPR 153
Left-handed 11, best RPR 153
Right-handed 1, best RPR 153

Three from three over fences up to the end of December and has the look of a strong stayer. Didn't have much to beat on his debut at Listowel in September and was allowed to coast home on his own in a time nearly 90 seconds slower than standard, but had to work harder for his next two wins when upped in grade. Jumped and battled well to beat Lyreen Legend in 2m6f Grade 2 at Punchestown in November and again showed a good attitude in the Grade 1 Topaz over 3m at Leopardstown under an inspired Ruby Walsh. Looked booked for second that day when stablemate Aupcharlie loomed alongside him turning for home and took a two-length lead jumping the last, but the latter's suspect stamina gave way close home. Has a good-ground action according to his trainer, but whether he has the speed for 3m on such a surface is debatable (beaten a long way over hurdles at Aintree on good, although was inexperienced and had a different trainer) and is on offer at a similar price for the the four-miler. Looks the right sort for this race if the ground stays on the soft side but could go up in trip if it dries out.

134

Hadrian's Approach
6 b g; Trainer Nicky Henderson
Chase form 1F22, best RPR 149
Left-handed F2, best RPR 149
Right-handed 12, best RPR 149

Connections wasted little time in sending this one over fences after just two runs over hurdles and he looked like he was crying out for a longer trip when just getting up on his debut over 2m3f at Ascot in November (runner-up has shown fair level of form since). Unfortunately fell four out when still travelling within himself in Harry Topper's race at Newbury later that month, so was short of big-race experience when running into Dynaste in the Grade 1 Feltham at Kempton and staying on into a well-beaten nine-length second. Completed his preparation with a short-head second to Unioniste in February, when plenty will have argued he was unlucky after taking a bump from the winner late on. Never had much of a chance against Dynaste at Kempton, but Feltham form is often turned around, he is much more lightly raced than David Pipe's grey and runs as though a much stiffer test will suit, so hard to see why he's so much bigger than Unioniste in the ante-post market.

Rocky Creek
7 b g; Trainer Paul Nicholls
Chase form 2111, best RPR 155
Left-handed 11, best RPR 155
Right-handed 21, best RPR 142
Cheltenham form (hurdles) 8, best RPR 129
At the festival 16 Mar 2012: tracked leaders, ridden when outpaced before 4 out, stayed on to lead 2 out, met last wrong, soon headed, no extra, finished eighth, beaten 27 lengths by Brindisi Breeze in Albert Bartlett

Full-brother to the ill-fated Tell Massini, who was a Grade 2 winner on his second start over hurdles, but was always going to be a chaser and looks a pretty useful one. Was surprisingly beaten at evens on his debut at Exeter, but in hindsight he put up a good performance to be beaten just over a length by Harry Topper, who is unbeaten since and would be the clear second on RPRs for this race if trainer Kim Bailey had bothered to enter him. Rocky Creek made no mistake next time and was then an impressive 15-length winner from Fill The Power at Warwick in January. Considered very much one for the future and trainer is already talking in terms of next season's Hennessy, but surely earned his place here instead of the four-miler with Reynoldstown win from Houblon Des Obeaux at Ascot. One negative is that he didn't run well in last season's Albert Bartlett, but he was only lightly raced and should be more the finished article this time.

Lord Windermere
7 b g; Trainer Jim Culloty
Chase form 22123, best RPR 145
Left-handed 2123, best RPR 145
Right-handed 2, best RPR 142

Has five chase runs and only one minor win to his name but has put up a couple of creditable efforts in decent company on his last two. The first came at the end of January when he was a half-length second to Texas Jack in a 2m5f Grade 2 at Leopardstown and he finished the same distance behind that horse when they were second and third to Boston Bob in a blanket finish over the same course and distance a fortnight later. Has never run over 3m but trainer says he'll get it no problem and, while he was also in the Arkle and Jewson at the time of writing, the market suggests this is where he's going. Needs to improve but is not much worse than Boston Bob on the book.

Super Duty
7 b g; Trainer Donald McCain
Chase form 2212, best RPR 150
Left-handed 212, best RP 150
Right-handed 2, best RPR 128

Progressive as a novice hurdler and finished

a respectable, if distant, second to Simonsig at Aintree in April. Already better as a chaser after four starts, though, and showed much-improved form on the second of them after finding 2m too short the first time. Just gave best close home after a protracted battle with the talented Poungach over 2m6f at Haydock and then put in a strong staying performance to land a Class 2 over 2m5f at Cheltenham in December, although what he achieved following a damp squib of a performance from favourite Broadbackbob is hard to fathom and the runner-up has been well beaten since. Improved again, though, when upped to 3m1f at Wetherby, only just losing out to the promising Goulanes having poached a near three-length lead at the last. Below par only start on soft ground as a novice hurdler, but hasn't encountered anything better as a chaser so far and trainer reluctant to keep running him on a surface he doesn't like. Could well become a player if the ground dries out, but will it?

Houblon Des Obeaux (above, nearside)
6 b g; Trainer Venetia Williams
Chase form 114232, best RPR 149
Left-handed 142, best RPR 149
Right-handed 132, best RPR 149

Spent a couple of seasons over hurdles for Venetia Williams but was bought to be a chaser and has already achieved a better level of form in this discipline, although he obviously needs to take it to another level. Won his first two and impressive when slamming hesitant jumper Poungach at Wincanton in November, but four defeats since, the first when making a bad blunder two out and finishing a close fourth to Harry Topper at Newbury over 3m. Rallied but couldn't get to Court In Motion in four-runner chase at Lingfield in December and arguably put up a better performance when a close third to Captain Conan in the Grade 1 Scilly Isles at Sandown in February. Put in his place by Rocky Creek in the Reynoldstown, but best hurdles form was at Cheltenham (course winner, also fourth in last season's Pertemps) and that suggests he'll improve granted a bigger field and a stronger pace. Interesting at a big price if lining up on the day and, while shorter for the four-miler, he has run in five straight Graded races, so trainer clearly rates him.

OTHERS TO CONSIDER

According to Racing Post Ratings Dynaste has at least 10lb in hand of all his potential rivals and anything not already mentioned either has an awful lot more to find or is probably going somewhere else. **Goulanes** would be one of the more interesting ones as beating Super Duty in the Grade 2 Towton on his chase debut was impressive, but he's in the hands of Dynaste's trainer David Pipe, who has already earmarked him for the four-miler, for which he's a much shorter price. **Sire Collonges** has had problems and could not have been right when readily brushed aside by the subsequently disappointing Our Father at Cheltenham in November, but he hasn't run since, is also in the four-miler and trainer Paul Nicholls has two others shorter for this race. There are plenty more Irish runners who could make the trip, but **Tofino Bay** would have to find unusual improvement for a ten-year-old, **Aupcharlie** is almost certainly coming down in trip and the rest look exposed as not being good enough.

RSA Chase results and trends

	FORM	WINNER	AGE & WGT	Adj RPR	SP	TRAINER	C.Runs	BEST RPR LAST 12 MONTHS (RUNS SINCE)
12	1-132	**Bobs Worth** C, D	7 11-4	172⁻⁶	9-2	N Henderson	3⁽⁹ᴳ⁾	3rd Gd1 Feltham Nov Ch (3m) **(1)**
11	21411	**Bostons Angel** D	7 11-4	160⁻¹³	16-1	J Harrington (IRE)	5⁽¹²ᴳ⁾	won Gd1 Dr PJ Moriarty Nov Ch (2m5f) **(0)**
10	3F122	**Weapon's Amnesty** C, D	7 11-4	160⁻¹⁵	10-1	C Byrnes (IRE)	5⁽⁹ᴳ⁾	2nd Leopardstown Gd1 nov ch (3m) **(1)**
09	-8131	**Cooldine**	7 11-4	166⁻³	9-4F	W Mullins (IRE)	3⁽¹⁵ᴳˢ⁾	won Gd1 Dr PJ Moriarty Nov Ch (2m5f) **(0)**
08	-1211	**Albertas Run** CD	7 11-4	164⁻³	4-1F	J O'Neill	4⁽¹¹ᴳˢ⁾	won Gd2 Reynoldstown Nov Ch (3m) **(0)**
07	-1111	**Denman** C, D	7 11-4	170ᵀ	6-5F	P Nicholls	4⁽¹⁷ᴳˢ⁾	won Newbury class 2 nov ch (3m) **(0)**
06	-1231	**Star De Mohaison**	5 10-8	159⁻⁷	14-1	P Nicholls	4⁽¹⁵ᴳ⁾	3rd Cheltenham Gd2 nov ch (2m5f) **(1)**
05	P-122	**Trabolgan** BF	7 11-4	162⁻³	5-1	N Henderson	3⁽⁹ᴳ⁾	2nd Gd1 Feltham Nov Ch (3m) **(1)**
04	F1332	**Rule Supreme** D	8 11-4	159⁻⁶	25-1	W Mullins (IRE)	8⁽¹⁰ᴳ⁾	2nd Punchestown hcap ch (3m4f) **(0)**
03	-1311	**One Knight**	7 11-4	153⁻¹⁴	15-2	P Hobbs	4⁽⁹ᴳ⁾	won Chepstow Gd2 nov ch (2m3½f) **(3)**

WINS-RUNS: 5yo 1-4, 6yo 0-17, 7yo 8-55, 8yo 1-25, 9yo 0-13, 10yo 0-1, 11yo 0-1 **FAVOURITES:** £0.45

TRAINERS IN THIS RACE (w-pl-r): Nicky Henderson 2-2-9, Paul Nicholls 2-1-8, Willie Mullins 2-2-11, Charlie Egerton 0-1-2, Colin Tizzard 0-0-4, Dessie Hughes 0-0-4, David Pipe 0-0-2, Donald McCain 0-0-1, Gordon Elliott 0-1-1, Nigel Twiston-Davies 0-1-5, Noel Meade 0-0-1, Paul Webber 0-0-2, Sue Smith 0-1-2, Thomas Mullins 0-0-1, Tom George 0-0-1, Venetia Williams 0-0-1

FATE OF FAVOURITES: 532P111554 **POSITION OF WINNER IN MARKET:** 4840111572

Key trends

🏇Did not run on the Flat 10/10

🏇Finished first or second last time out, 10/10

🏇Last ran between 24 and 53 days ago, 10/10

🏇Ran at least three times over fences, 10/10

🏇Contested a Graded chase (six won, four placed), 10/10

🏇Rated less than 14lb off RPR top-rated, 10/10

🏇Nine to 12 hurdles and chase runs, 9/10

🏇Chase RPR of at least 150, 9/10

🏇Aged seven, 8/10

Other factors

🏇Six winners had won Graded races over trips ranging from 2m4f to 3m

🏇In 2008 Albertas Run became the first Reynolstown winner to follow up here since Killiney in 1973

🏇Of the combined 44 chase starts of winners, none had finished outside the first three (two had fallen). However, only Denman was unbeaten over fences

🏇Six winners had previously run at the festival and five had excellent form – two landed the Albert Bartlett, one was second and one was seventh in the Bumper and one finished second in the Neptune. The other was pulled up in the Albert Bartlett

🏇Eight five-year-olds have run in the last 20 years – one won, four were placed, one unplaced and two fell

Notes

Sprinter Sacre is set to go off the shortest-priced festival favourite in modern times. No wonder. A breathtaking winner of last year's Racing Post Arkle Chase, he has since stretched his unbeaten run over fences to seven races with flawless displays in the Tingle Creek at Sandown and a Victor Chandler Chase switched to Cheltenham, in both races looking utterly different class. The news that Flemenstar would miss the festival owing to a lung infection removed from calculations the one remaining feasible threat and defeat is almost unthinkable, even though he could still face the last two winners of this race, Sizing Europe and Finian's Rainbow, as well as old rivals Cue Card – one of only three opponents to finish within ten lengths of him over fences – and Sanctuaire. An absolute joy to watch, he might just be one of the all-time greats.

Sprinter Sacre *(right)*
7 b/br g; Trainer Nicky Henderson
Chase form 1111111, best RPR 178
Cheltenham form (all) 311, best RPR 178
At the festival 15 Mar 2011: Tracked leaders, led just before 3 out, joined 2 out but still going strongly, ridden when hit last, immediately headed and faded, finished third, beaten five and a quarter lengths by Al Ferof in Supreme Novices' Hurdle

13 Mar 2012: Jumped well, raced keenly in 3rd, quickened to lead on bridle 4 out, still on bit approaching 2 out, shaken up after last as 2nd tried to close, never any danger, eased closing stages, impressive, won Arkle Chase by seven lengths from Cue Card

There have been some exciting 2m chasers over the past ten or 15 years, but this one is threatening to leave them all behind in terms of brilliance. His only two defeats in 11 starts have come when second over a too-far 2m4f on his hurdling debut at Ascot in November 2010 and in the following March's Supreme Novices' Hurdle when he looked to be cantering over everything two out but failed to get up the hill. Trainer Nicky Henderson predicted he would be a much better chaser and stronger for another season and he proved spot on as Sprinter Sacre has so far toyed with everything put in front of him, winning all seven chases by an aggregate of 95 lengths. His novice highlights included a 16-length defeat of the previous season's Champion Hurdle runner-up Peddlers Cross at Kempton, an on-the-bridle defeat of more experienced rivals in the Game Spirit at Newbury and an eased-down seven-length success from subsequent 26-length

Haldon Gold Cup winner Cue Card (Edgardo Sol, runner-up in that race, was a close third in this season's Game Spirit). Bare reading of his defeats of the 143-rated Kumbeshwar (15 lengths) and 138-rated Mad Moose (14 lengths) in two starts this campaign suggest he's done nothing more than he should have, but he had even better horses further behind and only once in his seven chase starts has he had the reins so much as shaken at him. That happened in last season's Arkle, but only very briefly and it's hard to think of a horse with a more bombproof profile at the festival. For all that, his best effort on Racing Post Ratings (178) is still short of the likes of Master Minded (186), Moscow Flyer (182), Azertyuiop (179) and Well Chief (179) in recent seasons, but that may simply be because there's nothing around who can get him out of a canter. Shame Nicky Henderson can't show us just how good he is even if he wanted to as there is no suitable handicap for him to run in nowadays.

Sizing Europe
11 b g; Trainer Henry de Bromhead
Chase form 11111322312121121111, best RPR 176
Left-handed 11121, best RPR 176
Right-handed 1113223212111111, best RPR 176
Cheltenham form 10112, best RPR 176
At the festival 11 Mar 08: Chased leaders, driven to challenge 2 out, weakened quickly before last, virtually pulled up before run-in, finished 14th, beaten 101l by Katchit in Champion Hurdle

16 Mar 2010: Took keen hold early, with leaders, went 2nd 9th and pressed leader, going easily when left in lead 2 out, 2 lengths up last, driven flat, held on near

finish, beat Somersby three-quarters of a length in Arkle Chase

16 Mar 2011: Tracked leader, led 7th, driven from 2 out, half-length lead last, ridden and stayed on strongly to go clear run-in, won Champion Chase by five lengths from Big Zeb

14 Mar 2012: Tracked leader until left in lead 4th, driven approaching last, joined by winner and bumped approaching bypassed final fence, headed final 120yds, no extra under pressure, finished second, beaten one and a quarter lengths by Finian's Rainbow in Champion Chase

Brilliantly consistent performer who has never been out of the front three in 21 chase starts (has been third only twice), has an Arkle and Champion Chase to his name and probably would have also won a Champion Hurdle had he not broken down in 2008. Lost his crown in somewhat controversial circumstances last season as looked to be cruising in front turning in but was run out of it close home by Finian's Rainbow after the omission of the last fence, which did not look unsafe to jump, made it a desperately long run-in. Since then he has arguably been in the form of his life, winning five on the spin at 2m-2m4f and looking as good as ever despite turning 11 in January. His very best falls a couple of pounds short of Sprinter Sacre and it's hard to ask him to improve again at his age, but in many respects it will be a shame if he sidesteps this for the Ryanair.

Mail De Bievre

8 b g; Trainer Tom George
Chase form (all left-handed) 12222115, best RPR 144

Showed some promise in bumpers for Alan King a few years ago but spent most of his time since in France, winning a Grade 2 and a Grade 3 over fences. Form hard to put a figure on but Racing Post Ratings gave him a best of 144 for running second to regular 3m4f winner Rubi Ball over 2m5f and official handicapper put him on 160. Had first outing for best part of 18 months when fifth in the Denman Chase for Tom George, but while he impressed plenty with his jumping from the front, he basically ran too free and finished knackered. Potentially better than that but requires bigger leap of faith than some imagine for him to turn into a Champion Chase prospect (only 16-1 in places, but still needs to be supplemented) over a trip he hasn't tried for four years.

Cue Card

7 b g; Trainer Colin Tizzard
Chase form 1U212151, best RPR 170
Left-handed 1U212, best RPR 167
Right-handed 151, best RPR 170
Cheltenham form (all) 1124U2, best RPR 167
At the festival 17 Mar 2010: Took keen hold, held up well in rear, scythed through field from 5f out, tracked leader over 2f out and still cruising, led over 1f out, hung left briefly but romped clear, won Champion Bumper by eight lengths from Al Ferof

15 Mar 2011: Took keen hold, held up in midfield, progress before 3 out, joined leader 2 out, ridden soon after, hanging and not quicken before last, faded, finished fourth, beaten six and a half lengths by Al Ferof in Supreme Novices' Hurdle

13 Mar 2012: Led until mistake and headed 9th, chased winner from 4 out, stayed on well to try and close on winner after 2 out and 4 lengths down soon after, readily outpaced from last but stayed on well for clear 2nd, beaten seven lengths by Sprinter Sacre in Racing Post Arkle Chase

Only horse to get Sprinter Sacre off the bridle, albeit only briefly in last season's Arkle, but after 2m5½f Ascot Chase victory in February was cut to as short as 3-1 favourite for the Ryanair and looks almost certain to go there. Dealt with in more detail in Thursday's preview.

OTHERS TO CONSIDER

Only nine horses remained among the entries for this race in mid-February and all of Sprinter Sacre's possible rivals either have better chances in another race or no hope at all. One who may fall into the latter category is last year's winner **Finian's Rainbow**, who hasn't beaten a rival in two runs this term, a wind operation in between seemingly not helping at all. **Sanctuaire** began the season looking Sprinter Sacre's most likely danger following his breathtaking Sandown success in April but has run two stinkers behind him this season and is untrustworthy. He seems better in the spring but will need to be. **Somersby** has been found out in this contest before and **Wishfull Thinking** shortened to 20-1 following his success in a dreadful Game Spirit only because he's one of the few who looks certain to line up. The only other possibles are **Realt Dubh**, who hasn't run to his best for nearly a year, and **Tataniano**, who was once very promising but has had loads of problems and has left Paul Nicholls.

Champion Chase results and trends

	FORM	WINNER	AGE & WGT	Adj RPR	SP	TRAINER	C.Runs	BEST RPR LAST 12 MONTHS (RUNS SINCE)
12	21-12	Finian's Rainbow D, BF	9 11-10	171-9	4-1	N Henderson	7(8G)	2nd Gd1 Victor Chandler Ch (2m1f) (0)
11	3-223	Sizing Europe CD	9 11-10	170-9	10-1	H De Bromhead (IRE)	9(11G)	3rd Punchestown Gd2 ch (2m) (0)
10	-2141	Big Zeb D	9 11-10	171-19	10-1	C Murphy (IRE)	13(9G)	won Navan Gd2 ch (2m) (2)
09	12-11	Master Minded CD	6 11-10	191T	4-11F	P Nicholls	12(12GS)	won Gd1 Champion Chase (2m) (3)
08	-2U11	Master Minded D	5 11-10	173-4	3-1	P Nicholls	8(8GS)	won Gd2 Game Spirit Ch (2m1f) (0)
07	2-21U	Voy Por Ustedes CD	6 11-10	174-9	5-1	A King	9(10GS)	won Kempton Gd2 ch (2m) (1)
06	-5431	Newmill D	8 11-10	159-23	16-1	J Murphy (IRE)	8(12G)	won Thurles Gd2 ch (2m4f) (0)
05	-1111	Moscow Flyer CD	11 11-10	185T	6-4F	J Harrington (IRE)	22(8G)	won Gd1 Tingle Creek Chase (2m) (1)
04	-U221	Azertyuiop CD	7 11-10	178-2	15-8	P Nicholls	8(8G)	2nd Victor Chandler Ch Gd2 hcap (2m) (1)
03	-1U11	Moscow Flyer CD	9 12-0	165-8	7-4F	J Harrington (IRE)	11(11G)	won Down Royal Gd3 ch (2m2f) (3)

WINS-RUNS: 5yo 1-1, 6yo 2-10, 7yo 1-8, 8yo 1-25, 9yo 4-25, 10yo 0-17, 11yo 1-10, 12yo 0-1 **FAVOURITES:** -£3.39

TRAINERS IN THIS RACE (w-pl-r): Paul Nicholls 3-2-18, Alan King 1-1-3, Henry de Bromhead 1-1-2, Nicky Henderson 1-1-5, Noel Meade 0-0-2, Philip Hobbs 0-2-4

FATE OF FAVOURITES: 1U1FF21402 **POSITION OF WINNER IN MARKET:** 1216321452

Key trends

🏇Won over at least 2m1f, 10/10

🏇At least seven runs over fences, 10/10

🏇No older than nine, 9/10

🏇Within 10lb of RPR top-rated, 8/10

🏇Grade 1 chase winner, 8/10

🏇Adjusted RPR of at least 170, 8/10

🏇Won Graded chase last time out, 7/10

🏇Course winner, 6/10

🏇Previous festival winner, 6/10

Other factors

🏇The four winners aged seven or younger were all French-breds. In the past ten years 30 French-breds have run, yielding another two seconds and four thirds

🏇Six winners had contested the Tingle Creek, in which they finished U21214

🏇Nine Tingle Creek winners (four of whom started favourite) have run, finishing 3U1F61P82. The two to succeed were Moscow Flyer (2005) and Master Minded (2009)

Notes

4.00 Coral Cup (Handicap Hurdle)   C4/RUK
🏇2m5f 🏇Grade 3 🏇£80,000

Older handicappers dominated this race in the early years, but increasingly the winners come from the younger age range – seven of the past 12 have been aged five or six, and six of the last eight winners were second-season hurdlers.

In-form runners do best, with ten of the winners in the race's 19-year history having scored on their previous run and three more finishing in the first three. Good handicap form is essential and three winners have come out of the past seven runnings of the Betfair Hurdle. On the Irish front the Boylesports.com Handicap Hurdle and the Boyne Hurdle over this trip at Navan in mid-February are worth checking.

Only one favourite has won, but the form factor means seven of the past ten winners were in the first six in the betting. Ten of the winners had landed a handicap that season and most weren't overraced (two to four runs). This is a high-quality handicap and six winners were rated at least 137 – in the past decade it is notable that three of the five winners rated 140-plus were Irish-trained. High weights are not necessarily a barrier to success, although none of the British-trained winners carried more than 11st 2lb.

Ireland has had seven winners and only Xenophon, 4-1 favourite in 2003, was strongly fancied. The other six Irish winners were returned at between 11-1 and 16-1.

Willie Mullins is the Irish trainer most likely to have the right type. On the British side, Philip Hobbs has had two high-class winners.

Coral Cup results and trends

FORM	WINNER	AGE & WGT	OR	SP	TRAINER	H.Runs	BEST RPR LAST 12 MONTHS (RUNS SINCE)
12	-9090 Son Of Flicka	8 10-6	135^T	16-1	D McCain	22$^{(28G)}$	2nd Martin Pipe Cond Hcp Hdl (2m4½f) (5)
11	2-102 Carlito Brigante (2ow)	5 11-0	142^{10}	16-1	G Elliott (IRE)	9$^{(22G)}$	2nd Fairyhouse hdl (2m) (0)
10	1-510 Spirit River c,	5 11-2	141^1	14-1	N Henderson	5$^{(28G)}$	won Chelt class 3 hcap hdl (2m1f) (1)
09	-4511 Ninetieth Minute	6 10-3	140^T	14-1	T Taaffe (IRE)	8$^{(27GS)}$	won Thurles Listed hdl (2m) (0)
08	12-71 Naiad Du Misselot D,	7 10-13	130^7	7-1	F Murphy	5$^{(24GS)}$	won Haydock class 2 hcap hdl (2m4f) (0)
07	23521 Burntoakboy D,	9 9-12	128^T	10-1	R Newland	27$^{(28GS)}$	won Leicester class 3 hcap hdl (2m4½f) (0)
06	50121 Sky's The Limit	5 11-12	144^{12}	11-1	E O'Grady (IRE)	8$^{(30G)}$	won Fairyhouse hdl (2m2f) (0)
05	-1626 Idole First	6 10-10	131^1	33-1	V Williams	8$^{(29G)}$	2nd Uttoxeter class 3 hcap hdl (2m) (1)
04	34231 Monkerhostin	7 10-8	147^3	13-2	P Hobbs	21$^{(27G)}$	2nd Chelt class 2 hcap hdl (2m5½f) (2)
03	21-21 Xenophon	7 11-0	130^5	4-1F	A Martin (IRE)	5$^{(27G)}$	won Pierse Hcap Hurdle (2m) (0)

WINS-RUNS: 5yo 3-53, 6yo 2-71, 7yo 3-55, 8yo 1-43, 9yo 1-31, 10yo 0-12, 11yo 0-3, 12yo 0-2 **FAVOURITES:** -£5.00

FATE OF FAVOURITES: 130F000000 **POSITION OF WINNER IN MARKET:** 1304426677

OR 122-135 5-8-119, **136-151** 5-20-141, **152-165** 0-2-10

Key trends

🏇Won between 2m2f and 2m6f over hurdles, 9/10

🏇Scored at Class 3 or higher, 9/10

🏇Carried no more than 11st 2lb, 9/10

🏇Not run for at least 32 days, 9/10

🏇Won a race earlier in the season, 9/10

🏇Officially rated 128 to 144, 9/10

🏇Aged five to seven, 8/10

🏇Top-six finish last time out, 8/10 (six won)

🏇Five to nine hurdle runs, 7/10

🏇No more than four runs that season, 7/10

Other factors

🏇None of the last ten winners was out of the handicap – the only two to do it were Olympian (1993) and Top Cees (1998)

🏇Only one outright and one joint-favourite have won in the race's 19-year history

4.40 Fred Winter Juvenile Handicap Hurdle   RUK

2m½f Grade 3 £75,000

This has quickly become a competitive contest, drawing the second rank of juvenile hurdlers from the Triumph Hurdle. Seven of the eight winners were rated between 124 and 133 (the exception was What A Charm off 115). Six of the winners were weighted to carry at least 10st 13lb.

Winning form is virtually essential, with only the two Irish-trained winners starting as maidens. Five of the other six winners had scored last time out (the two Irish winners were beaten in Grade 2 hurdles on their run before Cheltenham, as was Une Artiste last year). Six of the eight winners were having their fourth start over hurdles.

Getting a horse handicapped is the real skill and winning at a low level seems the key, with three of the winners coming off victories at Folkestone, Southwell and Taunton. Even 2007 winner Gaspara, who had just taken the Imperial Cup, was 8lb well in under her 4lb penalty.

French-breds have done well, with four victories in eight runnings. They mature early and generally need fewer runs to be ready.

David Pipe has had a winner, two runners-up, a third and a fourth from ten runners. Alan King, perennially well stocked in the juvenile department, has yet to win this race but has come close, having saddled three placed horses in the past two years (his last ten runners have finished 4003053230).

Fred Winter Handicap Hurdle results and trends

	FORM	WINNER	AGE & WGT	OR	SP	TRAINER	H.Runs	BEST RPR LAST 12 MONTHS (RUNS SINCE)
12	11114	**Une Artiste** D	4 10-8	127-6	40-1	N Henderson	3(24G)	won Haydock class 2 hdl (2m) (1)
11	757	**What A Charm**	4 10-6	115-3	9-1	A Moore (IRE)	3(23G)	7th Fairyhouse Gd2 nov hdl (2m) (0)
10	531	**Sanctuaire** D	4 11-2	127-9	4-1F	P Nicholls	3(24G)	3rd Auteuil hdl (2m2f) (1)
09	52111	**Silk Affair** (5x)	4 10-4	125-12	11-1	M Quinlan	5(22GS)	won Sandown cl 3 nov hcap hdl (2m4f) (1)
08	531	**Crack Away Jack** D	4 11-10	133-22	14-1	E Lavelle	3(22GS)	won Sandown class 3 nov hdl (2m½f) (0)
07	22111	**Gaspara**(4x) D	4 10-11	130-T	9-2J	D Pipe	10(24GS)	won Sandown Listed hcap hdl (2m½f) (0)
06	4P1	**Shamayoun** D	4 11-3	124-7	40-1	C Egerton	3(24G)	won Southwell class 4 nov hdl (2m) (0)
05	225	**Dabiroun**	4 11-4	124-4	20-1	P Nolan (IRE)	3(24G)	2nd Limerick mdn hdl (2m) (2)

FAVOURITES: -£0.25

FATE OF FAVOURITES: 00124143 **POSITION OF WINNER IN MARKET:** 90144150

OR 109-120 1-4-42, **121-133** 7-12-125, **134-145** 0-8-20

Key trends

🏇Yet to win over hurdles or beaten in first two starts over hurdles, 7/8

🏇By a sire who won a Group 1 on the Flat, 8/8

🏇Officially rated 124 to 133, 7/8

🏇Pre-race RPR of at least 112, 7/8

🏇Won last time out, 5/8 (all three exceptions were beaten in Grade 2 hurdles)

Set to carry at least 10st 13lb, 6/8 (two were ridden by conditionals)

Other factors

🏇Only five of the 42 horses rated 120 or less made the frame

🏇Four winners had earned a Flat RPR of at least 85; the other four were unraced on the level

🏇Four winners were French-bred

All eyes will be on Golantilla, who was bought for €375,000 by leading Irish owner Barry Connell a few days after his highly impressive bumper debut success at Cork in early January. Four weeks earlier he had announced himself as one of the hottest prospects on the Irish jumps scene with an equally dominant victory in a 3m point-to-point. He was trained by his breeder Sean O'Brien then but Connell moved him to Tony Martin. This is a late-closing race but, in the annual search for Willie Mullins's likely representatives, early attention focused on Clondaw Court and Union Dues. Other leading Irish hopes include Le Vent D'Antan and Moyle Park, while the British challenge seems set to be headed by the Jeremy Scott-trained Empiracle.

Golantilla
5 b g; Trainer Tony Martin
Bumper form 1 (right-handed), best RPR 127

Has long been a huge gossip horse and it was a brave call by former owner-trainer Sean O'Brien to turn down £190,000 at the sales in December before he had even made his bumper debut. That decision paid off, though, as he picked up almost double that following a deeply impressive performance at Cork in the first week of January. Golantilla was always cantering over his field and was pushed into a 13-length lead by the line. The form received a boost when the third won by six lengths at Limerick next time. Could be anything, but the same can be said about a lot of these.

Empiracle
6 ch g; Trainer Jeremy Scott
Bumper form (right-handed) 1 , best RPR 120

By Derby winner Kris Kin out of a sister to former Christmas Hurdle winner Mighty Mogul, this is another about whom there has been plenty of gossip. Has not been since a debut sucess at Huntingdon in October, when he won hard-held by seven lengths from a previous winner who has gone in again since, as has the third. Said to work all over the up-and-coming stable's Supreme Novices' Hurdle hope Melodic Rendezvous at home, but doubtful they've had anything like full 2m workouts. Purely on Racing Post Ratings he's achieved a fair bit less than many at bigger odds, but trainer knows a good horse when he sees one.

Clondaw Court *(right)*
6 b g; Trainer Willie Mullins
Bumper form (right-handed) 1, best RPR 127

At the time of writing the shortest in the betting for Willie Mullins, who has won seven of the 20 runnings of this race. Really hard to put a finger on what he achieved at Punchestown in November as he beat only five rivals by upward of 27 lengths and only one of those has shown anything worth reporting since. That was fourth-placed Mister Hotelier, who has won a maiden hurdle, but was a mile below what he'd previously shown in bumpers when running against Clondaw Court. Mullins's son Patrick has been on the trainer's last two winners of this race, so it's well worth taking note of what he chooses on the day.

Red Sherlock
4 ch g; Trainer David Pipe
Bumper form (right-handed) 11, best RPR tbc

Out of the terrific racemare Lady Cricket, which makes him a half-brother to Swing Bowler, who ran up a sequence over hurdles before finishing third to My Tent Or Yours in this season's Betfair Hurdle. Has obviously inherited at least some of that talent as he was a hugely impressive 23-length winner of a big-field Towcester bumper at the end of January. Made harder work of better race at Ascot in February, flashing his tail furiously at times, and while bookies were quick to cut him after that win, jockey Timmy Murphy suggested the four-year-old would benefit from missing the festival this year.

Union Dues
5 b g; Trainer Willie Mullins
Bumper form (left-handed) 11, best RPR 127

The shortest in the betting mid-February to
have had more than one run Picked up at the
sales for what Willie Mullins considered was a
"very cheap" £41,000 following his victory at
Killarney in July and made some inroads on
that price tag when winning a valuable Grade
2 bumper at Navan in December, comfortably
seeing off four previous winners. What the
form amounts to in a race run nearly a minute
slower than standard is hard to gauge (none of
his victims has run since) but promising and in
the right yard.

Le Vent D'Antan
4 b g; Trainer Elizabeth Doyle
Bumper form (left-handed) 1, best RPR 124

Four-year-old who was an easy winner of a

slowly run bumper at Leopardstown towards the end of January but is highly regarded by his trainer, who says he will prefer better ground and works "as well as Cheltenian", the 2011 Champion Bumper winner she handled before passing him on to Philip Hobbs. Most of his rivals were unraced, but the third gives the form some substance, having been fourth in a competitive event on his previous run.

Moyle Park
5 ch g; Trainer David Kelly
Bumper form (left-handed) 1, best RPR 125

Flemensfirth gelding who made quite an impression on his debut at the Leopardstown Christmas festival, staying on strongly for a four-length win over the Tony Martin-trained Blackmail, who had been a good second on his debut the time before and has subsequently won in the style of an above-average performer. Looks promising.

Regal Encore
5 b g; Trainer Anthony Honeyball
Bumper form (left-handed) 11, best RPR 125

Trainer makes a habit of winning bumpers and this one was subsequently bought by JP McManus after a winning debut at Southwell in February 2012. Again ran out a very impressive winner of a Chepstow bumper under a penalty in October (second has since won), after which his trainer said he would be kept to bumpers as he could be a festival horse despite having schooled over hurdles and been "arrow-straight" at them. Hasn't run since, but lengthy absences no worry for this race.

Oscar Rock
5 b g; Trainer Harry Fry
Bumper form 211, best RPR 131
Left-handed 11, best RPR 131
Right-handed 2, best RPR 103

Point-to-point winner who didn't look a superstar when only second on his Taunton debut in October but improved dramatically for soft ground when winning at Newbury the following month and was most impressive in an often informative Listed bumper at Newbury on Betfair Hurdle day, winning by eight lengths. Originally not considered for this and may still not go, but trainer keeping options open just in case he gets the soft ground he needs. The top dog on Racing Post Ratings.

Sgt Reckless
6 b g; Trainer Mick Channon
Bumper form 11, best RPR 112
Left-handed 1, best RPR 112
Right-handed 1, best RPR 112

Well backed when landing a Wincanton bumper in May 2012, but in hindsight didn't beat much as his eight rivals are 0-19 since. Again quickened up well to score under a penalty on Polytrack at Lingfield in January, although the three-and-a-quarter-length fourth was beaten 26 lengths into third by Red Sherlock later that month, suggesting this one has plenty to find.

Owen Mc
5 b g; Trainer Noel Meade
Bumper form (right-handed) 11, best RPR 130

Dual Fairyhouse winner in November and December and made a big impression both times. Has an "explosive turn of foot" according to his trainer and showed that first time, although he had to work harder to win a better race next time. Right up there on RPRs but trading at a good deal bigger on Betfair than he was with the bookmakers in mid-February, suggesting either a problem or that connections are undecided, so not an ante-post proposition, as if anything is.

OTHERS TO CONSIDER

You could go on and on for a race like this as there are no end of once- or twice-raced winners who could be targeted here. Nicky Henderson always says he is not the biggest fan of this race, but he has run a few in the past and his **Captain Cutter** is better than when third to Red Sherlock at Ascot in February as he was held up off a funereal pace. **Sizing Tennessee** is another from the Willie Mullins stable who could make the trip, having improved dramatically in his second season. Ted Walsh has a decent performer on his hands in **Champagne James**, whose colours were lowered by the Mullins-trained Union Dues at Navan but who was odds-on for that Grade 2 and was not at all suited by the slow pace.

Champion Bumper results and trends

	FORM	WINNER	AGE & WGT	Adj RPR	SP	TRAINER	B.Runs	BEST RPR LAST 12 MONTHS (RUNS SINCE)
12	21	Champagne Fever D	5 11-5	144-1	16-1	W Mullins (IRE)	2(20G)	won Fairyhouse bumper (2m) (0)
11	21	Cheltenian D	5 11-5	126-13	14-1	P Hobbs	2(24G)	won Kempton cl 5 mdn bumper (2m) (0)
10	1	Cue Card	4 10-12	126-15	40-1	C Tizzard	1(24G)	won Fontwell class 6 bumper (1m6f) (0)
09	2-11	Dunguib D	6 11-5	147T	9-2	P Fenton (IRE)	3(24GS)	won Navan Gd2 bumper (2m) (0)
08	1	Cousin Vinny	5 11-5	118-23	12-1	W Mullins (IRE)	1(23GS)	won Punchestown bumper (2m) (0)
07	111	Cork All Star CD	5 11-5	145T	11-2	J Harrington (IRE)	3(24GS)	won Cheltenham Lstd bumper (2m½f) (0)
06	2131	Hairy Molly	6 11-5	126-9	33-1	J Crowley (IRE)	4(23G)	won Naas bumper (2m3f) (0)
05	011	Missed That D	6 11-5	135-14	7-2F	W Mullins (IRE)	3(24G)	won Naas bumper (2m) (0)
04	311	Total Enjoyment D	5 10-12	138T	7-1	T Cooper (IRE)	3(24G)	won Leopardstown bumper (2m) (0)
03	21-12	Liberman D	5 11-6	135-11	2-1F	M Pipe	4(25G)	2nd Cheltenham Lstd bumper (2m½f) (0)

WINS-RUNS: 4yo 1-37, 5yo 6-137, 6yo 3-61 **FAVOURITES:** -£2.50

TRAINERS IN THIS RACE (w-pl-r): Willie Mullins 3-1-36, Alan King 0-0-4, David Pipe 0-0-6, Nicky Henderson 0-1-7, Nigel Twiston-Davies 0-0-5, Noel Meade 0-1-4, Ted Walsh 0-0-1

FATE OF FAVOURITES: 1010033062 **POSITION OF WINNER IN MARKET:** 1210252060

Key trends

🏇Won a bumper with at least 13 runners, 9/10

🏇Aged five or six, 9/10 (six aged five)

🏇Pre-race RPR of at least 118, 8/10 (exceptions were once-raced winners)

🏇Won a bumper worth at least 4k (pounds or euros) to the winner, 8/10

🏇Off the track for at least 33 days, 8/10 (four not seen since Christmas or earlier)

🏇Bred in Ireland, 7/10

Other factors

🏇Cue Card is the only winning 4yo since Dato Star in 1995, with 51 beaten in the interim

🏇Two winners had won their only previous start but six winners had run at least three times

🏇Ireland has won seven of the last ten and 15 of the 20 ever run

🏇Willie Mullins has the best record with seven victories (three in the last eight years) but is often mob-handed. On four of the occasions he has won it, he saddled just one runner. On the other three, the winner traded at a bigger price than at least one stablemate

🏇The 20 winners have been sired by 20 different stallions. Those successful so far are Montelimar, Where To Dance, Strong Gale, Accordion, Welsh Term, Florida Son, Glacial Storm, Mister Lord, River Falls, Broken Hearted, Teenoso, Flemensfirth, Overbury, Shernazar, Fasliyev, Bob Back, Presenting, King's Theatre, Astarabad and Stowaway

Notes

Thursday, March 14 (New Course)

Jewson
Novices' Chase

Pertemps Final
Handicap Hurdle

Ryanair Chase

Ladbrokes
World Hurdle

Byrne Group
Plate Handicap
Chase

Fulke Walwyn
Kim Muir
Handicap Chase

1.30 Jewson Novices' Chase C4/RUK
2m4f   *Grade 2*   *£100,000*

This race offers an opportunity for leading novice chasers at the intermediate distance of 2m4f and it seems set to become a Grade 1 soon judging by the quality it has attracted already. Ireland has provided both previous winners, most notably with this year's leading Gold Cup hope Sir Des Champs. His trainer Willie Mullins looks set to field a strong representative again – with the choice appearing to lie between Aupcharlie, Arvika Ligeonniere and Boston Bob – although running plans will depend on what the top yards send to the Arkle and RSA. Other possibles are Captain Conan for Nicky Henderson, Fago and Unioniste for Paul Nicholls and Dynaste for David Pipe, while the Tom George-trained Module is one of the shorter-priced hopefuls from a smaller yard.

Captain Conan
6 b g; Trainer Nicky Henderson
Chase form 111, best RPR 152
Left-handed 1, best RPR 151
Right-handed 11, best RPR 152
Cheltenham form 1, best RPR 151

Promising gelding who has been successful in four of his seven starts in Britain and Ireland, three of them Grade 1s at Sandown. Won last season's Tolworth Hurdle and, although he probably wouldn't have done if runner-up Colour Squadron hadn't hung all over the place, he proved it was no fluke with a couple of Grade 2 seconds to Tap Night and Darlan in the spring. Chase career could not have started more promisingly as he readily outpointed previous scorer Sire De Grugy at Cheltenham in November and then ran out a comfortable winner of the Henry VIII at Sandown from Hinterland. The runner-up was a useful hurdler but has been disappointing for Paul Nicholls this season, showing nothing against Simonsig in a slowly run race at Kempton and then getting beaten at odds of 30-100 in a jumpers' bumper, so the form may not be that solid. Third-placed Third Intention almost reversed the form in the 2m4½f Scilly Isles Chase in February, but the quirky six-year-old waited in front, thus gifting Captain Conan another Grade 1 success at his luckiest course. The winner did not jump or travel as well as he had at 2m, which was something of a surprise, so maybe Nicky Henderson did not have him as fit as he thought. Whatever the case, he arguably sets the standard here, but not at a level that will have anyone running scared.

Aupcharlie
7 b g; Trainer Willie Mullins
Chase form 122, best RPR 153
Left-handed 22, best RPR 153
Right-handed 1, best RPR 140
Cheltenham form (bumper) 3, best RPR 126
At the festival 16 Mar 2011: Held up well in rear, good progress on wide outside from 5f out to dispute lead over 3f out, headed and faded well over 1f out, finished third, beaten nine and a half lengths by Cheltenian in Champion Bumper

Finished third in the 2011 Champion Bumper but didn't make the festival as a hurdler, twice getting turned over at long odds-on before finally winning his maiden last January. Seems an altogether different proposition over fences, though, and was an easy winner on his November debut over 2m4f at Gowran before being thrown straight into Grade 1 company in the 3m Topaz at Leopardstown. Though only second string to the stable's Back In Focus, he looked much the classier of the pair and appeared set to win easily until his stamina gave way close home and he was caught on the line. Next run was almost a carbon copy as he was nutted by Tofino Bay and this strong traveller looks certain to be better suited by dropping in trip here. Big player for last year's winning trainer.

Module
6 b g; Trainer Tom George
Chase form F11, best RPR 143
Left-handed 1, best RPR 143
Right-handed F1, best RPR 130

Lightly raced gelding who was an easy winner of a fair Cheltenham handicap hurdle on

his British debut for Tom George (favourite Hinterland in third, second-placed Art Professor went on to be fifth in the Martin Pipe race) but then not seen until tipping up on his chasing debut in October. Showed no ill effects, though, as he ran out an impressive winner of a decent 2m3f chase at Newbury before completing his prep with a straightforward win in an easier race at Leicester. Going the right way according to his trainer, who seems to like him a fair bit. Also in the Arkle but much shorter for this.

Boston Bob

8 b g; Trainer Willie Mullins
Chase form (both left-handed) 11, best RPR 146
Cheltenham form (hurdle) 2, best RPR 152
At the festival 16 Mar 2012: Held up, hit 6th, headway approaching 2 out, ridden to chase winner before last, stayed on for pressure run-in, no impression close home, finished second, beaten two lengths by Brindisi Breeze in Albert Bartlett

Is a much shorter price for the RSA, but worth mentioning here because trainer was still leaning towards this after his last-gasp Dr P J Moriarty win at Leopardstown in February, especially if the ground is soft. Is 2-2 over fences but had to work had both times and doesn't quite look the horse he did when he lined up a short-priced favourite for last season's Albert Bartlett.

Argocat

5 b g; Trainer Tom Taaffe
Chase form (all right-handed) 7121, best RPR 137
Cheltenham form (hurdle) 9, best RPR 130
At the festival 14 Mar 2012: In touch, ridden approaching 3 out, weakened from next, finished ninth, beaten 13 lengths by Une Artiste in Fred Winter Juvenile Handicap Hurdle

Didn't quite make the grade as a hurdler but has made steady improvement since being sent over fences and has won both his starts over the Jewson trip of 2m4f. The latest was in a Grade 2 at Limerick over Christmas, after which his trainer said he'd put him away for this race. The Irish handicapper seems to like him as a mark of 146 puts him just 6lb shy of Captain Conan but Racing Post Ratings say the difference is more like a stone.

Benefficient

7 ch g; Trainer Tony Martin
Chase form 21241, best RPR 153
Left-handed 2241, best RPR 153
Right-handed 1, best RPR 132
Cheltenham form (hurdle) 0, best RPR 116
At the festival 14 Mar 2012: Chased leaders, ridden 3 out, weakened rapidly 2 out, finished tenth, beaten 48 lengths by Simonsig in Neptune

Also in the Arkle and won the Irish version by 20 lengths from Oscars Well in a strange race at Leopardstown. Favourite Arvika Ligeonniere fell four out and then Oscars Well, who traded at 1.01 on Betfair, clouted the last and stopped to a walk. Bennefficient looked the likely winner by then anyway, but does seem to save his best for Leopardstown and soft ground. Form claims all the same and market makes him slightly more likely to go for this race.

Tap Night *(left)*
6 ch g; Trainer Lucinda Russell
Chase form 141, best RPR 142
Left-handed 11, best RPR 142
Right-handed 4, bestRPR 133

Decent novice hurdler who came out roughly the same horse as Captain Conan in that discipline, having beaten him two lengths in receipt of 3lb in a Kelso Grade 2 last March. Hasn't achieved quite so much over fences and ran abysmally on his second start, but won the other two in good style, proving he stayed this sort of trip when winning at Ayr in February. In the Arkle as well, but shorter for this and wouldn't be out of place in making the line-up, although handicaps could be an option.

Third Intention
6 b g; Trainer Colin Tizzard
Chase form 23332, best RPR 151
Left-handed 23, best RPR 141
Right-handed 332, best RPR 151
Cheltenham form (chases) 23, best RPR 141
At the festival 18 Mar 2011: Mistake 1st, held up, headway approaching 2 out, ridden between last 2, stayed on run-in, not pace to reach leaders, finished seventh, beaten nine and three-quarter lengths by Zarkandar in Triumph Hurdle
14 Mar 2012: In touch, chased leaders after 4 out, effort and well there 2 out, ridden and beaten approaching last, finished eighth, beaten 17 lengths by Son Of Flicka in Coral Cup

Is a big price for a horse who came within a neck of beating favourite Captain Conan in the Scilly Isles at Sandown last time, but that's

because he always seems to keep a bit for himself and did just that when letting Captain Conan get up to beat him. Has plenty of talent when on a going day, as he proved when nine-length winner of the National Spirit Hurdle at Fontwell last season, and he's one of those with the talent to cause an upset if he wants to, although he would become the first maiden chaser to win this. Also in the RSA but weak effort when fading into third behind Dynaste in the Feltham and this is the most likely target.

OTHERS TO CONSIDER

Hard to pin down the likely final field for this race. While it's a Grade 2, that won't necessarily stop trainers from running their best horses, as Willie Mullins showed last term when winning the race with Gold Cup fancy Sir Des Champs. Dynaste is a hot favourite for the RSA after winning the Feltham in a similar style to stablemate Grands Crus last season and he would be a short price if getting the nod for this race. Trainer David Pipe says everything will rest on the state of the ground, but the odds suggest strongly he will be in the RSA anyway. Mullins has a potentially strong hand already but could also run **Arvika Ligeonniere** if he doesn't want to take on Simonsig and Overturn in the Arkle, while **Oscars Well** is another who could step up in trip. Those who could step down include **Unioniste** and **Hadrian's Approach**, but again the market strongly suggests otherwise. **Molotof** was fairly impressive when beating a progressive handicapper at Warwick in February and has the form to take a hand if joining stablemate Captain Conan, although he was beaten soundly on both previous visits to the festival.

Jewson Novices' Chase results

FORM	WINNER	AGE & WGT	Adj RPR	SP	TRAINER	C.Runs	BEST RPR LAST 12 MONTHS (RUNS SINCE)
12	1-111	Sir Des Champs C, D	6 11-4	161-8	3-1	W Mullins (IRE)	3(10G)	won Limerick Gd2 nov ch (2m3½f) (1)
11	4-122	Noble Prince D	7 11-4	164-6	4-1	P Nolan (IRE)	3(11G)	2nd Leopardstown Gd1 nov ch (2m1f) (0)

WINS-RUNS: 6yo 1-8, 7yo 1-9, 8yo 0-3, 9yo 0-1 **FAVOURITES:** -£2.00

TRAINERS IN THIS RACE (w-pl-r): Willie Mullins 1-0-2, David Pipe 0-0-2, Donald McCain 0-0-1, Henry de Bromhead 0-1-1, Nicky Henderson 0-0-3, Nigel Twiston-Davies 0-0-1, Paul Nicholls 0-0-2, Philip Hobbs 0-1-1

FATE OF FAVOURITES: 20 **POSITION OF WINNER IN MARKET:** 22

This lacks the quality of some of the other festival handicaps and, as a big-field 3m handicap hurdle, has a specialist element – dual winner Buena Vista had previously finished second and fifth and Creon, the 2004 winner, had been sixth the year before.

Good recent form has been less important in recent years, with five of the past nine winners having failed to make the first four on their previous outing, but over the longer term last-time-out winners have a strong record (nine winners in the past 17 years).

Favourites have a poor record and Inching Closer in 2003 is the only market leader to have won in the past 15 runnings – every winner since has started at double-figure odds.

The bottom weight tends to run off a mark around the mid-130s nowadays and the best place to find the winner is up to 144 – last year's first four ran off 142, 140, 139 and 140. The vast majority of winners carried between 10st 2lb and 11st 2lb.

Trainers renowned for stayers do well, such as Jonjo O'Neill (three winners) and Nigel Twiston-Davies (two). Irish runners are always to be noted, with three seconds and two thirds in the six runnings since their last success.

Qualifiers at Cheltenham (especially the October one), Leopardstown (December) and Haydock (February) are worth checking.

Pertemps Final results and trends

	FORM	WINNER	AGE & WGT	OR	SP	TRAINER	H.Runs	BEST RPR LAST 12 MONTHS (RUNS SINCE)
12	5P504	Cape Tribulation D	8 10-11	142-3	14-1	M Jefferson	10(24G)	5th Haydock Gd3 hcap hdl (3m) (1)
11	28700	Buena Vista CD	10 10-3	138-4	20-1	D Pipe	29(23G)	won Pertemps Final (3m) (6)
10	-8508	Buena Vista	9 10-1	133-1	16-1	D Pipe	22(24G)	5th Haydock Listed hcap hdl (3m1f) (2)
09	26211	Kayf Aramis D	7 10-5	129-7	16-1	V Williams	9(22GS)	won Warwick class 3 nov hdl (3m1f) (0)
08	-1271	Ballyfitz D	8 10-8	132-3	18-1	N Twiston-Davies	6(24GS)	won Haydock class 2 hcap hdl (3m) (0)
07	2-2F0	Oscar Park	8 10-9	140-T	14-1	D Arbuthnot	9(24GS)	2nd Newbury class 2 hcap hdl (3m½f) (2)
06	58505	Kadoun D	9 11-7	142-2	50-1	M O'Brien (IRE)	25(24G)	8th Fairyhouse hcap hdl (2m) (2)
05	21102	Oulart D	6 10-2	121-11	10-1	D Hughes (IRE)	6(22G)	won Leopardstown hcap hdl (3m) (2)
04	380P6	Creon (2oh)	9 10-0	120-3	50-1	J O'Neill	25(24G)	6th Chepstow class 3 hcap hdl (2m4f) (0)
03	710-1	Inching Closer	6 11-2	130-4	6-1F	J O'Neill	7(24G)	won Haydock class 3 hcap hdl (2m4f) (0)

WINS-RUNS: 5yo 0-26, 6yo 2-48, 7yo 1-60, 8yo 3-52, 9yo 3-22, 10yo 1-13, 11yo 0-11, 12yo 0-1, 13yo 0-2 **FAVOURITES:** -£3.00

FATE OF FAVOURITES: 1000020000 **POSITION OF WINNER IN MARKET:** 1050700596

OR 119-131 4-11-79, **132-144** 6-17-132, **145-157** 0-2-24

Key trends
- Aged six to nine, 9/10
- Off track between 20 and 48 days, 9/10
- Won at Class 3 or higher, 9/10
- Carried no more than 11st 2lb, 9/10
- Officially rated 129 to 142, 8/10
- Won over at least 3m, 8/10
- Winning form between 2m4f and 2m6f, 8/10
- Six to ten runs over hurdles, 6/10 (exceptions 22-plus)

Other factors
- Only one winner was out of the handicap (Creon 2lb wrong in 2004)
- Seven winners had run at the festival before – including three who had recorded a top-six finish in this race the previous year
- The Irish winners had all finished unplaced in the Leopardstown qualifier
- Two winners were novices
- Eight winners started at 14-1 or bigger
- Only one five-year-old has won the race

2.40 Ryanair Chase
2m5f Grade 1 £275,000

C4/RUK

As with other races at an intermediate distance, the final line-up will be dictated by running plans in the shorter and longer (and in this case more prestigious) alternatives – the Queen Mother Champion Chase and the Cheltenham Gold Cup. With Sprinter Sacre having scared away virtually all the opposition in the two-mile championship, this race could become a cracker with Finian's Rainbow and Sizing Europe (the last two Champion Chase winners) among those who could step up. Riverside Theatre, last year's winner, and Cue Card are two who look ideally suited by this distance, while Irish hopefuls First Lieutenant and Sir Des Champs could drop down from the Gold Cup. In the absence of some of those big names, opportunity would knock louder for Champion Court, Menorah, For Non Stop and China Rock.

Cue Card

7 b g; Trainer Colin Tizzard
Chase form 1U212151, best RPR 170
Left-handed 1U212, best RPR 167
Right-handed 151, best RPR 170
Cheltenham form (all) 1124U2, best RPR 167
At the festival 17 Mar 2010: Took keen hold, held up well in rear, scythed through field from 5f out, tracked leader over 2f out and still cruising, led over 1f out, hung left briefly but romped clear, won Champion Bumper by eight lengths from Al Ferof

15 Mar 2011: Took keen hold, held up in midfield, progress before 3 out, joined leader 2 out, ridden soon after, hanging and not quicken before last, faded, finished fourth, beaten six and a half lengths by Al Ferof in Supreme Novices' Hurdle

13 Mar 2012: Led until mistake and headed 9th, chased winner from 4 out, stayed on well to try and close on winner after 2 out and 4 lengths down soon after, readily outpaced from last but stayed on well for clear 2nd, beaten seven lengths by Sprinter Sacre in Racing Post Arkle Chase

Still only seven but has performed with great credit in three different Cheltenham Festival races already and will line up as favourite for a fourth if connections decide to come here instead of taking on Sprinter Sacre in the Champion Chase. That possibility was made all the more likely when he proved his stamina by landing the 2m5½f Ascot Chase in February, although the result was in doubt when Captain Chris loomed up to challenge two out only to take off too early and land on top of the fence. Cue Card didn't finish like a tired horse but most people thought Captain Chris had his measure (he was 1-2 on Betfair at the time). Still, that's top-class form for

the distance despite some erratic jumping. Talking of jumping, he seems to be more prone to errors when left alone to make up his own mind and it would be good to see him ridden more aggressively at his fences. This race is likely to attract a big field this year with everyone running scared of Sprinter Sacre in the Champion Chase and dominating won't be easy unless he jumps better than he did at Ascot.

First Lieutenant

8 ch g; Trainer Mouse Morris
Chase form 121P2234232, best RPR 168
Left-handed 12232, best RPR 168
Right-handed 21P342, best RPR 165
Cheltenham form 12, best RPR 164
At the festival 16 Mar 2011: Chased leaders, ridden from 2 out, not much room last, 2 lengths down on leader soon after, rallied gamely under pressure run-in, led last stride, won Neptune Novices' Hurdle by a short head from Rock On Ruby

14 Mar 2012: Prominent, went 2nd after 7th, led 8th, headed narrowly 4 out, regained lead on bend before 2 out, ridden and headed just before last, one pace and well held towards finish, finished second, beaten two and a half lengths by Bobs Worth in RSA Chase

Has the Gold Cup as another possible target and he's a genuine contender for that on his latest two efforts this term. The market suggests he's also very much under consideration for this race, perhaps on account of stamina worries if the ground is testing, and he'd obviously be a major player. Doesn't like bad ground but has improved on it this season, so could be about to do something big if it dries out.

Sizing Europe

11 b g; Trainer Henry de Bromhead
Chase form 111113223121211211111, best RPR 176
Left-handed 11121, best RPR 176
Right-handed 1113223212111111, best RPR 176
Cheltenham form 10112, best RPR 176
At the festival 11 Mar 08: Chased leaders, driven to challenge 2 out, weakened quickly before last, virtually pulled up before run-in, finished 14th, beaten 101l by Katchit in Champion Hurdle

16 Mar 2010: Took keen hold early, with leaders, went 2nd 9th and pressed leader, going easily when left in lead 2 out, 2 lengths up last, driven flat, held on near finish, beat Somersby three-quarters of a length in Arkle Chase

16 Mar 2011: Tracked leader, led 7th, driven from 2 out, half-length lead last, ridden and stayed on strongly to go clear run-in, won Champion Chase by five lengths from Big Zeb

14 Mar 2012: Tracked leader until left in lead 4th, driven approaching last, joined by winner and bumped approaching bypassed final fence, headed final 120yds, no extra under pressure, finished second, beaten one and a quarter lengths by Finian's Rainbow in Champion Chase

Appears as good as ever and may well come here instead of taking on Sprinter Sacre in the Champion Chase. No shame in that as he's already got the T-shirt and is getting on in years to be winning the two-mile championship, which has been taken by just four horses aged in double figures in the past 30 years. Three ten-year-olds have taken this in eight runnings, though, and there's no doubt it usually takes a lesser performance to win this than the Champion Chase or Gold Cup.

Riverside Theatre

9 b g; Trainer Nicky Henderson
Chase form 115F12111P6, best RPR 172
Left-handed 151P, best RPR 171
Right-handed 1F12116, best RPR 172
Cheltenham form 51, best RPR 171
At the festival 16 Mar 2010: Held up in rear, lost touch after 8th, last and looked like tailing off after next, still last 2 out, bounded up run-in, nearest finish, fifth, beaten eight and three-quarter lengths by Sizing Europe in Arkle Chase

15 Mar 2012: Tracked leaders, jumped slowly 3rd and 5th, pushed along 10th, hit 13th, stayed on well from 3 out, chased leader 2 out, challenged last, upsides under pressure with 1f to run, led final 50yds, gamely, won Ryanair Chase by half a length from Albertas Run

High-quality chaser with a good win record who always seemed best going right-handed until winning this race last year in a three-horse war with Albertas Run and Medermit.

Even so, he never really travelled like a Cheltenham horse and he ended up having a really hard race, so it was no surprise he flopped as favourite at Aintree next time. More worrying is the fact he was in trouble by halfway on his return in the King George and there remains the suspicion that last year's Ryanair bottomed him.

Champion Court

8 b g; Trainer Martin Keighley
Chase form U123122242, best RPR 161
Left-handed 123122, best RPR 161
Right-handed U242, best RPR 161
Cheltenham form (chases) 2312, best RPR 161
At the festival 18 Mar 2011: Raced keenly, held up, headway approaching 3 out, tracked leaders before 2 out, ridden between last 2, outpaced by front trio before last, beaten and no impression after, finished fourth, beaten 13 and a half lengths by Bobs Worth in Albert Bartlett

15 Mar 2012: Led until narrowly headed 5th, stayed upsides, slight lead next but hard pressed to 12th, asserted 4 out, ridden before 2 out, soon joined, headed with 1f to run, soon outpaced but kept on strongly for clear 2nd, beaten four and a half lengths by Sir Des Champs in Jewson Novices' Chase

Consistent performer who has won only two of his ten chases but finished second in five others, often in top company, and was the only one to make a race of it with Sir Des Champs in last season's Jewson. Found concession of 20lb to William's Wishes too much to handle on his return at Ascot, but that was hardly a surprise given the winner's progress and they were 17 lengths clear of the rest. He ran a far better race in the King George than the form book records, as he had most of the field well beaten heading out of the back straight but failed to stay. Was surprisingly beaten a neck by Alasi when a 4-9 chance back at Kempton in February but obviously had a hard race the time before and may not have fully recovered. There are plenty of horses among the entries rated a good deal higher than he is, but suspicion remains that he has a big run in him.

Menorah

8 b g; Trainer Philip Hobbs
Chase form U11F314313, best RPR 167
Left-handed F313, best RPR 164
Right-handed U11431, best RPR 167
Cheltenham form (chases) 3, best RPR 150
At the festival 16 Mar 2010: Tracked leaders, driven to challenge and went left 2 out, led soon after, wandered under pressure approaching last, hard ridden

run-in, held on all out, won Supreme Novices' Hurdle by a head from Get Me Out Of Here

15 Mar 2011: Chased leaders, hit 4 out, ridden to stay right there 2 out, one pace when hit last, weakened run-in, finished fifth, beaten nine and a half lengths by Hurricane Fly in Champion Hurdle

13 Mar 2012: In touch, headway to track leading duo after 4 out, ridden and hit 3 out, 7 lengths 3rd and ridden when blundered and weakened 2 out, finished third, beaten 29 lengths by Sprinter Sacre in Racing Post Arkle Chase

Former Supreme Novices' Hurdle winner who was making a right hash of his novice chasing campaign until finally getting it right with a Grade 1 victory at Aintree in April, beating the useful Cristal Bonus by seven lengths. Clumsy jumping returned to haunt him when he finished a distant third to Cue Card in the Haldon Gold Cup on his return, but he proved he's still a high-class performer when beating Hunt Ball at Kempton over Christmas, again confirming his suitability for the Ryanair trip. Clearly didn't stay (or jump well) when third in the Denman Chase and will be more at home coming back in trip. Tends to be better in the spring and an error-free round would put him right in the mix.

Grands Crus

8 gr g; Trainer David Pipe
Chase form 1114P3P, best RPR 168
Left-handed 114PP, best RPR 163
Right-handed 13, best RPR 168
Cheltenham form (chases) 14PP, best RPR 160
At the festival 17 Mar 2011: Held up in last early, headway after 3 out, going well tracking leaders before 2 out, ridden and chased winner approaching last, challenging run-in, not quicken and held final 100yds, finished second, beaten a length and three-quarters by Big Buck's in World Hurdle

14 Mar 2012: Held up, headway 13th (water), tracked leaders going well after 4 out, upsides 3 out, under pressure approaching 2 out, soon lost ground on front duo, weakened after last, finished fourth, beaten 18 lengths by Bobs Worth in RSA Chase

Taken out of the Gold Cup after another dreadful effort at Cheltenham in the Argento Chase on trials day in January. Was well backed that day following an encouraging third to Long Run in the King George, but never travelled and it was obvious he wasn't going to play a part long before his stamina was tested. Said to be back on target either for this race or the World Hurdle but it now takes a leap of faith to believe he'll ever return to the

form that saw him toy with Silviniaco Conti and Bobs Worth in the 2011 Feltham.

For Non Stop

8 b g; Trainer Nick Williams
Chase form F2213125, best RPR 167
Left-handed F2131, best RPR 167
Right-handed 225, best RPR 164
Cheltenham form (chases) F3, best RPR 154
At the festival 16 Mar 2011: Chased clear leader and clear of rest to 5th, led 3 out, ridden and headed before last, 2 lengths down when fell last in Coral Cup won by Carlito Brigante

15 Mar 2012: In rear, hit 3rd, in touch 6th, headway 12th, went 3rd 3 out, kept on under pressure but never any chance of reaching leading duo, finished third, beaten 13 and a half lengths by Sir Des Champs in Jewson Novices' Chase

Strong traveller who can look brilliant when it all comes together, as it did when the leaders went off at a suicidal pace in the Old Roan Chase at Aintree in October and he sluiced through the field to thrash Wishfull Thinking by 23 lengths off a mark of 151. Wasn't far off that form a month later despite some sloppy jumps when second to Captain Chris at Ascot, but then ran abysmally behind Menorah in the rescheduled Peterborough Chase at Kempton over Christmas. Was a well-backed favourite for that, so something must have been amiss as yard rarely gets it that wrong. Is another who could do with brushing up his jumping, but goes well fresh and has the talent to be a player.

Rubi Light

8 b g; Trainer Robbie Hennessy
Chase form 111721331215432, best RPR 168
Left-handed 13252, best RPR 168
Right-handed 1172131143, best RPR 168
Cheltenham form 35, best RPR 166
At the festival 17 Mar 2011: With winner, led 8th to 10th, headed next, stayed challenging, hit 7th, led next, headed 9th, led 10th, ridden, headed and blundered 3 out, lost 2nd next, chased winner again last, no impression, one pace into 3rd run-in, finished third, beaten three lengths by Albertas Run in Ryanair Chase

15 Mar 2012: Pressed leaders, led 8th to 10th, challenged from 11th, led 4 out, headed next, stayed right there until weakened approaching last, finished fifth, beaten seven and a half lengths by Riverside Theatre in Ryanair Chase

Classy and consistent eight-year-old who has already had two pops at this, doing best when third to Albertas Run two years ago. Below par on return this season when distant last of

three behind Flemenstar at Punchestown but, only 18 days later, was right back to his best when second to Sizing Europe in a 2m1f Grade 1 at Leopardstown in December. Very much at home on soft ground but hasn't yet had it at Cheltenham and no reason why he can't prove a major player in the right conditons. Due to run in the rescheduled Red Mills Chase at Navan in mid-February, a race normally run at Gowran and won by him in 2011 and 2012.

Albertas Run *(above)*

12 b g; Trainer Jonjo O'Neill
Chase form 1211134P2393P1362114FP12123, best RPR 171
Left-handed 2113P9311412123, best RPR 170
Right-handed 11423P1362FP, best RPR 171
Cheltenham form 0119112, best RPR 170
At the festival 15 Mar 2006: Prominent until niggled along and weakened 6f out, finished 15th, beaten 17 and a half lengths by Hairy Molly in Champion Bumper

13 Mar 2008: Held up but never very far away, tracked leaders 15th, shaken up 3 out, stayed on to track leader from 2 out, led approaching last, soon clear, comfortably, won RSA Chase by four and a half lengths from Roll Along

13 Mar 2009: In touch, headway to chase leaders 13th, ridden and hit 4 out, soon weakened, finished ninth, beaten 48 lengths by Kauto Star in Gold Cup

18 Mar 2010: Tracked leader, led 5th to 6th, stayed challenging until led 4 out, driven to assert approaching 2 out, stayed on strongly, won Ryanair Chase by four and a half lengths from Poquelin

17 Mar 2011: Led to 3rd, stayed pressing leader, slight lead 4th to 8th, headed 10th, stayed challenging, hit 13th, ridden after 4 out, led 3 out, hard driven and stayed on under pressure run-in, held on well, won Ryanair Chase by one length from Kalahari King

15 Mar 2012: Led to 4th, stayed challenging until led again 7th, headed 8th, led again 10th to 4 out, led 3 out, hard pressed soon after, joined last, edged right run-in, headed and no extra final 50yds, finished

second, beaten half a length by Riverside Theatre in Ryanair Chase

Legend of a horse who has achieved much more than most and yet doesn't quite get the credit he deserves. If he makes the festival it will be his seventh crack at the meeting at which he has won three times, almost making it four when second in this race last year. Is 12 now, however, and niggling problems mean he has yet to make it to the track this season, although he did figure among the five-day entries for the Ascot Chase in February. Has always been at his best on good ground, which he may not get this season, so a fairytale third Ryanair win looks unlikely

Somersby

9 b g; Trainer Mick Channon
Chase form 112233253122417234, best RPR 169
Left-handed 12235373, best RPR 167
Right-handed 1321224124, best RPR 169
Cheltenham form 323573, best RPR 167
At the festival 10 Mar 2009: In touch on outside, lost position after 3 out, pushed along after 2 out, ridden and kept on well run-in to take 3rd last strides but no impression on leading duo, finished third, beaten three lengths by Go Native in Supreme Novices' Hurdle

16 Mar 2010: Held up in midfield, progress 8th, pushed along in 4th after 3 out, stayed on from next to close on leading pair last, took second final 100yds, not reach winner, finished second, beaten three-quarters of a length by Sizing Europe in Arkle Chase

16 Mar 2011: Chased leaders, went 2nd 4 out, blundered next, stayed in touch with leaders under pressure until weakened before last, finished fifth, beaten 12 and a half lengths by Sizing Europe in Champion Chase

15 Mar 2012: In rear but in touch, headway 9th, chased leaders 4 out, weakened 3 out, finished seventh, beaten 17 lengths by Riverside Theatre in Ryanair Chase

Won the Grade 1 Victor Chandler Chase

last year and has always gone best at Ascot, which is worrying as he didn't really show enough behind Cue Card in the Ascot Chase in February to suggest he has any chance of reversing the form. That was his second poor performance in two runs this season and he managed only a well-beaten seventh in this race last year, so he has plenty to prove.

Mail De Bievre
8 b g; Trainer Tom George
Chase form (all left-handed) 12222115, best RPR 144

Showed some promise in bumpers for Alan King a few years ago but spent most of his time since in France, winning a Grade 2 and a Grade 3 over fences. Form hard to put a figure on but Racing Post Ratings gave him a best of 144 for running second to regular 3m4f winner Rubi Ball over 2m5f and official handicapper put him on 160. Had first outing for best part of 18 months when fifth in the Denman Chase for Tom George, but while he impressed plenty with his jumping from the front, he basically ran too free and finished knackered. Potentially better than that but requires bigger leap of faith than some imagine for him to turn into a Champion Chase prospect (only 16-1 in places, but still needs to be supplemented) over a trip he hasn't tried for four years.

Finian's Rainbow
10 b g; Trainer Nicky Henderson
Chase form 11121121146, best RPR 175
Left-handed 1112111, best RPR 175
Right-handed 1246, best RPR 167
Cheltenham form 521, best RPR 175
At the festival 17 Mar 2010: Slightly hampered 2nd, soon tracking leaders, travelling well approaching 2 out, soon ridden and found no extra before last, finished fifth, beaten six and three-quarter lengths by Peddlers Cross in Neptune Investment Management Novices' Hurdle

15 Mar 2011: Disputed 2nd, slight lead 7th, ridden 2 out, joined and hit last, headed soon after, kept on but no impression on winner, finished second, beaten two and three-quarter lengths by Captain Chris in Arkle Chase

14 Mar 2012: Raced in 3rd until left tracking leader from 4th, driven to close approaching last, ridden and bumped approaching bypassed final fence when challenging, stayed upsides and asserted under pressure final 120yds, all out, won Champion Chase by a length and a quarter from Sizing Europe

Wind operation following poor return at Ascot in November didn't seem to make any difference as he was even worse back there in February when tailed off behind Cue Card. Sad to see a Champion Chase winner in such rapid decline but hard to see how anyone could back him for any race little more than three weeks later.

OTHERS TO CONSIDER

There aren't really many more worth mentioning here as **China Rock** was said to be on target for the Gold Cup despite missing the Hennessy at Leopardstown and there has been no mention of coming here instead despite a quote of only 14-1 in places. **Call The Police** was cut to just 12-1 by Betfred in February, which seems an amazingly short price for a ten-year-old with an official mark 21lb lower than the highest-rated in the field, even allowing for the fact he's won two small-field races this year. He's double that with several firms but not exactly begging to be backed at those odds.

Ryanair Chase results and trends

FORM	WINNER	AGE & WGT	Adj RPR	SP	TRAINER	C.Runs	BEST RPR LAST 12 MONTHS (RUNS SINCE)
12	121-1	Riverside Theatre D	8 11-10	176^T	7-2F	N Henderson	8$^{(12G)}$	won Gd1 Ascot Chase (2m5½f) (0)
11	1-4FP	Albertas Run CD	10 11-10	176^{-1}	6-1	J O'Neill	22$^{(11G)}$	won Gd1 Melling Chase (2m4f) (3)
10	P1362	Albertas Run C, D	9 11-10	171^{-3}	14-1	J O'Neill	17$^{(13G)}$	won Ascot Gd2 chase (2m3f) (3)
09	14-16	Imperial Commander C, D	8 11-10	165^{-19}	6-1	N Twiston-Davies	5$^{(10GS)}$	won Paddy Power Gold Cup (2m4½f) (1)
08	23-22	Our Vic CD, BF	10 11-10	176^{-2}	4-1	D Pipe	17$^{(9GS)}$	2nd Gd1 King George VI Chase (3m) (1)
07	-1F31	Taranis CD	6 11-0	169^{-13}	9-2	P Nicholls	7$^{(9GS)}$	3rd Gd3 Boylesports Gold Cup (2m5f) (0)
06	-4B13	Fondmort CD	10 11-0	179^T	10-3J	N Henderson	27$^{(11G)}$	won Cheltenham Listed hcap ch (2m5f) (1)
05	2-222	Thisthatandtother C, BF	9 11-3	173^{-3}	9-2	P Nicholls	11$^{(12G)}$	2nd Paddy Power Gold Cup (2m4½f) (2)

WINS-RUNS: 6yo 1-5, 7yo 0-9, 8yo 2-23, 9yo 2-24, 10yo 3-16, 11yo 0-7, 12yo 0-2, 13yo 0-1 **FAVOURITES:** -£1.33

TRAINERS IN THIS RACE (w-pl-r): Jonjo O'Neill 2-1-3, Nicky Henderson 2-1-9, Paul Nicholls 2-2-11, David Pipe 1-1-4, Nigel Twiston-Davies 1-0-2, Alan King 0-2-3, Colin Tizzard 0-0-1, Evan Williams 0-0-1, Nick Williams 0-0-1, Noel Meade 0-0-1, Philip Hobbs 0-1-3, Robbie Hennessy 0-1-2, Sue Smith 0-0-1, Tom George 0-0-1, Willie Mullins 0-1-5

FATE OF FAVOURITES: P1452241 **POSITION OF WINNER IN MARKET:** 21322821

Run as a Grade 2 from 2005 to 2007

Key trends

🐎Pre-race RPR of at least 158, 8/8

🐎Officially rated at least 152, 8/8

🐎Course winner, 7/8

🐎From the first three in the market, 7/8

🐎No more than four runs since October, 7/8

🐎Top-three finish last time out, 6/8

🐎At least 11 runs over fences, 5/8

🐎Won or placed in the Paddy Power or December Gold Cup, 5/8

Other factors

🐎Four of the six beaten favourites had won a Grade 1 chase last time out

🐎Four winners had recorded at least a top-four finish in a Grade 1 or 2 chase over 3m-plus – the other four achieved that subsequently

Notes

3.20 Ladbrokes World Hurdle — C4/RUK
🏇3m   🏇Grade 1   🏇£275,000

Injury has robbed Big Buck's of the opportunity to make another piece of festival history with a fifth consecutive win, but in his absence the race is much more open and still has several high-class contenders. Reve De Sivola has stepped into the breach to take the Long Walk and Cleeve – two of the races usually reserved for Big Buck's – in his first season back over hurdles after disappointing over fences. Oscar Whisky, an apparent non-staying fifth last year, gave trainer Nicky Henderson more encouraging signs of his staying power when runner-up to Reve De Sivola in the Cleeve and is set to reoppose. The 2011 Champion Hurdle runner-up Peddlers Cross is another trying a different avenue, while Monksland has been the shortest-priced Irish contender in the ante-post market.

Reve De Sivola
8 b g; Trainer Nick Williams
Hurdles form 6332612121211, best RPR 167
Left-handed 63326121221, best RPR 167
Right-handed 11, best RPR 166
Cheltenham form (hurdles) 326221, best RPR 167
At the festival 13 Mar 2009: Prominent, stumbled when not much room on bend after 2 out, one pace from before last, finished sixth, beaten 11 and a half lengths by Zaynar in Triumph Hurdle

17 Mar 2010: Chased leaders, hit 6th, challenging when hit 3 out, upsides when left in lead 2 out, narrowly headed last, stayed on and switched left run-in but no impression on winner near finish, finished second, beaten a length and a half by Peddlers Cross

15 Mar 2011: Tracked leaders, hampered 3rd, went 2nd and blundered 12th, mistake 4 out, mistake 3 out and dropped to 4th, slightly hampered 2 out, faded, finished third, beaten 11 and a half lengths by Bensalem in Stewart Family Spinal Research Handicap Chase

Never ran on the Flat, so the fact he spent two seasons as a novice hurdler should not be held against him, especially as he was Grade 1-placed as a juvenile hurdler, finished sixth in the Triumph on only his fifth start and the following year was second to Peddlers Cross in a red-hot Neptune, finishing ahead of a subsequent Ascot Gold Cup winner, Champion Chase winner and Gold Cup runner-up. A season and a half spent chasing proved a bit of a waste as he never looked happy jumping fences, but a year off the track and a return to hurdles appears to have been the making of him as he has taken his form to a new level this term. A laboured second to the sadly now sidelined Big Buck's at Newbury hardly hinted at a revival, but Reve De Sivola was electric in the Long Walk at Ascot next time, winning by an eased-down 14 lengths, and he cemented his position at the top of the market when just outbattling Oscar Whisky by a neck in the Cleeve on trials day at Cheltenham. His chequered history masks the fact that he has been a remarkably consistent hurdler who hasn't finished out of the first two over hurdles since the 2009 Triumph, winning three of the four Grade 1s he has contested since then.

Oscar Whisky
8 b g; Trainer Nicky Henderson
Hurdles form 1141131F1151112, best RPR 170
Left-handed 141131115112, best RPR 170
Right-handed 1F1, best RPR 170
Cheltenham form 41311512, best RPR 170
At the festival 16 Mar 2010: Chased leaders, mistake 4th, right there when not much room 3 out, staying on same pace when not fluent last, no impression on leading trio run-in, finished fourth, beaten four lengths by Menorah in Supreme Novices' Hurdle

15 Mar 2011: Hit 2nd, chased leaders, not fluent 3rd, chased leader 3 out, led next, headed soon after, kept on gamely for 3rd but no chance with leading duo, finished third, beaten six and a quarter lengths by Hurricane Fly in Champion Hurdle

15 Mar 2012: Tracked leaders, not fluent 5th, close up after 3 out, not fluent 2 out, soon stalked winner, shaken up and weakened before last, finished fifth, beaten 13 and a half lengths by Big Buck's in World Hurdle

Nicky Henderson's remarkable win machine has looked as good as ever this term, adding two more easy victories to his tally over 2m4f-2m5f, distances over which he would arguably be unbeaten but for falling at the last when closing in on Overturn at Ascot last season. That form, giving the winner 8lb, gave him fine Champion Hurdle credentials, but connections opted to take on Big Buck's in the World Hurlde instead and it looked a clear case of him not staying when he faded quite badly after the last to finish fifth. Trainer was not convinced, however, expressing the belief there was something wrong, although his assertion that Oscar Whisky would not have won anything even at his preferred distance of 2m4f doesn't tally with the visual evidence. Still, with Big Buck's out of the way another crack at 3m was perfectly reasonable and it's hard to argue he didn't stay when he finished a neck second to Reve De Sivola in the Cleeve. However, while the bare form was not a mile off his best at 2m4f, that best came on the bridle in victory, so it's still easy to argue that 3m isn't really his trip. Class might get him there, but the Cleeve was run at a slow pace and it remains to be seen whether having to run the same distance nearly 50 seconds faster on better ground in March will prove more stamina sapping.

Monksland
6 b g; Trainer Noel Meade
Hurdles form 113121, best RPR 161
Left-handed 1131, best RPR 156
Right-handed 12, best RPR 161
Cheltenham form 3, best RPR 148
At the festival 14 Mar 2012: In touch, not fluent 4 out, headway next, hampered 2 out, rallied to retake 3rd soon after, kept on but never any chance with leading duo, finished third, beaten 18 lengths by Simonsig in Neptune

Proved a decent novice in only three runs, finishing a creditable if distant third to Simonsig in last season's Neptune on the last of them. He seems to have progressed again this season, winning a 2m Grade 2 at Down Royal on his return and then running second to Zaidpour in the Grade 1 Hatton's Grace over 2m4f at Fairyhouse before reversing form with that rival upped to 3m at Leopardstown. He looked beaten turning for home that day but stayed on really strongly, which is a good sign, although what the form amounts to is highly questionable as Zaidpour has never run Leopardstown particularly well and is 1-8 going left-handed compared with 6-8 the other way round. Would be slightly less

experienced than most recent winners of this and, on Racing Post Ratings, that sole 3m run gives him at least 10lb to find to play a hand, so he arguably looks short enough.

Bog Warrior
9 b g; Trainer Tony Martin
Hurdles form F1111, best RPR 164
Left-handed F, best RPR 123
Right-handed 1111, best RPR 164

Hugely talented hurdler/chaser who didn't see a racecourse until his seventh birthday but, having run in a bumper and a hurdle, was a Grade 1-winning chaser before his eighth. The wheels came off his chasing career last March, though, when he finished tailed off behind Flemenstar at Naas and he was switched back to hurdles after falling when beaten at the last on his return at Down Royal. Three easy successes have followed, the latest when he comfortably accounted for Zaidpour, whose only other defeat on a right-handed track came against Hurricane Fly, over 3m at Gowran. Fragile horse who needs plenty of dig and probably won't travel unless the ground is soft. Looks a massive player if it is, though.

Quevega
9 b m; Trainer Willie Mullins
Hurdles form 11931139111111, best RPR 159
Left-handed 319111, best RPR 157
Right-handed 1913111, best RPR 159
Cheltenham form 1111, best RPR 157
At the festival 10 Mar 2009: Held up in midfield, jumped slowly 2nd, closed on leaders from 3 out, led soon after 2 out, drew right away, impressive, won David Nicholson Mares' Hurdle by 14 lengths from United

16 Mar 2010: Held up in midfield, smooth progress to track leaders 3 out, decisive move from 2 out to lead well before last, shaken up and ran on strongly, won David Nicholson Mares' Hurdle by four and half lengths from Carole's Legacy

15 Mar 2011: Held up towards rear, steady headway 3 out, tracked leader 2 out, led on bit well before last, soon clear, impressive, won David Nicholson Mares' Hurdle by ten lengths from Sparky May

13 Mar 2012 Held up in mid-division, good headway 2 out, quickened to lead before last, driven clear run-in, readily, won David Nicholson Mares' Hurdle by four lengths from Kentford Grey Lady

Brilliant mare and one of several horses to take brief ante-post favouritism for this race after Big Buck's was ruled out. Reality has set in to a certain extent since, as she remains on course for a fifth consecutive Mares' Hurdle crown. She stands head and shoulders above all the other mares around and there has been talk of an audacious bid for a double 48 hours later, but realistically you'd have to think it doubtful. In any case, she has never run to a Racing Post Rating above 159, so with her 7lb mares' allowance would be no more than a strong contender and would probably have to run a career best to win. Can easily see her doing that if coming straight here, but that won't happen.

....

Peddlers Cross

8 b g; Trainer Donald McCain
Hurdles form 111111271, best RPR 170
Left-handed 11111127, best RPR 170
Right-handed 1, best RPR 139
Cheltenham form (hurdles only) 12, best RPR 170
At the festival 17 Mar 2010: Chased leaders, hard driven from 2 out, slight lead last, edged right under pressure run-in, all out, won Neptune Hurdle by a length and a half from Reve De Sivola

15 Mar 2011 Tracked leaders, led 4th, narrowly headed 2 out, driven to lead soon after, narrowly headed last but upsides, carried right run-in and kept on gamely under pressure, not pace of winner final 50yds, finished second, beaten one and a quarter lengths by Hurricane Fly in Champion Hurdle

15 Mar 2012: In rear but in touch, jumped right 7th, ridden and beaten 12th, no chance when blundered 4 out, finished eighth, beaten 73 lengths by Sir Des Champs in Jewson Novices' Chase

....

Top-class novice hurdler who won a vintage running of the Neptune in 2010 from this race's ante-post favourite Reve De Sivola and then gave the brilliant Hurricane Fly a fright in the following season's Champion Hurdle before running his only below-par race over hurdles when down the field at Aintree. Chasing career started well enough with two comfortable wins, but put firmly in his place at Kempton by Sprinter Sacre when not jumping well on his third outing and ran a stinker when well backed for the Jewson, having reportedly

been working all over Overturn, who ran second in the Champion Hurdle two days earlier. That prompted a change of plan and a return to hurdles for this campaign, but so far we have seen him only in a jumpers' bumper at Kempton, where he travelled like a class act but was run out of things by current Pertemps Final favourite Sam Winner, and a minor hurdle race at Musselburgh. He jumped with all his old aplomb then but didn't win as easily as the figures suggested he should, so the jury is out as to how much ability remains. Arguably the form horse if he returns to his best.

....

Solwhit

9 b g; Trainer Charles Byrnes
Hurdles form 15112111131162122221
Left-handed 113116221, best RPR 165
Right-handed 51121112122, best RPR 165
Cheltenham form 6, best RPR 153
At the festival 16 Mar 2010: Held up in midfield, close enough after 5th, lost place downhill before 3 out, struggling next, no chance after, plugged on, finished sixth, beaten 18 lengths by Binocular in Champion Hurdle

....

Really good two-miler a few seasons back and went off second favourite for the 2010 Champion Hurdle despite an interrupted prep. Below best there and spent the next year or so getting a good view of Hurricane Fly's backside before injury ruled him out for the best part of two years. Fine effort on return when running second to Bog Warrior over 2m4f in December, arguably achieving more then than when hacking up 19 days later from So Young at Naas. Clearly still has plenty of ability but yet to run beyond 3m and rated no better than 50-50 to turn up.

....

Grands Crus

8 gr g; Trainer David Pipe
Hurdles form 212111226, best RPR 171
Left-handed 1111226, best RPR 171
Right-handed 22, best RPR 119
Cheltenham form (hurdles) 112, best RPR 171

At the festival 17 Mar 2011: Held up in last early, headway after 3 out, going well tracking leaders before 2 out, ridden and chased winner approaching last, challenging run-in, not quicken and held final 100yds, finished second, beaten one and three-quarter lengths by Big Buck's in World Hurdle

14 Mar 2012: Held up, headway 13th (water), tracked leaders going well after 4 out, upsides 3 out, under pressure approaching 2 out, soon lost ground on front duo, weakened after last, finished fourth, beaten 18 lengths by Bobs Worth in RSA Chase

High-class grey who had a brilliant hurdles campaign two seasons ago, winning two decent handicaps and following up by taking the Grade 2 Cleeve in a canter by ten lengths. Was made the only danger to Big Buck's in the World Hurdle on the strength of that and though not up to that particular task was hardly disgraced in second. Last season he took like a duck to water over fences and looked to be heading right to the top following a deeply impressive victory in the Feltham at Kempton from Silviniaco Conti and Bobs Worth, both now leading contenders for the Gold Cup. Unfortunately nothing has gone right since as he was well beaten in the RSA, pulled up in the Paddy Power, gave a glimmer of hope with a distant third in the King George after a wind operation, but then was pulled up again in the Argento. Trainer took him out of the Gold Cup and it's either here or the Ryanair, but hard to back him with much confidence for anything.

Get Me Out Of Here *(above)*

9 b g; Trainer Jonjo O'Neill
Hurdles form 111127682P5222114P, best RPR 159
Left-handed 11112682P5222, best RPR 159
Right-handed 7114P, best RPR 157
Cheltenham form 26222, best RPR 159

At the festival 16 Mar 2010: In touch, headway on inside 3 out, tracking leaders when hampered 2 out, chased winner soon after, soon ridden, went left under pressure after last, stayed on well under pressure, not quite get up, finished second, beaten a head by Menorah in Supreme Novices' Hurdle

18 Mar 2011: Held up towards rear, good headway 2 out, hard driven to challenge last, led soon after, stayed on well under pressure run-in, headed last stride, finished second, beaten a nose by Final Approach in County Handicap Hurdle

14 Mar 2012: In touch, ridden to chase winner approaching last, stayed on under pressure, held final 100yds, finished second, beaten three and a half lengths by Son Of Flicka in Coral Cup

Useful and consistent hurdler when he gets his conditions and has a first and second in the Betfair (Totesport) Hurdle plus three runner-up spots at the Cheltenham Festival to his name. Looked on good terms with himself when winning over 2m at Kempton in October, but unfortunately he can't go a yard on heavy ground and finished tailed off and pulled up on his last two starts. Won't be winning anything if there's much cut in the ground but arguably one of the more interesting outsiders based on his Cheltenham record if the ground dries out.

OTHERS TO CONSIDER

Smad Place is the most likely winner out of those not mentioned. He was third last year but hasn't exactly covered himself in glory this term with a distant third to Tidal Bay at Wetherby and a 14-length second to Reve De Sivola in the Long Walk. There's a suspicion that, Big Buck's aside, last year's World Hurdle was not up to scratch, so he has plenty to prove.

World Hurdle results and trends

	FORM	WINNER	AGE & WGT	Adj RPR	SP	TRAINER	H.Runs	BEST RPR LAST 12 MONTHS (RUNS SINCE)
12	1-111	Big Buck's CD	9 11-10	182ᵀ	5-6F	P Nicholls	28⁽¹¹ᴳ⁾	won Gd1 Liverpool Hurdle (3m½f) (3)
11	11-11	Big Buck's CD	8 11-10	180ᵀ	10-11F	P Nicholls	23⁽¹³ᴳ⁾	won Gd1 World Hurdle (3m) (3)
10	11-11	Big Buck's CD	7 11-10	180ᵀ	5-6F	P Nicholls	19⁽¹⁴ᴳ⁾	won Gd1 Liverpool Hurdle (3m½f) (2)
09	1-U11	Big Buck's CD	6 11-10	170⁻⁷	6-1	P Nicholls	15⁽¹⁴ᴳˢ⁾	won Gd2 Cleeve Hurdle (3m) (0)
08	13-11	Inglis Drever C, D	9 11-10	174ᵀ	11-8F	H Johnson	20⁽¹⁷ᴳˢ⁾	won Newb Gd2 Long Dist Hdl (3m½f) (1)
07	1F-12	Inglis Drever CD	8 11-10	171⁻²	5-1	H Johnson	16⁽¹⁴ᴳˢ⁾	2nd Gd2 Cleeve Hurdle (3m) (0)
06	2-211	My Way De Solzen D	6 11-10	161⁻⁸	8-1	A King	10⁽²⁰ᴳ⁾	won Gd1 Long Walk Hurdle (3m) (1)
05	-2211	Inglis Drever	6 11-10	166⁻¹⁴	5-1	H Johnson	9⁽¹²ᴳ⁾	won Gd2 Kingwell Hurdle (2m) (0)
04	121-2	Iris's Gift CD, BF	7 11-10	177⁻³	9-2	J O'Neill	8⁽¹⁰ᴳ⁾	won Gd1 Sefton Novices' Hurdle (3m½f) (1)
03	11-12	Baracouda CD, BF	8 11-10	180ᵀ	9-4J	F Doumen (FR)	17⁽¹¹ᴳ⁾	won Gd1 Stayers' Hurdle (3m) (2)

WINS-RUNS: 5yo 0-7, 6yo 3-31, 7yo 2-36, 8yo 3-27, 9yo 2-18, 10yo 0-9, 11yo 0-7, 13yo 0-1 **FAVOURITES:** -£0.43

TRAINERS IN THIS RACE (w-pl-r): Paul Nicholls 4-0-7, Alan King 1-3-11, Jonjo O'Neill 1-1-11, Charlie Egerton 0-0-1, Colin Tizzard 0-0-1, David Pipe 0-1-6, Donald McCain 0-0-1, Emma Lavelle 0-0-2, Jennie Candlish 0-0-2, Malcolm Jefferson 0-0-1, Nicky Henderson 0-1-7, Noel Meade 0-0-1, Oliver McKiernan 0-0-1, Philip Hobbs 0-0-3, Tom George 0-0-1, Willie Mullins 0-2-13

FATE OF FAVOURITES: 1223F14111 **POSITION OF WINNER IN MARKET:** 1234313111

Key trends

🏇 Top-two finish last time out, 10/10

🏇 Ran no more than four times since August, 10/10

🏇 Won a Graded hurdle over at least 3m, 9/10

🏇 Not out of the first two all hurdle starts that season, 9/10

🏇 RPR of at least 165, 9/10

🏇 Ran between eight and 20 times over hurdles (Big Buck's in the past two years is the only exception), 8/10

🏇 Aged six to eight, 8/10

🏇 Previously ran at the festival, 8/10

Other factors

🏇 The last four winners aged nine or more were previous winners of the race

🏇 A five-year-old has never won this race. However, four of the six to have run in the past ten seasons were placed

🏇 Seven winners had finished first or second in this race before

🏇 All four Irish winners since the mid-1980s prepped in the Boyne Hurdle at Navan

🏇 Four winners contested the Long Walk Hurdle, where they finished 2111

🏇 The previous year's winner has returned six times in the past decade. The overall record is five wins and one second

Hunt Ball could try for another festival success here after last year's Pulteney win

The David Pipe-trained Salut Flo last year became the first successful favourite in this race since the 1999 victory of Majadou, who perhaps not coincidentally was trained by Pipe's father Martin. Apart from that pair, only one other winner in the past 14 runnings has gone off shorter than 12-1 and overall this race (established in 1951 and traditionally known as the Mildmay of Flete) has been the biggest graveyard for favourites at the festival with just four winning.

In past years this was one of the best weight-carrying races at the festival, with several winners scoring under 11st-plus, but the recent trend has been towards the bottom end of the handicap. Fourteen of the past 17 winners have carried 10st 10lb or less – including all of the first three in the past four years. Since the 141-rated Majadou, ten of the past 12 winners have been in the ratings band from 128 to 139.

Cheltenham form is important, with most of the recent winners having run at the festival before, but Salut Flo was a rare winner to emerge from the big December handicap chase (known this season as the Paul Stewart Ironspine Charity Challenge Gold Cup) – likewise, the Paddy Power Gold Cup tends to be a poor guide. Form at Warwick, Sandown and Kempton in February is worth noting.

The bigger stables struggle to get runners in the race at the lower end of the handicap and Paul Nicholls has not won in 22 attempts (second and fourth are his best showings). Nicky Henderson has been more successful, with two winners and a third from his last 11 runners that have been in the ideal ratings band. Another trainer to note is Venetia Williams, who has form figures of 221PP17F0 since 2005 with runners in the ideal ratings band.

There has been a single Irish-trained winner in the long history of this race.

Byrne Group Plate results and trends

	FORM	WINNER	AGE & WGT	OR	SP	TRAINER	C.Runs	BEST RPR LAST 12 MONTHS (RUNS SINCE)
12	112/0	Salut Flo	7 10-10	137-5	9-2F	D Pipe	6(22G)	12th Atlantic4 Gold Cup hcap ch (2m5f) (0)
11	152F1	Holmwood Legend (5x) D	10 10-6	130-5	25-1	P Rodford	12(20G)	won Sandown class 3 hcap ch (2m4½f) (0)
10	-3144	Great Endeavour D	6 10-1	135-11	18-1	D Pipe	3(24G)	4th Fontwell class 3 nov ch (2m6f) (1)
09	20272	Something Wells	8 10-7	139-1	33-1	V Williams	10(23GS)	2nd Ascot class 2 hcap ch (2m5½f) (2)
08	547U5	Mister McGoldrick D	11 11-7	145-6	66-1	S Smith	33(22GS)	4th Wetherby class 2 hcap ch (2m½f) (2)
07	6-134	Idole First C, D	8 10-7	136T	12-1	V Williams	8(23GS)	won Kempton class 3 hcap ch (2m4½f) (2)
06	0-433	Non So	8 11-3	137T	14-1	N Henderson	10(24G)	3rd Wetherby class 2 hcap ch (2m4½f) (0)
05	-2384	Liberthine	6 10-1	128-6	25-1	N Henderson	6(22G)	3rd Kempton class 2 hcap ch (2m4½f) (2)
04	22141	Tikram (8oh) D	7 10-0	133-9	12-1	G Moore	5(16G)	2nd Cheltenham class 2 nov ch (2m½f) (3)
03	/376-	Young Spartacus C, D	10 10-9	147-9	16-1	H Daly	14(19G)	3rd Peterborough Chase (2m4f) (0)

WINS-RUNS: 5yo 0-3, 6yo 2-22, 7yo 2-37, 8yo 3-60, 9yo 0-38, 10yo 2-33, 11yo 1-17, 12yo 0-2, 13yo 0-3 **FAVOURITES:** -£4.50

FATE OF FAVOURITES: U24F0F2231 **POSITION OF WINNER IN MARKET:** 0606500001

OR 120-134 3-13-73, **135-149** 7-15-125, **150-164** 0-2-17

Key trends

🐎Won at Class 3 level or higher, 10/10

🐎Won between 2m3f and 2m5f, 9/10

🐎Ran within the last 40 days, 8/10

🐎Top-five finish last time out, 8/10

🐎Ran between three and 14 times over fences, 9/10

🐎Carried no more than 10st 10lb, 8/10

🐎Officially rated 128 to 139, 8/10 (both exceptions in the mid-140s)

🐎Ran at a previous festival, 7/10 (three had run in the County Hurdle)

Other factors

🐎None of the last ten winners had figured prominently in one of the big 2m4f handicaps run at Cheltenham earlier in the season

🐎The two novices to win were rated 133 and 135

🐎Ireland has not won this Double-U-Again in 1982

🐎Last year Salut Flo was the first winning favourite since Majadou (1999), who was also the last winner before him to be sent off at shorter than 12-1

Notes

Sunnyhillboy (3) comes from the clouds to win last year's Kim Muir

This is a highlight of the season for amateur riders and the best jockeys are in big demand – the non-claiming amateurs Jamie Codd, Richard Harding and the now retired Richard Burton have each had two victories in the past eight runnings.

With little between most of the runners nowadays (few get in off a mark in the 120s), the significant ratings bands appear to be moving upwards. The top-weight won in 2009 and 2010, Junior was successful under 11st 6lb in 2011 and last year the first four came from the highest four marks in the handicap – the last four winners account for all but one of the top five weight-carrying performances in the past 30 years.

A number of shrewd trainers target this race and their runners merit plenty of respect. Seven of the past 11 winners have come from the Pipe stable, Nicky Henderson and Donald McCain. David Pipe, whose father Martin won this race on three occasions, had the first two in 2011. Henderson has had three successes in all, including a couple of 1-2s, while McCain has had two winners (Ferdy Murphy has also won twice).

In contrast, Paul Nicholls has had one placed horse from 14 runners and there has been only a single Irish-trained winner since the mid-1970s.

This can often be a plot race and punters should give consideration to runners with a light preparation and who may not have shown good recent form, with seven of the past ten winners unplaced last time out.

Eight- and nine-year-olds have done best in recent years, accounting for 15 of the past 19 winners from around half the total runners in that period. Only four of the last 33 winners were aged seven or younger, yet runners aged six and seven have been favourite in three of the past five years and second favourite on the other two occasions.

Since Glyde Court in 1985 only three novices have been successful, which is the lowest return for any long-term festival handicap. It appears many trainers don't want to risk the novice/amateur combination.

Kim Muir Handicap Chase results and trends

FORM	WINNER	AGE & WGT	OR	SP	TRAINER	C.Runs	BEST RPR LAST 12 MONTHS (RUNS SINCE)
12 -37P9	Sunnyhillboy C	9 11-11	142-1	13-2F	J O'Neill	11(23G)	3rd Irish Grand National (3m5f) (3)
11 31-32	Junior	8 11-6	134-4	10-3F	D Pipe	6(24G)	3rd Cheltenham Gd3 hcap ch (3m3½f) (0)
10 0-311	Ballabriggs D	9 11-12	140T	9-1	D McCain	10(24G)	won Ayr class 2 hcap ch (3m1f) (0)
09 14339	Character Building D	9 11-12	139-10	16-1	J Quinn	10(24GS)	3rd Cheltenham cl 2 hcap ch (3m2½f) (1)
08 1-43P	High Chimes	9 10-10	127-7	14-1	E Williams	7(24GS)	3rd Haydock class 2 hcap ch (3m) (1)
07 36120	Cloudy Lane D, BF	7 10-11	124T	15-2F	D McCain	5(24G)	2nd Newcastle class 3 nov ch (3m) (1)
06 3621P	You're Special C, BF	9 10-12	125-6	33-1	F Murphy	18(21G)	won Doncaster class 2 hcap ch (3m2f) (1)
05 31522	Juveigneur	8 11-7	128-6	12-1	N Henderson	19(24G)	2nd Newbury class 3 hcap ch (3m) (0)
04 -42P9	Maximize D	10 10-6	127-7	40-1	M Pipe	19(22G)	2nd Chelt class 4 am hcap ch (3m½f) (2)
03 P589-	Royal Predica	9 10-13	134-3	33-1	M Pipe	27(23G)	5th Wm Hill Handicap Chase (3m½f) (2)

WINS-RUNS: 5yo 0-1, 6yo 0-17, 7yo 1-49, 8yo 2-53, 9yo 6-51, 10yo 1-30, 11yo 0-18, 12yo 0-10, 13yo 0-4 **FAVOURITES:** £10.33

FATE OF FAVOURITES: 23001U0311 **POSITION OF WINNER IN MARKET:** 0050185311

OR 114-123 0-6-31, **124-133** 5-17-131, **134-143** 5-7-71

Key trends

🏇Rated within 8lb of RPR top-rated, 10/10

🏇Ran over at least 3m last time out, 10/10

🏇Officially rated 124 to 142, 10/10

🏇Aged seven to nine, 9/10

🏇Won a handicap chase, 8/10

🏇Won over at least 3m, 8/10 (both exceptions had placed over further)

🏇Finished in first three in either or both of last two starts, 7/10

🏇Had run at a previous festival, 6/10

Other factors

🏇Ireland has not won this since Greasepaint in 1983

🏇Four winners had run within the past 33 days, the other six had been off for at least 58

🏇None of the last six winners had more than 11 chase runs

🏇Three winners were ridden by claiming amateurs but seven of the last eight were ridden by non-claiming amateurs

🏇Three winners had recorded a top-three finish at Cheltenham earlier in the season

Notes

Friday, March 15

(New Course)

🐎 JCB Triumph Hurdle

🐎 Vincent O'Brien County Hurdle

🐎 Albert Bartlett Novices' Hurdle

🐎 Betfred Cheltenham Gold Cup

🐎 CGA Foxhunter Chase

🐎 Martin Pipe Conditional Jockeys' Handicap Hurdle

🐎 Johnny Henderson Grand Annual Chase

1.30 JCB Triumph Hurdle   C4/RUK
2m1f   Grade 1   £120,000

Countrywide Flame at 33-1 last year was a rare big-priced winner in the recent history of the Triumph, which has become a more predictable race dominated by the big stables since the expansion of the festival in 2005 and the addition of the Fred Winter as an alternative. It's not surprising therefore that early leaders in the ante-post market included Rolling Star (Nicky Henderson), Far West (Paul Nicholls), Diakali and Blood Cotil (Willie Mullins) and L'Unique (Alan King) – those trainers have won seven of the past ten runnings between them. The Dessie Hughes-trained Our Conor made a big splash with his victory in the Grade 1 Spring Juvenile Hurdle, while Swnymor (Tim Vaughan) and Kashmir Peak (for last year's winning trainer John Quinn) are other leading contenders.

Our Conor
4 b g; Trainer Dessie Hughes
Hurdles form 111, best RPR 146
Left-handed 11, best RPR 146
Right-handed 1, best RPR 132

Didn't see a racecourse until May last year but was progressing on the Flat before trainer Dessie Hughes switched his attention to hurdles and he's carried on doing so in three starts since. Was an easy winner of a maiden and a Grade 3 before lining up at Leopardstown for the Grade 1 Spring Juvenile Hurdle, Ireland's best trial, and he cut down the leader and 7-4 favourite Diakali going to the last before extending his advantage all the way to the line. Historically this is Ireland's worst novice hurdle at the festival, but Finale winner Ruacana finished nine and a quarter lengths back in third, so there's every reason to think this one is a particularly strong contender this year. Sire only just got 1m but dam responsible for a few middle-distance winners on the Flat and staying chaser Gidam Gidam and there's no doubt he saw out the 2m well, which augurs well for the stiffer test to come.

Rolling Star
4 b g; Trainer Nicky Henderson
Hurdles form (both left-handed) 11, best RPR 149
Cheltenham form 1, best RPR 149

Seven goes on the Flat in the French provinces without a win, but got the job done at the first time of asking over hurdles at Auteuil and soon found his way to Nicky Henderson after that. Showed plenty of speed to cut down odds-on

Irish Saint in the Triumph trial at Cheltenham in January, the pair having pulled 30 lengths clear of the rest, and looks highly promising, although the trainer of the runner-up sees his horse as a staying chaser of the future and if the Betfair market is right won't be taking the winner on again. Plenty of potential without really giving the impression he's another Zaynar or Soldatino for the stable.

Far West
4 b g; Trainer Paul Nicholls
Hurdles form 31111, best RPR 145
Left-handed 3111, best RPR 145
Right-handed 1, best RPR
Cheltenham form 11, best RPR 145

Unraced on the Flat, which would make him an unusual winner, but has been at the top of the tree at Paul Nicholls's yard all season and impressed on his second British start when a seven-length winner of a Grade 2 at Cheltenham in November, although there are question marks over the form with the Nicky Henderson-trained runner-up getting chinned at odds-on next time. Didn't have anything to beat when long odds-on back at Cheltenham in December but then saw off leading Supreme fancy River Maigue at Ascot in February, albeit in receipt of a handy 9lb. Has speed as well as stamina and very much a player.

Swnymor
4 b g; Trainer Tim Vaughan
Hurdles form (both left-handed) 1F, best RPR 135

Rated 87 on the Flat and was an impressive

odds-on winner on his first try for Tim Vaughan at Newbury in December, before heading to the Grade 1 Finale at Chepstow just over two weeks later. Was well backed to follow up and looked sure to do just that as he'd taken command going to the last but fell. That sort of form puts him right in the mix and there's no doubt he's going to stay the trip well, but could do with a confidence booster after what was quite a heavy tumble.

Kashmir Peak
4 b g; Trainer John Quinn
Hurdles form 11U, best RPR 129
Left-handed 1, best RPR 129
Right-handed 1U, best RPR 121

Represents last year's winning trainer John Quinn and received glowing praise from him when winning easily on his debut at Market Rasen in November (form nothing special). Duly improved on that when causing a minor surprise in a six-runner Grade 2 at Doncaster the following month (odds-on third had been second to Far West the time before). Runner-up Sametegal was well backed to turn that form around at Musselburgh next time on 3lb better terms but, while he duly won, Kashmir Peak unseated at the fourth-last when yet to be asked. Trainer said he has "one for good ground and one for soft" and this one is the good-ground performer despite a pedigree that suggests soft shouldn't be an issue.

Diakali
4 gr g; Trainer Willie Mullins
Hurdles form 112, best RPR 144
Left-handed 2, best RPR 140
Right-handed 11, best RPR 144

Looked like developing into Ireland's main hope after two front-running wins at Gowran and Punchestown, the latter in a Grade 3, but beat only eight rivals in all and on second start showed a tendency to get in a little close to his hurdles. That jumping was found out when he was upped in class again for the Grade 1 Spring Juvenile Hurdle on Leopardstown's trials day in February. Attempting to make all again, he was erratic at his hurdles and proved a stting duck for the smooth-travelling Our Conor. Hard to see him turning that form around and it won't be easy making all in a big-field Triumph, which this year's looks sure to be given the absence of a standout contender.

Lac Fontana
4 b g; Trainer Paul Nicholls
Hurdles form (left-handed) 2, best RPR 99

Must have impressed someone to be as short as 14-1 in mid-February as his debut over hurdles on Betfair Hurdle day left a lot to be desired. Well backed, he was given 16lb and a two-length beating by the year-older Chatterbox, who was well on top at the line. The winning time was pretty dreadful and this borderline Listed-class Flat performer may do better with a stronger gallop but he needs to as well as brushing up his jumping. Trainer talking of upping him in grade for his next outing, so clearly thinks a bit of him.

L'Unique
4 b f; Trainer Alan King
Hurdles form 411, best RPR 128
Left-handed 41, best RPR 128
Right-handed 1, best RPR 115

Represents a trainer who knows a thing or two about winning Triumph Hurdles and he clearly holds this filly in high regard. Sent off favourite for a Listed juvenile contest at Aintree in December, she sluiced home by 12 lengths and, while the race looked weak for the grade, the runner-up and distant third have both won races since. Faced a straightforward task at Kempton in January and again did it well. Jumping an asset, but trainer said he views her as a long-term chasing prospect and is not certain to run her. That said, he's also talking about the Adonis at Kempton, and if she wins that she'll have to run.

Hidden Justice *(below, left)*
4 b g; Trainer John Quinn
Hurdles form (both left-handed) 11, best RPR 125

The trainer's soft-ground horse for this, he ran his best-ever race off a mark of 69 on his final Flat start when second on heavy in October and made an immediate impact on his hurdles debut at Wetherby over Christmas, again on heavy ground. In a race that looked to have some interesting recruits (a rare Guillaume Macaire-trained 7-4 and a 13-8 favourite with experience and a much better Flat record), he bolted up by 15 lengths from Only Orsenfoolsies, who won by eight lengths

next time. Hidden Justice didn't need to be as good to follow up at Catterick next time, but it's encouraging he confirmed his original impression with a comfortable five-length win, again from a next-time-out winner. Seems to have impressed Ladbrokes more then everyone else as they were only 12-1 in mid-February compared with a general 25-1.

Chris Pea Green *(above)*
4 b g; Trainer Gary Moore
Hurdles form 11, best RPR 129
Left-handed 1, best RPR 111
Right-handed 1, best RPR 129

Speedily bred but didn't run on the Flat, instead making a winning bumper debut in November at Huntingdon before seemingly not handling Polytrack in his bid to double up two weeks later. Was then sent off 8-1 for a fairly dreadful six-runner maiden hurdle featuring a 4-11 favourite who could manage only fourth, but duly dotted up by 20 lengths. That form was nothing special and he was made a 12-1 chance for the old Chatteris Fen at Huntingdon before again spreadeagling the field. Topspeed figures pretty poor, though, and you'd have to worry about whether he could do it in a strongly run race over an extra furlong.

OTHERS TO CONSIDER

Rolling Star's Cheltenham victim **Irish Saint** boasts better form than most coming into this race, but his position in the Betfair market (on offer at 85 in mid-February) suggests connections are leaning towards missing out with a horse considered to have a big future as a chaser. **Blood Cotil** was considered by many to be more than just a second-string to Willie Mullins's Diakali in the Spring, but ran like one and has a lot of ground to make up. Third in that race, **Ruacana** won the Finale at Chepstow thanks to Swnymor's last-flight fall and he also has ground to make up, although he at least looks like he's going to appreciate an end-to-end gallop. **Sametegal** gives Paul Nicholls yet another string to his bow without looking anything special, while **Vasco Du Ronceray** looks to have been found out after two short-priced defeats. It's also worth noting that two of the last three winners weren't even seen in Britain until the Adonis at Kempton at the end of February, so the entries for that – at least from the likes of Nicholls and Henderson – need to be monitored.

Triumph Hurdle results and trends

	FORM	WINNER	AGE & WGT	Adj RPR	SP	TRAINER	H.Runs	BEST RPR LAST 12 MONTHS (RUNS SINCE)
12	12123	Countrywide Flame D	4 11-0	151-6	33-1	J Quinn	6(20G)	2nd Gd1 Finale Hurdle (2m½f) (1)
11	1	Zarkandar	4 11-0	155-2	13-2	P Nicholls	1(23G)	won Gd2 Adonis Nov Hdl (2m) (0)
10	4211	Soldatino D	4 11-0	150-6	6-1	N Henderson	2(17G)	won Gd2 Adonis Nov Hdl (2m) (0)
09	11	Zaynar D	4 11-0	152-6	11-2	N Henderson	2(18GS)	won Newb class 4 nov hdl (2m½f) (1)
08	12	Celestial Halo D, BF	4 11-0	145-11	5-1	P Nicholls	2(14GS)	won Newb class 3 nov hdl (2m½f) (1)
07	12111	Katchit CD	4 11-0	150-10	11-2	A King	6(23GS)	2nd Wetherby Listed nov hdl (2m) (3)
06	811	Detroit City D	4 11-0	152-2	7-2F	P Hobbs	3(17G)	won Sandown class 3 nov hdl (2m½f) (0)
05	111	Penzance D	4 11-0	137-13	9-1	A King	3(23G)	won won Gd2 Adonis Nov Hdl (2m) (0)
04	331	Made In Japan D	4 11-0	127-23	20-1	P Hobbs	3(23G)	won Sandown class 3 nov hdl (2m½) (0)
03	1841	Spectroscope	4 11-0	133-20	20-1	J O'Neill	4(27G)	won Kemp class 3 nov hdl (2m) (0)

FAVOURITES: -£5.50

TRAINERS IN THIS RACE (w-pl-r): Alan King 2-4-14, Nicky Henderson 2-1-11, Paul Nicholls 2-0-12, Philip Hobbs 2-2-6, John Quinn 1-0-2, Jonjo O'Neill 1-0-3, Brian Ellison 0-0-1, Charlie Longsdon 0-0-2, Colin Tizzard 0-0-1, Dermot Weld 0-2-3, Dessie Hughes 0-0-2, David Pipe 0-0-4, Donald McCain 0-0-2, Gary Moore 0-0-5, Gordon Elliott 0-0-4, John Ferguson 0-0-1, John Murphy 0-0-4, Sabrina Harty 0-1-1, Tim Easterby 0-0-1, Tim Vaughan 0-0-3, Tom George 0-0-2, Venetia Williams 0-1-7, Willie Mullins 0-1-9

FATE OF FAVOURITES: 3031022443 **POSITION OF WINNER IN MARKET:** 0041223330

Key trends

🏇Last ran between 19 and 55 days ago, 10/10

🏇Ran between two and six times over hurdles, 9/10

🏇Won at least 50 per cent of hurdle races, 9/10

🏇By Group 1-winning sire, 9/10

🏇Pre-race RPR of at least 127, 8/10

🏇Won last time out, 8/10

Other factors

🏇Zarkandar is the only once-raced hurdler to win in the past 30 years

🏇Only three winners were undefeated over hurdles

🏇Four had won Graded hurdle events (three had landed the Adonis at Kempton in February)

🏇The last winner of Chepstow's Finale Hurdle to win this race was Mysilv in 1994

🏇Of the seven who raced on the Flat in Britain and Ireland, six had recorded an RPR of at least 86

🏇Seven had won and three placed over middle distances (1m2f-1m6f)

🏇Since the introduction of the Fred Winter Hurdle in 2005, seven of the eight winners have come from the first four in the betting

Notes

In recent years this race has been won by Ireland or one of the big British stables (Paul Nicholls, Martin Pipe, Philip Hobbs and Jonjo O'Neill have saddled the only British winners since 2000). Nicholls formerly had some success controlling the handicap, winning in 2004, 2006 and 2009, but has found that more difficult in the face of the Irish onslaught.

Five of the last six winners have been from Ireland, and four of them were trained by a Mullins. Willie Mullins had his first festival handicap victory in this race with Thousand Stars in 2010 and followed up in 2011 with Final Approach (he didn't have a runner last year).

Alderwood last year was the seventh winner in a row rated in the 130s and, although at eight he was older than the recent norm (eight five-year-olds and two six-year-olds have won in the past 14 runnings), he was still a novice. That made him the eighth winner in the last nine runnings to have been a first-or-second season hurdler – a critical factor to consider nowadays.

In more than half a century only two winners have broken the effective ceiling weight of 11st 2lb – Blowing Wind carried 11st 8lb in 1998 and Spirit Leader 11st 7lb in 2003. What those two high-weight winners had in common was that they were coming off big handicap wins (the Imperial Cup for Blowing Wind and the Tote Gold Trophy for Spirit Leader).

The Betfair Hurdle and Boylesports.com Handicap Hurdle have been the key races in recent years – seven of the past 11 winners had run in one of those hot contests (as well as a runner-up and two thirds in the last two years). With such good form guides available, most of the winners have been prominent in the betting. Nine of the past 14 winners were in the first four in the market – although four of the last five were 20-1 (three times) and 50-1.

Another trainer to note is Philip Hobbs, whose two County winners had made the frame in the Betfair Hurdle. He didn't have a runner last year but in 2011 had the third and fourth at big prices. Nicky Henderson has not won this race since 1997 but is always likely to have the right type.

Abbey Lane looks a leading contender after winning the Boylesports

County Hurdle results and trends

FORM	WINNER	AGE & WGT	OR	SP	TRAINER	H.Runs	BEST RPR LAST 12 MONTHS (RUNS SINCE)
12	10120 Alderwood D	8 11-1	139-3	20-1	T Mullins (IRE)	12(26G)	won Killarney hcap hdl (2m6f) (2)
11	13-51 Final Approach	5 10-12	139-8	10-1	W Mullins (IRE)	4(26G)	won MCR Hcap Hurdle (2m) (0)
10	40110 Thousand Stars D	6 10-5	134-5	20-1	W Mullins (IRE)	14(28G)	14th MCR Hcap Hurdle (2m) (0)
09	1349 American Trilogy D	5 11-0	135-7	20-1	P Nicholls	4(27GS)	3rd Cheltenham Gd2 nov hdl (2m½f) (2)
08	22233 Silver Jaro BF	5 10-13	132-11	50-1	T Hogan (IRE)	10(22GS)	3rd Pierse Hcap Hurdle (2m) (1)
07	-1713 Pedrobob	9 10-0	135-10	12-1	A Mullins (IRE)	7(28GS)	3rd Gd3 Tote Trophy Hcap Hdl (2m½f) (0)
06	U1131 Desert Quest (4x) D	6 10-10	131-4	4-1J	P Nicholls	8(29G)	won Newbury class 3 hcap hdl (2m½f) (0)
05	60048 Fontanesi (5oh) D	5 10-0	128-2	16-1	M Pipe	16(30G)	2nd Aintree class 3 hcap hdl (2m½f) (9)
04	-1238 Sporazene	5 10-13	151-6	7-1J	P Nicholls	7(23G)	2nd Newbury Listed hcap hdl (2m½f) (2)
03	23151 Spirit Leader D	7 11-7	140-19	10-1	J Harrington (IRE)	14(28G)	won Gd3 Tote Trophy hcap hdl (2m½f) (0)

WINS-RUNS: 5yo 5-52, 6yo 2-80, 7yo 1-66, 8yo 1-34, 9yo 1-20, 10yo 0-10, 11yo 0-4, 12yo 0-1 **FAVOURITES:** -£3.50

FATE OF FAVOURITES: P101026000 **POSITION OF WINNER IN MARKET:** 4181407040

OR 122-134 4-15-111 **135-148** 5-14-144 **149-161** 1-1-12

Key trends

🐎Achieved career-best RPR of at least 129 on a left-handed track, 10/10

🐎Officially rated 128 to 144, 9/10 (last seven in the 130s)

🐎Ran between four and 14 times over hurdles, 9/10

🐎Carried no more than 11st 1lb, 9/10

🐎No previous festival form, 9/10

🐎Ran in the last 35 days, 8/10

🐎Aged five or six, 7/10

Other factors

🐎No winner was more than 5lb out of the handicap

🐎There have been three winning novices since 1996 – all were rated no higher than 135

🐎Eighteen of the 30 placed horses started 25-1 or bigger

🐎Three winners ran in the Betfair Hurdle (formerly Totesport Trophy), finishing 183; four ran in the Boylesports Hurdle (formerly MCR and Pierse), finishing 5301

🐎Paul Nicholls has had three winners, two seconds and a fourth in the past nine years

Notes

2.40 Albert Bartlett Novices' Hurdle — C4/RUK
3m — Grade 1 — £120,000

This is likely to have a fluid picture until close to the day, with running plans from the big stables for the Supreme and Neptune likely to dictate what ends up here. In particular, the targets for the Willie Mullins-trained Ballycasey, Pont Alexandre and Champagne Fever will have a major bearing on the market. At Fishers Cross appears to have a leading chance for Rebecca Curtis but also has alternatives – the Neptune or even the Pertemps Final. David Pipe also has handicap options with Gevrey Chambertin. Cloudy Copper and Taquin Du Seuil have been prominent in the betting for Jonjo O'Neill, who has won the race twice, and Charles Byrnes (who won with Weapon's Amnesty in 2009) has been eyeing this all season for Our Vinnie. Coneygree, half-brother to Hennessy winner Carruthers, would be a popular winner for Mark Bradstock.

Ballycasey
6 gr g; Trainer Willie Mullins
Hurdles form (both right-handed) 11, best RPR 144

Unbeaten in three starts for Willie Mullins. Landed a decent bumper from subsequent dual Grade 3-winning hurdler Our Vinnie on his debut in December 2011 and then was off the track for a year. Easy winner of a maiden hurdle at Clonmel on his return (form nothing special, with all his victims to run since largely well beaten) and seemed to improve on that when an unextended winner of a five-runner novice hurdle at Thurles. Has been brought along a lot more slowly than many of the Mullins novice hurdlers and will clearly be a chaser in time, but jumps very well and, as a son of Presenting, he ought to be better still when the ground dries out, if it ever does. Hasn't run anything approaching a fast time, but that is true of most this season.

At Fishers Cross
6 b g; Trainer Rebecca Curtis
Hurdles form 251111, best RPR 154
Left-handed 21111, best RPR 154
Right-handed 5, best RPR 110
Cheltenham form 11, best RPR 154

Dual bumper winner who was chinned at odds-on on his hurdling debut a day after this race was run last year and closed that season with a heavy defeat at Punchestown. Has obviously grown up a lot since, as he is unbeaten in four this season, taking sizeable steps up the ladder each time. Ready win in a 3m handicap hurdle at Cheltenham confirmed his stamina for this and he then surprised leading Neptune fancy The New One in a Grade 2 over 2m5f on trials day. The highly regarded runner-up looked to have left him for dead between the last two and may have gone too soon on the sticky ground, but the form is hot whatever way you look at it and the extra three furlongs in a strongly run race will play to his strengths. Trainer doesn't want the ground to dry out as the slower surface helps his sometimes suspect jumping. In the Neptune and very short for that with some firms (7-1) but nearly 300 on Betfair at the time of writing.

Gevrey Chambertin
5 gr g; Trainer David Pipe
Hurdles form 111, best RPR 147
Left-handed 11, best RPR 140
Right-handed 1, best RPR 147

Full-brother to 2011 Feltham Chase winner Grands Crus and has achieved a fair bit more as a novice hurdler than his three-year-older sibling did, winning all three at up to 2m4f. Had to battle to win under a penalty at Haydock in November but improved again when ready winner of a handicap at Wincanton, taking it up at the third and going clear in the straight for a seven-length win. Outsiders filled the places and both have been soundly beaten since, which makes you wonder what he beat, but he was backed as if defeat was out of the question and is clearly highly regarded. Also in the Neptune but shorter in the betting for this race, even though he needs to improve again and get the trip better than his brother.

Coneygree
6 b g; Trainer Mark Bradstock
Hurdles form (all left-handed) 1113, best RPR 148
Cheltenham form 113, best RPR 148

Bred by the late Lord Oaksey and a half-brother to popular Hennessy-winning chaser Carruthers. Could prove just as good too. Having adopted his sibling's heart-on-sleeve front-running tactics, he ran away with his first three starts over hurdles, including two Grade 2 affairs at Cheltenham. Was partiularly impressive when slamming 155-rated chaser Aerial upped to 3m in December but could not match that form when only third to At Fishers Cross and The New One dropped back to 2m5f on trials day. However, it's fair to say that the pedestrian pace set by Mattie Batchelor did not play to his strengths and he'll surely go a bit harder next time, even allowing for the extra three furlongs. Is probably always going to be at his best in deep ground, but may get it this year.

African Gold
5 b g; Trainer Nigel Twiston-Davies
Hurdles form 21111, best RPR 133
Left-handed 1111, best RPR 133
Right-handed 2, best RPR 110

Has won five of his six starts overall, as he began his career with a bumper success in May. Trainer decided to take the handicap route after he was awarded a mark of 118 for his novice win at Wetherby and he won his next two, albeit having to work hard both times, the second off 129. Was put back into novice company at Doncaster, comfortably seeing off the Nicky Henderson-trained favourite Close Touch, but arguably didn't have to improve. Has an official mark of 135, which means he'd be getting 17lb off At Fishers Cross in a handicap, so not easy to see why he's as short as 12-1 with Hills, especially as trainer has nominated the Pertemps as an option.

Our Vinnie
6 b/br g; Trainer Charles Byrnes
Hurdles form 72113, best RPR 141
Left-handed 723, best RPR 136
Right-handed 11, best RPR 141
Cheltenham form 2, best RPR 136

Has plenty of experience and shrewd trainer gave him an early look at Cheltenham when he was well backed to win a staying novice in October, which he would have done but for mistakes at the last two flights (jumped second-last too well and nearly slipped, made a right hash of the last). Showed a fine attitude to get within a head of the now 140-rated winner and those battling qualities again in evidence for wins in two Grade 3s on bad ground in Ireland, both at 3m. Couldn't live with the drop back to 2m4f behind Pont Alexandre in January, but that was to be expected as he's a proper stayer. Will relish a strongly run race and better ground if he gets it and one of the more interesting ones at a double-figure price.

Taquin Du Seuil
6 b/br g; Trainer Jonjo O'Neill
Hurdles form 1211, best RPR 150
Left-handed 11, best RPR 150
Right-handed 21, best RPR 139

Is also in the Neptune and is a shorter price for that with most firms but, for the conspiracy theorists among you, in mid-February he was only 6-1 with Ladbrokes for this (compared with 16-1 generally) yet a top-priced 10-1 for the Neptune. Wherever he ends up he's going to warrant plenty of respect as his only defeat in four hurdles starts came against My Tent Or Yours over 2m at Ascot. Since stepping up to 2m4-2m5f he's been an easy winner of his last two, a Grade 2 at Sandown and then the Grade 1 Challow at Newbury, for which he was heavily backed and ran out a nine-length winner. Will have a leading chance if he comes here.

Inish Island
7 ch g; Trainer Willie Mullins
Hurdles form 463343121, best RPR 144
Left-handed 642, best RPR 143
Right-handed 433311, best RPR 144
Cheltenham form 2, best RPR 143

Didn't get off the mark until seventh start over hurdles but has improved again since, although was a well-held second to At Fishers Cross in a handicap at Cheltenham when getting 3lb. Trainer suggested owners might like to come here following Clonmel success in February, but seemed keener to stay at home himself.

Road To Riches *(above)*
6 b g; Trainer Noel Meade
Hurdles form (both right-handed) 11, best RPR 141

One defeat, when falling at the first on his debut in a point-to-point in April, but otherwise won one of those and has been odds-on winner of three starts under rules, the first a Naas bumper. Was a 1-6 chance to win his maiden hurdle at Punchestown and did so by a comfortable two and a quarter lengths from Pride Ofthe Parish, who won next time and then ran Our Vinnie to a short head in a Grade 3. Again won easily enough upped to Grade 3 company at Cork over 3m despite a last-flight blunder and clearly has immense promise. Trainer called him a "horse for next year really", so whether he travels is another matter.

Utopie Des Bordes
5 b m; Trainer Nicky Henderson
Hurdles form 262289311, best RPR 136
Left-handed 26228931, best RPR 120
Right-handed 1, best RPR 136

Mare who had a typically hectic start to life in France, running 17 times in 14 months, and perhaps it shouldn't be held against her that she failed to win in seven hurdles runs. Waved goodbye to France in the best possible fashion, however, when beating the now Paul Nicholls-trained Fago in a Grade 1 chase at Auteuil over 2m6f. Has since won both hurdles starts for Nicky Henderson, the second coming in a Listed race over 2m4f in heavy ground at Sandown, after which Barry Geraghty said she wouldn't have a problem with 3m. Trainer indicated this is the most likely target as owner Simon Munir has Une Artiste to pit against Quevega in the Mares' Hurdle.

OTHERS TO CONSIDER

There are plenty of horses among the entries who would be far shorter in the betting on the day than some of those mentioned here, but they have largely been dealt with in the Neptune section as that is where they are more likely to head. **Pont Alexandre**, for instance, would probably be favourite if Willie Mullins has a change of heart, but the trainer was strongly leaning towards the shorter race, hence a much-inflated price for this on Betfair. **Cloudy Copper** was impressive in deep ground at Kempton in January and only has this as an entry, but he is said to take plenty of time to get over his races and the latest exchange moves lean towards him being a non-runner. **Rule The World** is only 8-1 in places but was 60-plus on Betfair at the time of writing, while others who would be of interest but were considerably bigger on the exchange include **Busty Brown, Defy Logic and Shutthefrontdoor**.

Albert Bartlett Hurdle results and trends

	FORM	WINNER	AGE & WGT	Adj RPR	SP	TRAINER	H.Runs	BEST RPR LAST 12 MONTHS (RUNS SINCE)
12	2111	Brindisi Breeze D	6 11-7	157^{-6}	7-1	L Russell	$3^{(20G)}$	won Haydock Gd2 nov hdl (3m) (0)
11	1-111	Bobs Worth C	6 11-7	160^{T}	15-8F	N Henderson	$3^{(18G)}$	won Cheltenham Gd2 nov hdl (2m4½f) (0)
10	12F34	Berties Dream	7 11-7	155^{3}	33-1	P Gilligan (IRE)	$14^{(19G)}$	3rd Cheltenham Gd2 nov hdl (2m5f) (1)
09	-5112	Weapon's Amnesty D, BF	6 11-7	150^{-12}	8-1	C Byrnes (IRE)	$4^{(17GS)}$	2nd Leopardstown Gd2 nov hdl (2m4f) (0)
08	1-212	Nenuphar Collonges CD	7 11-7	146^{-12}	9-1	A King	$4^{(18GS)}$	2nd Warwick Gd2 nov hdl (2m5f) (0)
07	-1211	Wichita Lineman C	6 11-7	161^{T}	11-8F	J O'Neill	$4^{(20GS)}$	won Gd1 Challow Hurdle (2m5f) (1)
06	1-111	Black Jack Ketchum CD	7 11-7	161^{T}	EvensF	J O'Neill	$3^{(19G)}$	won Cheltenham Gd2 nov hdl (3m) (0)
05	62162	Moulin Riche	5 11-7	149^{-8}	9-1	F Doumen (FR)	$8^{(18G)}$	2nd Haydock Gd2 nov hdl (2m7½f) (0)

WINS-RUNS: 5yo 1-28, 6yo 4-62, 7yo 3-43, 8yo 0-15, 9yo 0-1 **FAVOURITES:** -£0.75

TRAINERS IN THIS RACE (w-pl-r): Jonjo O'Neill 2-0-2, Alan King 1-1-9, Charles Byrnes 1-2-4, Lucinda Russell 1-0-1, Nicky Henderson 1-1-5, Charlie Egerton 0-0-2, Charlie Longsdon 0-0-1, Colin Tizzard 0-1-3, Dessie Hughes 0-0-2, David Pipe 0-0-3, Emma Lavelle 0-1-3, Evan Williams 0-0-2, Gordon Elliott 0-0-1, John Quinn 0-0-1, Mouse Morris 0-0-2, Mark Bradstock 0-0-3, Martin Keighley 0-0-3, Mags Mullins 0-1-1, Nigel Twiston-Davies 0-0-7, Noel Meade 0-0-6, Pat Fahy 0-0-1, Paul Nicholls 0-3-7, Paul Nolan 0-0-2, Paul Webber 0-0-1, Philip Hobbs 0-0-2, Rebecca Curtis 0-0-3, Tom Hogan 0-0-1, Tim Vaughan 0-0-1, Tom George 0-0-2, Willie Mullins 0-2-11

FATE OF FAVOURITES: 31132P12 **POSITION OF WINNER IN MARKET:** 51154012

Key trends

🏇Pre-race RPR of at least 139, 8/8

🏇At least three runs over hurdles, 8/8

🏇Top-two finish in a Graded hurdle last time out, 7/8 (four won)

🏇Won over at least 2m5f, 7/8

🏇Aged six or seven, 7/8

🏇Course winner, 4/8

Other factors

🏇Six of the British and Irish-trained winners had won a Graded hurdle, while the French-trained victor had won a Listed handicap hurdle

🏇Five winners had raced at least twice around Cheltenham

Notes

3.20 Betfred Cheltenham Gold Cup C4/RUK
3m2½f Grade 1 £550,000

Bobs Worth has been solid favourite since his impressive victory in the Hennessy on December 1, even though he has not run again after a poor tracheal wash scuppered plans for a prep in the Argento Chase. With Kauto Star and Denman retired, Paul Nicholls has turned to Silviniaco Conti in his bid for a fifth Gold Cup and has guided him through an unbeaten build-up. Willie Mullins is aiming for his first Gold Cup with Sir Des Champs, winner of the Irish Hennessy and like Bobs Worth twice victorious at the festival already. Long Run and Imperial Commander, the winners in 2011 and 2010 respectively, try to emulate Kauto Star by regaining the cup, while The Giant Bolster will be out to show last year's second place at 50-1 was no fluke.

Bobs Worth
8 b g; Trainer Nicky Henderson
Chase form 13211, best RPR 174
Left-handed 111, best RPR 174
Right-handed 32, best RPR 162
Cheltenham form 1111, best RPR 166
At the festival 18 Mar 2011: Midfield, headway approaching 7th, led between last 2, jumped left and tried to assert last, edged right towards finish, driven out and stayed on well, won Albert Bartlett Novices' Hurdle by two and a quarter lengths from Mossley

14 Mar 2012: Held up in midfield, headway to go prominent 8th, led narrowly when stretched for 4 out, headed on bend approaching 2 out, regained lead just before last, ridden run-in, stayed on well and drew away towards finish, won RSA Chase by two and a half lengths from First Lieutenant

Looked to have his flaws as a novice when beaten in the Feltham at Kempton and Reynoldstown at Ascot, but he got it right when it mattered in the RSA Chase as he powered away from First Lieutenant after the last with favourite Grands Crus well beaten off. That took his record on left-handed tracks to a perfect five-from-five, with four of those successes coming at Cheltenham, and he maintained his unbeaten profile going anti-clockwise when winning the Hennessy under 11st 6lb on his return. That form arguably makes him no better than runner-up Tidal Bay, who was giving him 6lb, but he won with a bit in hand and the form has been well franked with Tidal Bay winning the Lexus at Leopardstown by a head from First Lieutenant, who had been third at Newbury. Sixth-placed Teaforthree, who was getting a stone and was beaten more than 25 lengths, nearly won the Welsh National, so it's hard to put the Hennessy down as anything

other than a top-class piece of handicap form and a level that makes Bobs Worth a worthy Gold Cup favourite. He was withdrawn from his intended prep in the Argento in January after a tracheal wash revealed all wasn't quite right, but that was seen as a potential positive to some given the state of the ground at Cheltenham. It could also be argued, however, that any sort of interrupted prep cannot be seen as an advantage. As far as recent trends are concerned he'd be the first winner for many years to come in on the back of just one run, while the last winner who didn't contest the King George or Lexus was Cool Dawn in 1998.

Sir Des Champs
7 b g; Trainer Willie Mullins
Chase form 11111241, best RPR 169
Left-handed 1141, best RPR 169
Right-handed 1112, best RPR 165
Cheltenham form 11, best RPR 168
At the festival 18 Mar 2011: Held up in rear, headway approaching 2 out, ridden and strong run approaching last, finished strongly to lead final 20 yards, won Martin Pipe Conditional Jockeys' Handicap Hurdle by half a length from Son Of Flicka

15 Mar 2012: Raced in 3rd early, steadied in touch, headway 10th, went 3rd again next, tracked leader 4 out, challenged travelling well 2 out, upsides last, shaken up to lead with 1f to run, quickened clear smartly, easily, won Jewson Novices' Chase by four and a half lengths from Champion Court

Top-class performer who completed a second consecutive unbeaten season for Willie Mullins when sent novice chasing last term, winding up with an easy win in the Grade 2 Jewson at the festival, his second straight success at the meeting. Was made ante-post favourite for the Gold Cup after that and his price has been pretty much static ever since, although this season's efforts have posed more questions than answers. Lost that unbeaten tag on his return when he appeared outclassed by Flemenstar over 2m4f at Punchestown and didn't make the vast improvement expected next time in the Lexus at Leopardstown, where he didn't travel that well and jumped poorly but stayed on to be a close fourth to Tidal Bay, one place behind Flemenstar. He finally got his revenge on Flemenstar back at Leopardstown in the Hennessy when all out to win by a length and three-quarters on a day when the hold-up tactics employed on the free-running second were questionable to say the least. It's true that Sir Des Champs put in his best round of jumping of the season, but the times of other races on the day suggest the ground was a good deal better than for the Lexus yet the Hennessy was run some eight seconds slower, so it's fair to say his jumping was hardly put under pressure. Scores highly on the key trends, except the one that says he hasn't yet achieved the level of form (172 RPR) of nine of the last ten winners going into it. That won't stop him winning if he's good enough, but he's had three goes as a second-season chaser without quite getting there, so is arguably a good deal shorter in the betting than he should be.

Silviniaco Conti

7 ch g; Trainer Paul Nicholls
Chase form 31241111, best RPR 175
Left-handed 31111, best RPR 175
Right-handed 124, best RPR 164
Cheltenham form (hurdles) 3, best RPR 156

Looked potentially high class in first season as a novice, losing no caste in defeat when second to Grands Crus in the Feltham, but swerved Cheltenham after a below-par performance in the Reynoldstown at Ascot. That proved a good move by Paul Nicholls as he hasn't looked back since, closing last term with a 13-length drubbing of Jewson second Champion Court at Aintree before going unbeaten in three this season. The first was in the Charlie Hall when he coasted home 11 lengths clear of Wayward Prince and he was then well backed to beat Long Run in the Grade 1 Betfair Chase, which he did in commanding fashion thanks to Ruby Walsh dictating a slow pace. Answered

questions about his ability in a stronger-run race when ultimately impressive winner of the Denman Chase at Newbury in his prep, giving 4lb and a seven-length beating to last season's Gold Cup runner-up The Giant Bolster when reportedly much in need of the run. If there is more to come after that he is going to be a huge player and he has clearly achieved a lot more than Sir Des Champs, yet is a bigger price. The one negative is his lack of chase form at Cheltenham, but he did finish third in a 2m Bula when giving weight to the first two, so it's hard to argue this strong stayer didn't handle the track.

Long Run

8 b g; Trainer Nicky Henderson
Chase form 1211113311221321, best RPR 181
Left-handed 121113312132, best RPR 181
Right-handed 1121, best RPR 181
Cheltenham form 3313, best RPR 181
At the festival 17 Mar 2010: Held up in last pair, blundered 6th, took keen hold and progress to track leaders 9th, mistakes 12th and 16th, soon pressed leader, led narrowly 3 out, mistake 2 out and soon headed, no chance with winner, lost second last stride, finished third, beaten seven lengths by Weapon's Amnesty in RSA Chase

18 Mar 2011: In touch, blundered 3rd, hit 10th, tracking leaders when blundered 12th, stayed there, not fluent 4 out, ridden before next, stayed on to challenge 2 out, led before last, driven and stayed on strongly run-in, won Gold Cup by seven lengths from Denman

16 Mar 2012: Tracked leaders, disputed 2nd 4 out, hit 3 out and dropped to close 3rd, rallied and hit 2 out, driven to challenge last, soon one pace under pressure and one pace into 3rd close home, finished third, beaten three lengths by Synchronised in Gold Cup

Has never been anything other than top class since arriving in Britain from France in December 2009 and by the time of his eighth birthday had won two King Georges and a Gold Cup. However, he has not always pleased everyone, his jumping being an issue almost as consistently as the choice of jockey, owner Robert Waley-Cohen's son Sam, who seems to get the plaudits when he wins but is offered up for crucifixion when he doesn't. The fact Waley-Cohen is an amateur riding against professionals is, of course, always going to be a disadvantage, but it's the owner's prerogative and it's about time everyone got used to it and focused simply on what the pair are capable of together – which is top-class form.

Admittedly, he hasn't seemed as good as when winning the Gold Cup two seasons ago, but he was perhaps a shade overrated at the time, with the measure of decline in Denman and an out-of-sorts Kauto Star not fully realised. Otherwise he's been exceptionally consistent, busting a 170 RPR on his last eight starts. More of an out-and-out stayer than when first coming to Britain, he was undone by a slow pace when second to Silviniaco Conti in the Betfair Chase on this season's return (his third seasonal debut defeat in a row) but battled home bravely in a brutal King George to nail Captain Chris on the line. Not as invincible as he once looked, but it should surprise no-one if he regains his title.

First Lieutenant
8 ch g; Trainer Mouse Morris
Chase form 121P2234232, best RPR 168
Left-handed 12232, best RPR 168
Right-handed 21P342, best RPR 165
Cheltenham form 12, best RPR 168
At the festival 16 Mar 2011: Chased leaders, ridden from 2 out, not much room last, 2 lengths down on leader soon after, rallied gamely under pressure run-in, led last stride, won Neptune Novices' Hurdle by a short head from Rock On Ruby

14 Mar 2012: Prominent, went 2nd after 7th, led 8th, headed narrowly 4 out, regained lead on bend before 2 out, ridden and headed just before last, one pace and well held towards finish, finished second, beaten two and a half lengths by Bobs Worth in RSA Chase

A record of just two wins in 11 chase starts masks the fact that this is a thoroughly genuine and still improving chaser, whose two previous Cheltenham Festival efforts – victory in the Neptune, runner-up in the RSA – suggest it would be folly to discount him. Indeed, he may not have won this season, but his last three runs have been his best, especially his Hennessy third and Lexus second. What's more, the form he displayed in November and December was way in advance of what he has ever shown at the same time of year as he normally comes into his own on better ground in the spring. Can't beat Bobs Worth on RSA or Hennessy form, but stranger things have happened and Mouse Morris will doubtless have him primed as usual.

Imperial Commander
12 b g; Trainer Nigel Twiston-Davies
Chase form 114161P251U1P2, best RPR 182
Left-handed 1141121U1P2, best RPR 182
Right-handed 6P5, best RPR 143
Cheltenham form (chases) 114111P2, best RPR 182
At the festival 14 Mar 2007: Chased leaders, not fluent 3rd, went 2nd 4 out to next, soon ridden, weakened after 2 out, finished seventh, beaten 14 lengths by Massini's Maguire in Ballymore Properties Novices' Hurdle

12 Mar 2009: Tracked leaders, led 9th, ridden 3 out, stayed on gamely run-in, won Ryanair Chase by two lengths from Voy Por Ustedes

19 Mar 2010: Tracked leaders, went 2nd 4 out, led 2 out, driven clear from last, won going away, won Gold Cup by seven lengths from Denman

18 Mar 2011: Chased leaders, mistake 13th, pressed leaders 16th, blundered 4 out, soon weakened, tailed off when pulled up before last, dismounted, finished lame in Gold Cup won by Long Run

Impressive winner of 2010 Gold Cup who has had his problems since, running only four times, and was off for nearly two years after going lame in Long Run's Gold Cup. Even allowing for his tendency to go well fresh, it was some training performance to get him back in such rude health for the Argento in January, when he almost made a fairytale return, having looked all over the winner until Cape Tribulation edged past him at the line. He is now as short as 16-1 to turn back the years in the big one itself, but it's hard to see if you take the time to put the Argento form into perspective. Imperial Commander was getting 6lb from the 151-rated winner and is going to have to improve at least a stone to be competitive. His past record suggests he's more likely to go backwards than forwards after a big run just a few weeks ago and the less romantic, more hard-nosed punters are likely to get stuck into laying him win and place. Surefire on-the-day drifter if he gets there.

Captain Chris
9 b g; Trainer Philip Hobbs
Chase form 222111U3P4122, best RPR 170
Left-handed 221P4, best RPR 168
Right-handed 211U3122, best RPR 170
Cheltenham form 121P4, best RPR 168
At the festival 15 Mar 2011: Tracked leaders, pushed along and stayed on well from 3 out, went 2nd before 2 out, ridden to challenge last, led soon after, stayed on strongly, won Arkle Chase by two and three-quarter lengths from Finian's Rainbow

15 Mar 2012: chased leaders until lost position 12th, plenty to do 3 out, stayed on well approaching 2 out, kept on well run-in but no impression on leading trio, finished fourth, beaten six lengths in Ryanair Chase by Riverside Theatre

1 MONTH FOR £1

START YOUR MEMBERS' CLUB TRIAL IN TIME FOR THE CHELTENHAM FESTIVAL

RACINGPOST.com/membersclub
THE PULSE OF THE FESTIVAL

Lexus finish: (from left to right) Sir Des Champs, First Lieutenant, Tidal Bay and Flemenstar fight it out, but only the Gigginstown pair are left standing now as sights are set on the Gold Cup

Much was expected of the 2010 Arkle winner last term but, while runner-up Finian's Rainbow went on to win the Champion Chase, he struggled. He started well enough as he looked all over the winner of the Haldon Gold Cup until over-jumping at the last and coming down, but after that was a distant, apparently non-staying third in the King George before being pulled up in the Argento after developing a tendency to jump sideways. The ability was still there, though, and he didn't run at all badly in the Ryanair two months later when, despite completely losing his position at the 12th, he ran on stoutly to be fourth. This year has been much more straightforward, with a comfortable win at Ascot and then a neck defeat by Long Run in the King George, when he was just outstayed. That represented a career-best on ground he hated and he could well have been in the process of bettering it when, not for the first time, he proved too brave for his own good at Ascot. That was in the Grade 1 Ascot Chase in February, when he looked to have the measure of Cue Card going to the second-last only to come up miles too soon and land on top of the fence. Should stay if the ground dries out and has a massive run in him if he can avoid race-ending errors.

The Giant Bolster *(below, leading)*
8 b g; Trainer David Bridgwater
Chase form 1F1UFU721423P2, best RPR 170
Left-handed 1F1UFU7214232, best RPR 170
Right-handed P
Cheltenham form (chase only) F1UU12, best RPR 170
At the festival 17 Mar 2010: Hampered 2nd, towards rear, ridden and hit 3 out, stayed on from 2 out and kept on run-in but never in contention, finished sixth, beaten seven lengths by Peddlers Cross in Neptune

16 Mar 2011: Last when mistake 5th and eventually unseated rider in RSA Chase won by Bostons Angel

16 Mar 2012: Tracked leaders, not fluent 15th, outpaced 17th, jumped slowly 4 out, good progress to chase leader after 3 out, led approaching 2 out, hard driven, joined last, soon headed and dropped to 3rd, rallied for 2nd close home in Gold Cup, beaten two and a quarter lengths by Synchronised

Has always had class but was clumsy as a novice chaser, failing to complete more often than not, and it's to David Bridgwater's huge credit that he turned him into such a sure-footed jumper in a second season that culminated in second place in the Gold Cup behind Synchronised. Third to Silviniaco Conti in the Betfair Chase first time up confirmed he belongs in the big league and he can be forgiven his King George flop as that was his first run over fences going right-handed and he was never travelling. Much more like it when second, again to Silviniaco Conti, in the Denman Chase at Newbury, although he has plenty to find off that, having been beaten seven lengths getting 4lb. Ran a similar race last term, though, and turned form around with Long Run at Cheltenham. Hard to see hi winning what might be a better Gold Cup this year, but no surprise if he places again.

Katenko
7 b g; Trainer Venetia Williams
Chase form 1F1134F84F211, best RPR 162
Left-handed 1F1134F84F1, best RPR 162
Right-handed 21, best RPR 151
Cheltenham form 1, best RPR 162

Grade 3 chase winner in France who made no show over the fixed brush hurdles on his debut for Venetia Williams in November but has made huge strides in three chase starts since. Second to Wyck Hill at Ascot was a good effort, but didn't really prepare us for what to come only two weeks later when he was heavily

backed late on and sauntered home from a last-time-out winner at Sandown. Sluiced up again in the 2m5f handicap that last year's Gold Cup runner-up The Giant Bolster took en route to the festival and has risen from 136 to 158 in a short space of time. Quite a while since the last winner went straight from handicaps into a Gold Cup and he needs to make another sizeable leap, but he's young, clearly ultra-progressive and his trainer doesn't tilt at windmills. May take in another handicap before the final decision is made.

Cape Tribulation

9 b g; Trainer Malcolm Jefferson
Chase form 1P22P5011, best RPR 166
Left-handed: 12P5011, best RPR 166
Right-handed P2, best RPR 151
Cheltenham form (chase only) 51, best RPR 166
At the festival 13 Mar 2009: Tracked leaders, went 2nd approaching 2 out, upsides on long run to last before checked slightly, soon ridden, no extra run-in, finished fifth, beaten ten and a half lengths by Weapon's Amnesty in Albert Bartlett

18 Mar 2010: Held up, hit 8th, dropped away before 2 out, never on terms, finished 13th, beaten 78 lengths by Big Buck's in World Hurdle

15 Mar 2012: Held up in midfield, progress from 9th, tracked leaders 2 out, smooth headway to go 2nd on long run after, led last, driven out flat, won Pertemps Final, beating Catch Me by three-quarters of a length

Has always been highly regarded by Malcolm Jefferson but had largely underachieved until make enormous strides over the past 12 months. Did not go unbacked when winning the Pertemps Final over hurdles last season off a mark of 142 and then defied top weight off 8lb higher at Aintree. He seemed to revert to type after that, though, being well beaten when favourite on the Flat, finishing tailed

off behind Thousand Stars in a Grade 1 at Auteuil, and again well beaten by Tidal Bay at Wetherby. Switching back to fences has transformed him, though, and he followed an easy win off 142 in the Rowland Meyrick at Wetherby over Christmas with a battling half-length success from Imperial Commander in the Argento in January. Hard to know what he achieved in desperate conditions against a runner-up making his comeback after nearly two years off and the chances are he needs to take another big step. Still, he's a strong traveller who clearly handles the mud.

OTHERS TO CONSIDER

We're running out of time for anything else to make an impact on the market, although a few others will probably line up. **Mail De Bievre** looked a chaser of huge potential at Newbury behind Silviniaco Conti but ended up beaten miles having run far too free and will probably contest the Champion Chase or Ryanair. **Wyck Hill** has a victory over Katenko to his name, but he has stayed in his box since, while the runner-up has improved dramatically. Bottomless ground would obviously suit the likes of **Quito De La Roque**, **Teaforthree** and **Monbeg Dude**, but none looks anywhere near good enough even with conditions in their favour, while **Bog Warrior** will probably contest the World Hurdle if making the trip. At the Grand National weights lunch Willie Mullins claimed **Prince De Beauchene** was better than his previous winner Hedgehunter, who also finished second in a Gold Cup, so he wouldn't be out of place if lining up just a few weeks before his big target.

Gold Cup results and trends

	FORM	WINNER	AGE & WGT	Adj RPR	SP	TRAINER	C.Runs	BEST RPR LAST 12 MONTHS (RUNS SINCE)
12	-P731	Synchronised	9 11-10	175-12	8-1	J O'Neill	8(14G)	won Gd1 Lexus Chase (3m) (0)
11	13-31	Long Run	6 11-10	184-2	7-2F	N Henderson	9(13G)	won Gd1 King George VI Chase (3m) (0)
10	1-P25	Imperial Commander C	9 11-10	181-15	7-1	N Twiston-Davies	9(11G)	2nd Gd1 Betfair Chase (3m) (1)
09	2-1U1	Kauto Star CD	9 11-10	188-1	7-4F	P Nicholls	20(16GS)	won Gd1 King George VI Chase (3m) (0)
08	1-111	Denman C, D	8 11-10	184-5	9-4	P Nicholls	8(12GS)	won Gd3 Hennessy Gold Cup (3m2½f) (2)
07	11111	Kauto Star	7 11-10	188T	5-4F	P Nicholls	10(18GS)	won Gd1 Betfair Chase (3m) (3)
06	11152	War Of Attrition	7 11-10	168-7	15-2	M Morris (IRE)	9(22G)	2nd Gd1 Lexus Chase (3m) (0)
05	B1211	Kicking King	7 11-10	181T	4-1F	T Taaffe (IRE)	11(15G)	won Gd1 King George VI Chase (3m) (0)
04	11-21	Best Mate CD	9 11-10	182T	8-11F	H Knight	12(10G)	won Gd1 Ericsson Chase (3m) (0)
03	21-11	Best Mate CD	8 12-0	176T	13-8F	H Knight	9(15G)	won Gd1 Cheltenham Gold Cup (3m2½f) (2)

WINS-RUNS: 6yo 1-3, 7yo 3-21, 8yo 2-44, 9yo 4-33, 10yo 0-27, 11yo 0-14, 12yo 0-3, 13yo 0-1 **FAVOURITES:** £8.85

TRAINERS IN THIS RACE (w-pl-r): Paul Nicholls 3-6-27, Jonjo O'Neill 1-2-7, Mouse Morris 1-0-3, Nicky Henderson 1-1-6, Nigel Twiston-Davies 1-0-5, Colin Tizzard 0-0-1, David Bridgwater 0-1-1, David Pipe 0-0-2, George Charlton 0-0-1, Philip Hobbs 0-0-3, Tom George 0-0-1, Venetia Williams 0-1-2, Willie Mullins 0-1-5

FATE OF FAVOURITES: 1110121F13 **POSITION OF WINNER IN MARKET:** 1113121313

Key trends

🏇Two to five runs that season, ten winners in last ten runnings

🏇Grade 1 chase winner, 10/10

🏇Aged between seven and nine, 9/10

🏇Won Graded chase that season, 9/10

🏇Ran between six and 12 times over fences, 9/10

🏇Achieved pre-race chase RPR of at least 171, 9/10

🏇Within 7lb of RPR top-rated, 8/10

🏇Finished first or second in any race at Cheltenham, 8/10

🏇Won or placed previously at the festival, 8/10

🏇Won over at least 3m, 8/10

Other factors

🏇Kauto Star is the only horse to regain the crown and also the only one since Bregawn in 1983 to improve on a placed effort from 12 months earlier

🏇In the past ten years horses starting 16-1 or bigger have finished in the top three 11 times (one win, five runners-up and five thirds)

🏇The last winner not to have contested either the King George or the Lexus was Cool Dawn in 1998

🏇Denman, War Of Attrition, Kicking King and Best Mate had made the frame in championship novice hurdles at the festival, suggesting an ability to travel and hold a position is a key attribute

Notes

4.00 CGA Foxhunter Chase   C4/RUK
🏇3m2½f   🏇Amateur riders   🏇£40,000

With almost two-thirds of the winners coming from pointing yards, this is not the strongest race for trends, although recently it has been the best festival race for front-runners.

Sixteen of the past 22 winners have been aged nine or younger – three of the first four last year were in that age bracket from a representation of half the runners.

The five biggest shocks of recent years (20-1 or bigger) have been since 2002 and, despite that, 11 of the past 20 winners were sent off at single-figure odds (six were favourite).

Since the first Irish-trained victory in 1983 there have been six subsequent wins, although Punchestown is often the main aim for Irish hunters.

Warwick is by far the best venue to find the winner. Since 1993 six of the nine British-based hunters had won at the Midlands track. The Raymond Smith Memorial Hunters Chase at Leopardstown in early February is the best Irish trial. Salsify won it last year, before his victory here, and this year he beat his main Irish rival, Tammys Hill, by a neck.

Foxhunter Chase results and trends

	FORM	WINNER	AGE & WGT	Adj RPR	SP	TRAINER	C.Runs	BEST RPR LAST 12 MONTHS (RUNS SINCE)
12	-11P1	Salsify	7 12-0	132⁻¹⁴	7-1	R Sweeney (IRE)	8(22G)	won Leopardstown hunt ch (3m) (0)
11	44-21	Zemsky	8 12-0	125⁻²³	33-1	I Ferguson (IRE)	6(24G)	won Musselburgh cl 6 hunt ch (3m½f) (0)
10	2-121	Baby Run	10 12-0	144⁻⁷	9-2J	N Twiston-Davies	9(24GS)	won Warwick class 6 hunt ch (3m1f) (0)
09	11	Cappa Bleu	7 12-0	130⁻¹⁴	11-2	S Crow	0(24GS)	won Chaddesley Corbett open (3m) (0)
08	-P211	Amicelli	9 12-0	128⁻⁶	33-1	C Coward	8(23GS)	won Brocklesby Park open (3m) (1)
07	19F0-	Drombeag	9 12-0	119⁻¹⁷	20-1	J O'Neill	8(24GS)	9th Foxhunter Chase (3m2½f) (2)
06	1-34U	Whyso Mayo	9 12-0	120⁻³⁰	20-1	R Hurley (IRE)	5(24G)	3rd Punchestown hunt ch (3m1f) (2)
05	5-1U1	Sleeping Night	9 12-0	150ᵀ	7-2F	P Nicholls	12(24G)	won Wetherby class 6 hunt ch (3m1f) (2)
04	-11P2	Earthmover CD, BF	13 12-0	140⁻³	14-1	P Nicholls	36(24G)	won Cheltenham cl 6 hunt ch (3m2½f) (3)
03	11-11	Kingscliff	6 12-0	143⁻⁶	11-4F	S Alner	1(24G)	won Wincanton cl 6 hunt ch (3m1½f) (0)

WINS-RUNS: 6yo 1-3, 7yo 2-24, 8yo 1-36, 9yo 4-39, 10yo 1-39, 11yo 0-49, 12yo 0-31, 13yo 1-12, 14yo 0-4 **FAVOURITES:** £1.00

TRAINERS IN THIS RACE (w-pl-r): Paul Nicholls 2-0-13, Sheila Crow 1-0-2, Rodger Sweeney 1-0-1, Jimmy Mangan 0-2-2, Richard Barber 0-1-5

FATE OF FAVOURITES: 1P1P2P0142 **POSITION OF WINNER IN MARKET:** 1519802103

Key trends

🏇Won over at least 3m, 10/10

🏇Aged ten or younger, 9/10

🏇Ran between 20 and 33 days ago, 9/10 (exception was having first start in nearly a year)

🏇Recorded a pre-race RPR of at least 130, 8/10

🏇Rated within 11lb of RPR top-rated, 8/10

🏇Won last time out, 7/10

Other factors

🏇Record of previous year's winner is P36204U; Double Silk doubled up in 1993 and 1994

🏇Three winners had competed at the festival before and all had been in the first four

🏇Six winners were former handicap chasers and four had come from point-to-points

🏇Four of the beaten favourites (including joint-favourites) were trained in Ireland

🏇Those aged 12 or older have had just one win and one place (47 have run)

Big prices have been the norm in the four runnings, with winners at 14-1, 20-1 and 25-1 – a sequence interrupted only by 9-2 winning favourite Sir Des Champs two years ago. All the winners have been aged five or six and it is notable that all four were in their second season over hurdles.

Nicky Henderson has been dangerous in every renewal, as he saddled the inaugural winner, three of the first five the next year and the third-placed horse in the past two years (from a total of 12 runners).

David Pipe has yet to win the race named in honour of his father, having had the beaten favourite twice and an unplaced second favourite.

Ireland has been a growing force in the County Hurdle and the same might happen here – in the past two years they have had only three runners but they finished 124.

Martin Pipe Handicap Hurdle results

	FORM	WINNER	AGE & WGT	OR	SP	TRAINER	H.Runs	BEST RPR LAST 12 MONTHS (RUNS SINCE)
12	135P1	**Attaglance**	6 11-3	139^T	20-1	M Jefferson	13$^{(24G)}$	won M Rasen class 3 hcap hdl (2m3f) (0)
11	1-1	**Sir Des Champs**	5 11-3	134^T	9-2F	W Mullins (IRE)	2$^{(23G)}$	won Navan hdl (2m) (0)
10	-445U	**Pause And Clause** D,	6 11-10	137^{-3}	14-1	E Lavelle	8$^{(24S)}$	4th Haydock Listed hcap hdl (3m1f) (2)
09	-4134	**Andytown** C, D,	6 11-2	133^{-6}	25-1	N Henderson	7$^{(23GS)}$	won Chelt class 3 cond hcap hdl (2m5f) (1)

WINS-RUNS: 4yo 0-1, 5yo 1-24, 6yo 3-30, 7yo 0-22, 8yo 0-9, 9yo 0-5, 10yo 0-2, 12yo 0-1 **FAVOURITES:** £1.50

FATE OF FAVOURITES: 3010 **POSITION OF WINNER IN MARKET:** 0610   **OR 127-132** 0-4-39, **133-139** 4-7-46, **140-145** 0-1-9

Saint Roque has been prominent in the ante-post lists for the Martin Pipe

Notes

5.15 Johnny Henderson Grand Annual H'cap Chase RUK
2m½f — Grade 3 — £90,000

This has become the 'getting out stakes' on the final day of the festival, but the last winning favourite was in 2004 and five of the subsequent eight winners have gone off at 12-1 or bigger.

A strong recent trend is that three of the last four winners were officially novices. This has been the best race for novices at the festival with 11 winners, rated from 129 to 138, since 1983.

The race's title has commemorated Nicky Henderson's father Johnny since 2005 and the trainer won the following year with Greenhope and again last year with Bellvano (both 20-1 shots). He has also had three runner-ups and two thirds from a total of 25 runners.

Paul Nicholls has had the top-weight in five of the past eight years and won twice, with runners carrying 10st 1lb and 10st 11lb, but he has also had four beaten favourites. His best prospect is likely to be getting a novice under the radar.

In the two decades up to 1998 the winners were almost evenly split between those carrying more than 11st and those carrying less, but the past 13 winners have all shouldered between 10st and 10st 13lb, with 61 unsuccessful runners under a bigger weight.

Oiseau De Nuit in 2011 was the highest-rated winner since Uncle Ernie in 1997 (both ran off a mark of 145) and broke a trend that had seen victory go to runners rated 129-134 in nine of the previous ten runnings (that narrow ratings range produced the first two in six of those years). Bellvano last year was also outside that range off a mark of 138 but he was one of the lowest-rated in the race (136 was the lowest).

Just six winners since 1973 had failed to make the first four last time out and 30 of the winners were aged seven to nine. Three of the four recent Irish-trained winners prepped over hurdles – the exception was the novice Fota Island. Seven of the last eight British-trained winners had won at Cheltenham before.

Bellvano (centre) was a 20-1 winner for Nicky Henderson last year

Grand Annual Handicap Chase results and trends

	FORM	WINNER	AGE & WGT		OR	SP	TRAINER	C.Runs	BEST RPR LAST 12 MONTHS (RUNS SINCE)
12	-1621	**Bellvano** D	8	10-2	138^T	20-1	N Henderson	5$^{(21G)}$	won Kelso class 2 nov ch (2m1f) (0)
11	U6483	**Oiseau De Nuit** CD	9	10-13	145^3	40-1	C Tizzard	20$^{(23G)}$	3rd Newbury Gd2 ch (2m1f) (0)
10	222F5	**Pigeon Island** C, D	7	10-1	129^T	16-1	N Twiston-Davies	7$^{(19S)}$	2nd Cheltenham Gd2 nov ch (2m5f) (2)
09	423F2	**Oh Crick** (1oh) C, D	6	10-0	130^{-13}	7-1	A King	6$^{(18GS)}$	2nd Hereford class 3 nov ch (2m3f) (0)
08	4P-36	**Tiger Cry** D	10	10-6	134^{-1}	15-2	A Moore (IRE)	12$^{(17GS)}$	3rd Ascot class 2 hcap ch (2m1f) (0)
07	3-333	**Andreas** CD, BF	7	10-11	143^{-1}	12-1	P Nicholls	11$^{(23GS)}$	3rd Sandown Gd3 hcap ch (2m) (0)
06	163-5	**Greenhope** C, D	8	10-11	132^9	20-1	N Henderson	5$^{(23G)}$	6th Grand Annual Hcap Ch (2m½f) (1)
05	33212	**Fota Island** (2oh) D, BF	9	10-0	130^{-6}	7-1	M Morris (IRE)	7$^{(24G)}$	2nd Navan ch (2m1f) (2)
04	4/61F	**St Pirran** C, D, BF	9	10-1	130^T	4-1F	P Nicholls	10$^{(21G)}$	won Sandown class 2 hcap ch (2m) (1)
03	-2231	**Palarshan** (4oh) C, D	5	10-0	134^{-10}	8-1	H Daly	4$^{(21G)}$	won Leicester class 4 nov ch (2m) (0)

WINS-RUNS: 5yo 1-6, 6yo 1-27, 7yo 2-37, 8yo 2-58, 9yo 3-40, 10yo 1-28, 11yo 0-14 **FAVOURITES:** -£5.00

FATE OF FAVOURITES: 510F620P00 **POSITION OF WINNER IN MARKET:** 5130422800

OR 125-136 7-11-98, **137-150** 3-17-98, **151-162** 0-2-14

Key trends

🐎Distance winner, 10/10

🐎No more than 12 runs over fences, 9/10

🐎Carried no more than 10st 11lb, 9/10

🐎Aged nine or under, 9/10

🐎Officially rated 129 to 138, 8/10 (exceptions 143 and 145)

🐎Course winner, 7/10 (two of the exceptions had finished second in this race)

🐎No more than four runs since August, 6/10

🐎Yet to win that season, 6/10

Other factors

🐎There have been five winning novices and all were rated between 129 and 138

🐎From a combined total of 42 outings prior to this race in the current season, the winners had finished out of the frame on only 12 occasions

🐎Seven winners had previous festival form, including three who had run in the race previously

🐎Two winners prepped for this race over hurdles

🐎Since 2005, when the race was renamed in honour of his father, Nicky Henderson's runners have finished 346, 180P, 800, 20, 3P, 20P, 60, 1240PF

🐎The record of the previous year's winner is 0045B

Notes